Freeing the
Natural Voice

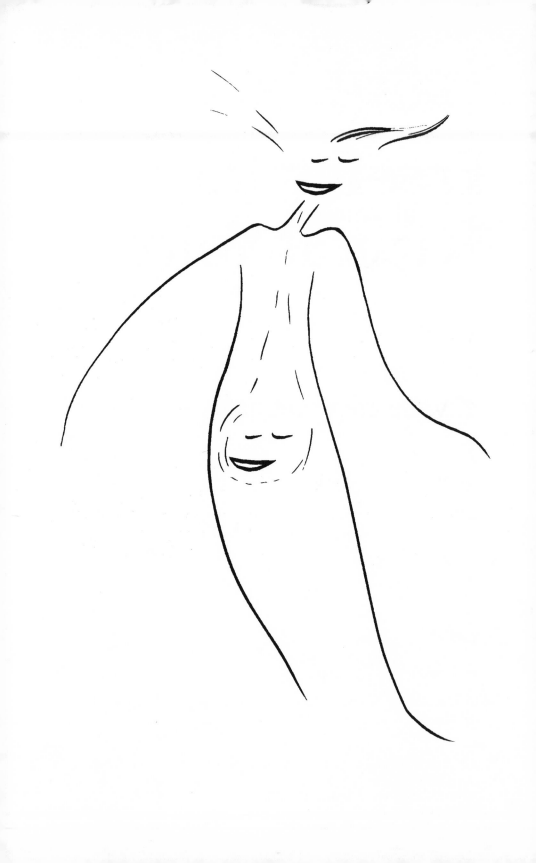

Freeing the Natural Voice

Imagery and Art in the Practice of Voice and Language

REVISED AND EXPANDED

by Kristin Linklater

Illustrations by Andre Slob

DRAMA PUBLISHERS
an imprint of Quite Specific Media Group Ltd.,
Hollywood

DRAMA PUBLISHERS
an imprint of
Quite Specific Media Group Ltd.
7373 Pyramid Place
Hollywood, California 90046
www.quitespecificmedia.com
e-mail: info@quitespecificmedia.com

This new edition of *Freeing the Natural Voice* is dedicated to the memory of Iris Warren, who was the originator of the idea contained in the first edition, published in 1976. Her work is maintained in this book and augmented with additional exercises that I have developed over the past twenty-five years.

Uttering a word is like striking a note on the keyboard of the imagination.

—Ludwig Wittgenstein
Philosophical Investigations
Part I section 6

Contents

Preface

I WAS LUCKY TO COME to the United States when I did. I came in response to the urgent encouragement of many American actors who came to the London Academy of Music and Dramatic Art (LAMDA) for a year of training during the years I taught there. They were usually on a graduate level or had been working professionally and came for further training. They told me that the kind of voice work that Iris Warren and I were teaching was unknown in the States at that time and could be immensely valuable to American actor training. When I arrived in New York in 1963 it seemed that I was bringing a method of work at exactly the right time to exactly the right place.

The search for an equilibrium between technique and emotional freedom occupied actor training from the 1920s on. Indeed, the search continues to this day; but in the history of actor development, both American and British, the search was consistently out of step throughout the 1930s, '40s, and '50s. Stanislavsky's books, the Group Theatre, and Lee Strasberg's Actors Studio moved American actors forward in psychological and emotional exploration to the point that they virtually abandoned the study of external skills. In Britain those skills reigned supreme. By the 1950s the influence of an emotionally vital American theatre had begun to inspire the British to fill out their technique with more gut content. By the 1960s, America, mushrooming with regional repertory companies, found its actors and directors crying out for technique to cope with a wide range of theatrical productions from classical to avant-garde.

When American actors tried to find teachers to help them meet their demands, they often found that technical skills were still being taught as they had been in the twenties through elocution, ballet, singing, gymnastics, and phonetics, making the gap between creation and communication unbridgeable. There was the creative, imaginative inner life and the skillful outer communicative one, with no connective tissue.

Meanwhile in London, methods—originated by Jacques Copeau, developed by Michel St. Denis and Litz Pisk, and nurtured at the Old Vic Theatre School—of developing the actor's being into a sensitive, integrated, creative instrument had grown. The spirit of the Old Vic Theatre was carried into LAMDA when Michael MacOwan took it over in 1954, beginning his collaboration in actor training with Iris Warren.

When I moved to America in 1963 to set up my own voice studio, I found that the voice work I brought with me had evolved over the years to the point at which it would marry well with American methods of acting. There was still an imbalance between the creative use of inner self and communicative skill in both America and Britain: British theatre was still suffering from a lack of emotional and psychological demands, while American theatre training placed little value on physical and vocal skills, but all this was changing. The language I had inherited from Iris Warren was easily translated into the emotional and psychological terminology of, for instance, the Method and other acting methodologies that had branched off from those of the Group Theatre.

I had much to learn, and the balance in my own work was immeasurably enhanced by my involvement, between 1964 and 1978, as vocal coach with various American acting companies, such as the Tyrone Guthrie Theatre under Sir Tyrone Guthrie, the Lincoln Center Repertory Company under Robert Whitehead, Harold Clurman, and Elia Kazan, and the Open Theater under Joseph Chaikin. Another strong influence on my development as a teacher was the acting teacher Peter Kass, with whom I worked in the New York University Graduate Theatre Program (now The Tisch School of the Arts) throughout that same period.

It was in America that I was introduced to the Alexander Technique (Judith Leibowitz was my teacher) that helped clarify the psychophysical nature of the voice work, and I benefited enormously during the sixties, seventies, and eighties from the growing psycho-therapeutic and general interest in the interdependence of the mind and body; more and more people were discovering that to unlock the mind, it was necessary to unlock the body and vice versa. The Alexander Technique, Feldenkrais work, Rolfing, T'ai Chi, Yoga, and now Body Mind Centering are all popular and effective physical disciplines that help to free the emotional and psychological self by ridding the body of habitual tensions. The turn of the twentieth to the twenty-first century found the world of neuroscience providing new insights into the workings of the mind, the emotions, the body, and consciousness. Books such as *Descartes' Error* and *The Feeling of What Happens* by Antonio Damasio offer scientific back up for the theories of those of us in the performance-training field who teach the wisdom of the body and the fundamental intelligence of the emotions.

Although I continue to attend relevant workshops and read appropriate books, I learn most from my students. Since my teaching days at New York University, I have trained, taught, and acted with Shakespeare & Company in Lenox, Massachusetts, freelanced across the United States, taught ongoing workshops for actors in Italy and guest workshops in other places around the world. I have also established workshops and teacher-training courses in Germany, a country that honors literature, language, and the art of speaking to an extent that I find humbling. I have taught undergraduate acting students at Emerson College and graduate acting students at Columbia University and coached theatre, film, and television professionals, both actors and singers. Hardly a teaching day passes without my receiving some small or large revelation about the complexity, resilience, and mystery of the human experience and its reflection in the voice. I have learned over the years which exercises work and which do not because my students tell me. Every exercise in this book has stood the test of repetition over many years, and each one produces results when practiced conscientiously, willingly, and with understanding.

This new edition of *Freeing the Natural Voice*, which was first published in 1976, offers some of the fruits of the deeper knowledge that I have accrued in the past three decades, and it also includes some of the physical exercises that are now part and parcel of my voice work but were not part of Iris Warren's original teaching.

I must acknowledge that very few of the physical exercises were created by me; I have appropriated and absorbed them from many different sources and married them with voice so that they have often undergone a sea change. Movements reminiscent of gym exercises may have been transformed by changing the goal from muscle development to that of energy flow. Yoga floor exercises have been customized for specific vocal purposes and may be almost unrecognizable as Yoga. While I have occasionally taken a Yoga class, I use and have adapted Yoga-based exercises that I learned from Ruth Solomons and Kelly Holt in their modern dance classes at NYU in the 1960s and '70s. The least reconstructed appropriations that have become integral to my voice work I learned from Trish Arnold, who was my movement teacher at LAMDA.

Tribute to Iris Warren

THIS BOOK CONTAINS A detailed series of exercises, combining imagery and imagination with technical information. The serious student will be led to an understanding of the psycho-physiology of his or her voice that allows a fundamental reconditioning of habitual ways of communicating. The framework of exercises is impeccably designed and has an enduring potency. Its architecture is the work of the late Iris Warren.

It was Iris Warren who moved the science of voice production for British actors into a new phase in the mid-twentieth century by adding psychological understanding to physiological knowledge. Voice work designed specifically for the actor began to be systematized with the pioneering studies of Elsie Fogerty during the first quarter of the twentieth century in London. She developed a method of speech and voice training that was based on the accurate physical mechanics of the voice. She was the principal of The Central School of Speech and Drama in London and was succeeded there by the equally influential Gwyneth Thurburn. The Central School, under the direction of both Fogerty and Thurburn, rivaled the Royal Academy of Dramatic Art (RADA) for distinction as London's best drama school. Clifford Turner, a graduate of Central School, taught voice and speech at RADA. Both schools, which based their actor training on voice and text, dominated the English-speaking actor-training arena for the first half of the twentieth century.

In the late 1930s, Iris Warren, working privately with actors in her own studio, began tackling actors' most common problem, that of straining their voice when expressing strong emotion. She did not deal directly with the suffering voice but with the physical and mental tensions caused by blocked emotions. She administered voice exercises, but she altered their nature by shifting the controls from external, physical muscles to internal, psychological impulses. The criterion for assessing progress lay in the answer to the question "How does it feel?" rather than "How does it sound?" The ultimate aim was, and is, to free oneself through the voice. Iris Warren's constant emphasis was "I want to hear you, not your voice." This was happening at a time when the "voice beautiful" was still very much in vogue, when pear-shaped vowels and technical skill were preferred to "vulgar" emotion.

My own work with Iris Warren began when I was an acting student at the London Academy of Music and Dramatic Art (LAMDA) in the 1950s. After completing the program, I spent two years acting in a repertory company and in 1957 was invited back to LAMDA as a student-teacher of voice production under Miss Warren. I worked with her, learning and teaching, for six years. In 1963 I decided to come to America to set up my own voice studio.

During the time that I was both student and teacher at LAMDA, the principal (director) of the school was Michael MacOwan, a visionary teacher whose artistic influence on me continues to this day. He had been a successful director in London's West End but was dissatisfied with the inconsistent quality of the actors with whom he had to work. He decided to remedy the problem at the root by taking over a failing drama school and completely redesigning it from mission to curriculum. He was my acting teacher and laid the foundation for my understanding of Shakespeare. With uncanny prescience, he saw my potential as a teacher and issued the invitation to me to learn Iris's approach to voice training.

More than forty years on, I marvel at the accuracy of Iris Warren's anatomical and psychological understanding of the voice. With the advance of technology, voice scientists began discovering in the 1970s and '80s what Iris knew intuitively. Thus far, no voice scientist has come up with procedures for enhancing voice production that perform better than the exercises Iris Warren devised in the middle of the last century.

My life-debt to my first, formative teachers, Michael MacOwan and Iris Warren, has, I think, been settled by my teaching. I will, however, always respect the memory of Michael and Iris and acknowledge with a degree of awe the long tradition to which I find I belong. I hope that Michael's devotion to truthful acting and Iris's unerring instinct for the sound of truth in the actor's voice have been preserved in me over the past several decades and have evolved into the version of those truths that I now teach, educated by the decades but fueled always by passion and tested by instinct.

An Introduction: The Approach to Vocal Freedom

THIS BOOK IS INTENDED FOR use by professional actors, student actors, teachers of acting, teachers of voice and speech, singers, singing teachers, and interested lay people. Its aims are to provide a series of exercises to free, develop, and strengthen the voice as a human instrument and to present a lucid view of the voice both in the general context of human communication and as a performer's instrument. For simplicity's sake I will address all readers as actors; perhaps those who are "interested lay people" might consider that you are in fact performers in the daily acts and scenes of your lives; as you train yourselves to pay attention to your habits of communication, you will find the same pleasurable state of self-awareness that actors develop as an essential part of their craft. As Jacques notes in Shakespeare's *As You Like It*, "All the world's a stage, and all the men and women merely players. . . ." Act II, scene 7.

This approach to voice is designed to liberate the natural voice and thereby develop a vocal technique that serves the freedom of human expression. The basic assumption of the work is that everyone possesses a voice capable of expressing, through a two- to four-octave natural pitch range, whatever gamut of emotion, complexity of mood, and subtlety of thought he or she experiences. The second assumption is that the tensions acquired through living in this world, as well as defenses, inhibitions, and negative reactions to environmental influences, often diminish the efficiency of the natural voice to the point of distorted communication. Hence, the emphasis here is on the removal of the blocks that inhibit the human instrument as distinct from, but not excluding, the development of a skillful musical instrument. I must underline at the outset that in our perception of our own voices there is a vital difference to be observed between what is "natural" and what is "familiar."

The result of the work will be to produce a voice that is in direct contact with emotional impulses, shaped by the intellect but not inhibited by it. Such a voice will be a built-in attribute of the body. It will have an innate potential for a wide pitch range, intricate harmonics, and kaledoscopic textural qualities and will be articulated into clear speech in response to clear thinking and the desire to communicate. The natural voice is transparent, it reveals, not describes, inner impulses of emotion and thought, directly and spontaneously. The person is heard, not the person's voice.

To free the voice is to free the person, and each person is indivisibly mind and body. Since physical processes generate the sound of the voice, the inner muscles of the body must be free to receive the sensitive impulses from the brain that create speech. The natural voice is most perceptibly blocked and distorted by physical tension; it suffers equally from emotional blocks, intellectual blocks, aural blocks, and psychological blocks. All such obstacles are psychophysical in nature, and once they are removed the voice is able to communicate the full range of human emotion and all the nuances of thought. The voice's limits lie only in the limits of desire, talent, imagination, or life experience.

Physical awareness and relaxation are the first steps in the work to be done on the voice. The mind and the body must learn to cooperate in activating and releasing inner impulses and dissolving physical inhibitions. Actors must develop bodies that are sensitive and integrated, rather than supercontrolled and muscular; and they must educate the voice into the union of self and body.

The voice communicates the inner world of the psyche to the outer world of attentive listeners both on the stage and in life.

The neuro-scientist Antonio Damasio reminds us that the word *psyche* originally meant "breath and blood": "I marvel at the ancient wisdom of referring to what we now call mind by the word psyche which was also used to denote breath and blood" (from *The Feeling of What Happens*, p. 30). *Psychology*, then, means the knowledge of breath and blood. Catharsis happens when the psyche of the *character* disturbs the breath, blood, and psyche of the *audience*. The original meaning of *catharsis*, according to Martha Nussbaum in *The Fragility of Goodness*, was "to shed light into dark places." The word could have been applied to cleaning the kitchen as much as to awakening the inner world of a listener. The voice of the actor should be the most potent theatrical element by which the light of a cathartic event illuminates the dark places, hidden stories, or pent-up emotions of the audience. To achieve that potency, the actor's voice must be rooted in neuro-physiological pathways of the body that are trained to pick up and transmit impulses of emotion, imagnation, psyche, and intellect. The actor must develop a body that sees, hears, feels, and speaks. The actor's brain must *be* his or her body.

The sensitivity with which the sound-waves of the actor's voice can tune into and transmit the brain and body waves of thought and feeling allows communication to emanate and envelop an audience in invisible streams of energy. The speaker is on the stage and in the auditorium at the same time. The voice that originates deep in the body will go beyond the body, enlarging the speaker. Often, a member of the audience will be astonished to see that the actor who seemed six feet tall on stage is, on the street, six inches shorter. When the actor plugs into the character's psyche, the electrical power of the imagination amplifies and activates the vibratory flow of voice so that it pours images and impulses directly into the receptors of the audience. It is the vibrations flowing out from the speaker's body that make the speaker seem larger than life-size.

The paradox is that actors must *train* their voices so that they can sacrifice them. Actors' voices must learn to be dissolved by the impulses of thought and feeling. Actors must not use their voices to describe and transmit the story, but their voices must be wide and long and strong and tender enough to reveal the breadth and depth of the imagination. If the voice is limited by habit and tension, it will limit the transmission of the imagination. The imagination must serve the text but can only partially do so with a limited voice. Let me emphasize here that imagination is not the same as fantasy. The actor's imagination must be trained with the fanaticism that an Olympic athlete trains his or her body to be precisely truthful to the exigencies of the text. This is particularly true of classical and poetic texts, but it is also true of contemporary texts where subtext is the chief informant. You cannot be sure of the accuracy of your subtext unless you can probe the text for its underlying story with laser precision. Indulgent is the actor who fantasizes around the text. An actor whose imagination is sparked and ignited by the text discards the first, second, or even third layers of information gleaned from the text and digs deeper into her or his own imaginative archaeology until the seed of the playwright's meaning impregnates and gestates and is reborn through a cellular metamorphosis in the actor's organism.

Perfect communication demands from the actor a balanced quartet of emotion, intellect, body, and voice. No one part can compensate with its strength for the weakness of another. The actor who plays Hamlet with his emotional instrument dominant but his voice and intellect underdeveloped will only communicate the generalized tone of Hamlet's pain and agony. The audience will think, "He's suffering a lot — but why?" The emotionally available actress who plays Ophelia may tap a vein of madness that is authentic, but without the voice and textual understanding to shed light onto the situation she will be dismissed by the audience as incidental to the story.

In contrast with these emotionally driven performances are those of two actors in whom the thought process dominates their work: a too-powerful intellect can also unbalance the actor's quartet. These actors intelligently argue the case for Hamlet and for Ophelia but fail to move their audience. They are bound to fail in fully communicating their characters if their emotions are not involved. A very athletic actor might dominate the quartet with his physical instrument: playing Henry V he might choose to do a back flip off the battlements and breathlessly launch into, "Once more unto the breach, dear friends, once more/Or close the wall up with your English dead..." The audience will be transfixed by his physical prowess but pay no attention to what he is saying. Without intellect, voice, and emotion, physical energy is mere flashiness. Communication is skewed because the quartet is again unbalanced.

The same kind of imbalance happens when an actor's voice is his strongest instrument: the audience may be moved by the sound and rhythm of his speech, but without physical embodiment, clear thought, and emotional truth that voice, despite its strength and beauty, is counter-productive to perfect communication.

The causal conductor of the actor's quartet is the creative imagination, and the actor's training must deliver to that conductor a voice, a body, intellect, and emotions that can serve the creative impulse without being distorted by personal habit. While this book focuses on the vocal instrument, its overall aim is not just to develop the voice but also to contribute to the development of an actor's quartet capable of creating unlimited characterizations.

In the following chapters I have tried to capture the work that Iris Warren said should never be written down and that I use daily in the classroom. It is intended, by its nature, to be conveyed orally, and it is dangerous to confine and define it in printed words. I resisted writing the original edition of this book for years, but its value has been proven over the past thirty years and the risk of its being misunderstood outweighed by the many experiences of understanding. The additional material must now stand the test of publication.

The obvious strength of the oral approach is in the one-to-one relationship between teacher and pupil. No two people, no less two voices, are the same, and each person's problems differ. How do you teach relaxation? By carefully laying a hand on the breathing area, on the shoulders, on the back of the neck or the jaw to feel whether the muscles are responding to the messages being sent to them. How do you induce a new use of the voice? By moving the body in new directions that break conditioned, habitual movements. How can the student know that a new experience is a constructive one without feedback from some external and trustworthy guide? To this last question I have no good answer, and do believe that a book is a poor substitute for a class.

It is also important to keep in mind that this book may be difficult to use because it requires dealing with cause rather than effect. The exercises are concerned more with re-thinking usage than with re-doing sounds. This is a book to be engaged in slowly. It is a practical book for practical use, not one to be skimmed for new ideas.

Whenever possible, I suggest that the serious student work with at least one other person, taking turns reading the instructions and checking the results. Mutual teaching can be very rewarding, and it incorporates the central point of voice work, namely communication.

If you have to work alone, you must sacrifice your desire for results to the experience of causes. Although you will need your intellect to understand the exercises, you must abandon it when *doing* them in favor of feelings and sensory impressions. You must not jump to conclusions as to what is right or wrong because you are already a well-developed censor of self. Nor can you trust your judgment, since it is biased by habitual ideas of good and bad and wary of new experiences.

You will be reconditioning a way of communicating that has served you, for better or worse, all your life, so in order to effect real change you must plan regular and committed work for at least a year. Also, realize that you are using your voice throughout the day, and that your exercises can, and should, be practiced continually. Even if you do work regularly, progress is slow; in the beginning there can be marked improvement, but this will level off for a time. Most important of all, you must have patience. Even after you understand and practice the exercises, it may take time before you can experience the promised freedom in performance. But when you do, the results will be enormously satisfying.

Throughout the book I suggest the amount of time it might take to learn an exercise and the length of time you should practice and absorb it before moving on to the next one. These times are offered as a guide and will undoubtedly be adapted to each person's capability.

This introduction offers a general context for the ensuing work. Before proceeding to the exercises, however, you must have some theoretical knowledge of how your voice works and some psychophysical understanding of what may be preventing it from working to its full potential.

How the Voice Works

Here is a simple physiological outline of the mechanics of speaking:

(1.)   There is an impulse in the motor cortex of the brain.

(2.)   The impulse stimulates breath to enter and leave the body.

(3.)   The outgoing breath makes contact with the vocal folds creating oscillations.

(4.)   The oscillations create frequencies (vibrations).

(5.)   The frequencies (vibrations) are amplified by resonators.

(6.)   The resultant sound is articulated by the lips and tongue to form words.

This picture is easily grasped. It is, unfortunately, a gross over-simplification of an infinitely intricate human process.

Here now is a more scientific description:

(1.).   A series of impulses are generated in the motor cortex of the brain and sent through neural pathways to the speech structures.

(2.)   The impulses are timed to arrive at the different locations in the body so that a smooth, coordinated set of actions takes place.

(3.)   First the vocal tract from the lips and nose to the lungs is opened up and the inspiratory muscles of respiration contract to lower pressure in the thorax so that air can rush into the lungs relatively unimpeded.

(4.)   When sufficient air has been inspired for the desired utterance, the respiratory system reverses itself and by a combination of elastic recoil of distended tissue and by abdominal and thoracic muscle contraction, forces are developed to push air back up the vocal tract and out through the mouth and nose.

(5.)   In the larynx, however, the vocal folds have at least partially closed at the beginning of exhalation so that the air stream is now impeded in its upward path.

(6.)   The pliable vocal folds are set into quasi-synchronous oscillation as the air passes between them.

(7.)   These oscillations break up the outgoing breath stream into puffs of air that are released into the vocal tract above.

(8.)   These puffs of air activate the air in the resonation cavities of the pharyngeal, oral, and nasal passages, producing sound in the upper vocal tracts.

(9.)   The shape, volume, and opening of the resonators determine the overtone structure of the sound, while the basic pitch is determined by the rate at which the vocal folds vibrate.

(10.) Resonation comes in two types: the first shapes or colors the voice generated at the larynx, regardless of the speech sound intended (i.e., creates the timbre or tonal qualities of the voice). The second type modifies the larynx-generated sound for a specific speech sound. The first type of sound is always present for the speaker, and the second type depends on what the speaker wants to say— the movements involved in this comprise what is called articulation.

Dr. Robert Sataloff has contributed an elegant and extended account of the anatomy and physiology of the voice that is included as an Appendix to this book.

From this point on, I shall make minimal use of exact scientific terminology. I have outlined the physical anatomy faithfully, but I have chosen to describe the voice by its perceivable features in metaphor and in analogy. This simplification may make the voice scientist quail, but it has proven to be the best approach for the voice user.

Most of the time my references to, and images of, the voice and breath mechanisms are anatomically accurate. But there are instances when a rigorous devotion to anatomical exactness would be counterproductive to the freedom of vocal function. Let me give an example of this: it is an anatomical fact that the voice originates in the larynx; that the voice box is in the throat. If, in working on your voice, you focus on that anatomical truth, you will end up with monochromatic, forced voice production or, at best, a voice devoid of personality. For the development of an artistic and personally expressive voice, you must refocus your attention on the source of breath and the resonators.

Here is another example of the reductive effect of being faithful to pure anatomy: the anatomically accurate fact is that breath goes into and out of the lungs and that the lungs exist in the space between the collarbone and the bottom of the ribcage. But when the imagination extends the dwelling-place of breath to the pelvic floor or even to the legs and feet, the actual lungs respond with an expansion of their capacity. Even more important, the image of breath entering and filling spaces in the pelvic basin, the hip sockets, and the thighs stimulates deep involuntary breathing musculature and connects the mind to primal energy sources in the sacral nerve plexi. The power of the imagination, properly used, can stimulate breathing on a profound level and enhance the function of the voice to maximum effect.

Returning now to the six-point outline of How the Voice Works, I will translate the first point, "There is an impulse in the motor cortex of the brain" into "there is a need to communicate." This need becomes an electrical impulse that travels via the spinal cord to the nerve endings that govern the speech and breathing muscles. According to the stimulus, this impulse will contain greater or lesser voltage. If someone you see daily and have no particular regard for says "good morning" to you, you will have a slight reaction in the breath and larynx muscles creating just enough vibration to serve the need of a dutiful response. If, on the other hand, the speaker is someone whom you love, whom you are delighted and surprised to see, the stimulus may arouse you emotionally; your solar plexus nerve endings will glow with warmth, your breath will react with vitality and play vigorously on your vocal folds, making the vibrations dance out through the resonators, thus serving your need to communicate your feelings. There are infinite varieties of external stimuli and internal reactions, and impulse, arousing the reflex musculature of speech, controls their expression.

Step 2, which states, "the impulse stimulates breath to enter and leave the body," means that countless muscles throughout the torso perform an extraordinary number of coordinated movements that expand the rib cage, contract and lower the diaphragm, move the stomach down, and shift the intestines to make room for the expanding lungs, allowing the air cells to suck in air and then, reversing the action, to expel it. All this is easy involuntary reaction.

Next in the physiological picture comes the play of breath on the vocal folds, Step 3. In fact, the respiratory and laryngeal actions are simultaneous; the same impulse that stimulates the breathing musculature activates the laryngeal musculature to stretch the vocal folds so that they offer enough resistance to the breath to oscillate on impact. A gentle pressure of breath meeting relatively relaxed vocal folds creates slower oscillations and the resultant vibrations of sound are of a low frequency. A strong pressure of air finds greater resistance in folds stretched and expanded by the stronger impulse, and a higher frequency of vibration results in a higher pitch. (The vocal folds are between thirty and fifty millimeters in length, and are lengthened and shortened by the cartilage to which they are attached. Involuntary muscles reacting directly to motor impulses from the brain govern the movement.)

In Step 4 the initial vibrations of sound are no more recognizable as sound than the vibrations created on piano strings if the hammer were to strike them without a sounding board behind them. But as soon as the breath oscillates the folds, the vibrations that occur re-sound off the nearest sounding boards, which are found in the cartilage of the larynx.

In Step 5 "the vibrations are amplified by resonators." Voice practitioners have conflicting opinions about how the resonating system works and what approach to take in describing it: indeed, it may only be adequately described in terms of advanced physics. For working purposes I use the following practical, tangible description. The nature of vibrations is that they multiply as they meet appropriately resistant textures. They sound again as they bounce off different surfaces, with different quality and quantity determined by the texture of the surface and the shape of the cavity. The re-sounding (resonating) surfaces within the body, available to the initial vibrations of sound, are virtually uncountable considering that bone, cartilage, membrane, and muscle can all serve as amplifiers and conductors.

The harder the surface, the stronger the resonance: bone is best, cartilage is very good, and toned-up muscle can provide a good resonating surface, but a flabby, fleshy, nonresistant area will only muffle and absorb vibrations (like heavy velvet or a sponge). The voice finds its most satisfying resonators where there are clearly defined hollows and empty tunnels in the architecture of the body, such as the pharynx, the mouth, the nose; but the bony structure of the chest, the cheekbones, the jawbone, the acoustically powerful sinus hollows, the skull, the cartilage of the larynx, and the vertebrae of the spine all demonstrably contribute resonance.

The relationship between pitch and resonators has to do with suitable apertures, appropriate shapes, and large or small cavities. The muscle lining of the pharynx and the mouth also provides subtle tuning as it tenses and relaxes.

For working purposes, the pattern of resonating response to changing pitch can be observed as follows: the low sounds get resonance from the chest

and lower throat (pharynx); the lower-middle part of the range is amplified from the back wall of the throat up through the soft palate, the teeth,
the jawbone, and the hard palate; moving upward through the middle voice,
resonance comes in from the mid-sinuses, the cheekbones, the nose; finally,
the upper-middle and high voice resonate in the upper sinuses above the
nose, and in the skull. All the pitches and resonance spill into one another's
precincts, creating harmonics and overtones.

The final stage of vocal communication, Step 6, shows the stream of
vibrations, flowing unimpeded through richly resonating chambers and out
through the mouth, being formed into words. There are ten general areas
of articulation in the mouth: two lips, the tip of the tongue, the teeth, the
front or blade of the tongue, the upper gum ridge, the middle of the tongue,
the roof of the mouth, the back of the tongue, and the back of the hard
palate, which can include activity in the soft palate. Consonants are formed
when two articulating surfaces meet, or almost meet, interrupting or modi-
fying the flow of breath or sound. Vowels are formed as the lips and tongue
move to mold the flow of vibrations into different shapes. It is the economy
with which words are formed that creates the accuracy with which they
realize thought.

■ AN IDEAL COMMUNICATION

In order to demonstrate how this sophisticated musical instrument becomes human in its response to the impulse to communicate, I would like to posit an idea of how the natural voice would ideally function to communicate the thoughts and a continuum of feelings of a hypothetical human being who is uninhibited, open, sensitive, emotionally mature, intelligent, and uncensored.

When such a person is feeling relaxed, warm, comfortable, and content, the muscles are loose, the breathing is undisturbed, and the energies flow easily. If there is an impulse to transmit this state through words, it generates just enough extra energy to send breath gently onto the vocal folds, which, while remaining relatively relaxed, produce a low sound that resonates through the chest and lower pharynx. A change in mood from lazy contentment to positive happiness, or surprise, or impatience, increases the causal energy that then dispatches the breath with greater vigor onto tighter folds, producing a higher frequency of vibrations that ring into the middle resonators of the face. The muscle tissue lining the corridors and caverns of the throat, mouth, and mask simultaneously responds to the mood change and involuntarily tightens and relaxes, helping to tune the resonators to the pitch generated by the increased energy. As excitement grows, the breath becomes still more stimulated and the folds tighten more, producing higher sounds; correspondingly, muscles in the upper pharynx stretch and tone up, the soft palate lifts higher, and the sound is released into the upper sinuses. Finally, if excitement reaches a pitch commonly regarded as hysterical (perhaps because most people are unaccustomed to operating at that level), the pressure on the folds and their responsive tension will send a scream into the head, which is a superb acoustic dome with a bony resilience capable of dealing with the pressure of such a sound.

This pattern of emotional energy and resonating response is, as I have said, hypothetical and too simple to encompass habitually aggressive or habitually passive behavior, defense mechanisms, or neuroses, but it can offer some landmarks in the foggy geography of how we communicate what we feel.

Why the Voice Does
Not Work

THE VOICE IS PREVENTED from responding with ideal spontaneity because that spontaneity depends on reflex action, and most people have lost the ability and, perhaps, the desire to behave reflexively. Except when pushed beyond control by extreme pain, extreme fear, or extreme ecstasy, nearly all reflexive vocal behavior is short-circuited by secondary impulses.

These impulses, in general, are protective, and at best give one time to think. When, however, the secondary impulses are so well developed that they blot out the impact of the primary, or reflex, impulse, a habit has formed. Habits are a necessary part of one's being able to function: some are consciously chosen (what route to take to work every day; a shower in the morning or a bath at night). But most mental and emotional habits ("I never cry," "I always think that . . . ," "I can't sing," "I always cry when they play the national anthem") have been formed unconsciously and by people other than oneself. There is no choice attached to such conditioning. Behavior that is suggested or demanded from outside responds *only* to secondary impulses rather than primary ones. "Stop that screaming or you get no ice cream." "Shut your mouth right now or you'll get a spanking." "Big boys don't cry." "Nice little girls don't shout." "That's not funny; that's rude." Or, in extreme cases, "Take that; that'll teach you." And, "Sssh . . . you mustn't giggle in church, God is looking at you."

Deep in the unconscious mind, the animal instinct to respond emotionally to stimulus is largely conditioned out of us as children. There should, of course, be a balance of instinctual response and conscious control in mature behavior, but much human behavior is unconsciously controlled by habits conditioned in childhood by arbitrary influences, such as parents (or lack of them), teachers, peers, fellow gang members, movie stars, or pop stars. If we come to a point in our lives where we, as actors, want access to the primitive sources of laughter, sorrow, anger, joy, we may find that the emotions themselves have been civilized or brutalized out of us. The nervous system impulses are blocked, rerouted, or crossed with countermanding impulses.

Here now is a simple story that illustrates the idea of primary and secondary impulse conditioning. I call it the "Chocolate-Chip Cookie Story." The story is a very simple emblematic outline of the complex psychophysical development of the voice from birth to adulthood. It differs in detail from individual to individual but is applicable in general to most human beings.

When a baby is born, a battalion of primary impulses is instantly activated to perform the body's essential first job, which is to make the baby live. Life stirs as breath pumps in and out of the baby's lungs, and a myriad other life-giving operations kick into action. That is the first experience—life or death. Breath gives life.

But life is not enough; survival is necessary. The baby's body experiences something deep in the interior of the tiny belly that we might label the Pang. The Pang signals the need for sustenance, without which life will not continue. The Pang in the middle of the belly has a built-in neural union with the baby's breathing mechanism, and the breath that has been experienced as life-giving now becomes the instrument of survival. The Pang simultaneously acts upon the lungs and larynx to produce a wail. The baby produces a cry that is astonishingly powerful for such a small agent. And the crying and wailing continue until heard. Miraculously the wail is translated by those who hear it as a cry for hunger. Warm milk is introduced to the tiny body, and the pain, the contraction, and the Pang dissolve in the comfort and warmth of sustenance. Breath and voice have been deployed in the service of survival. The first experience of the baby's voice is in response to a life-or-death need. Need, Pang, Voice, Response, Survival.

This cardinal experience is repeated countless times in the ensuing months. The baby's organism is imprinted with the experience delivered by its primary impulses: the Pang, the wail, the milk, and the comfort are all necessary for survival. The baby's organism has learned a fundamental lesson of communication, which is that it must communicate if it is to survive and that communication begins with the Pang. This is a life-or-death lesson. Wailing works!

We can see that from this first simple physical pang of hunger and the contrasting warmth and contentment that come when the pang is removed, the roots of all later emotional feelings, from sadness, anger, and fear to happiness, joy, and love, are formed.

This first conditioning works well for the baby's survival. Lessons are also absorbed that modify the primary impulse response mechanism but the impulse has, by and large, remained the engine of the child's life. But then comes a major new phase.

Imagine the little girl or boy at two to three years old. Many words have been acquired. Many of these words are attached to food—a subject of primary interest. But the Pang still rules. Imagine the three-year-old playing with his or her toys late one afternoon while Mom or Dad or caregiver is in the kitchen preparing supper. The child feels a life-or-death *need* for a chocolate-chip cookie. The child runs into the kitchen with all the force of the Pang fueling his or her body and voice. *"I want a chocolate-chip cookie! Gimme a chocolate-chip cookie! Chocolate-chip cookie! Chocolate-chip cookie!"*

As can easily be imagined, Mom or Dad or caregiver may not respond positively to this onslaught. The reaction is likely to be some variation on, "Stop that horrible noise. You will certainly *not* get a chocolate-chip cookie. Not until you learn to ask nicely. When you stop screaming and say 'please' and 'thank you' in a nice voice then perhaps you can have a cookie."

Unfortunately this phase in learning new rules of communication may continue for some time and may include physical punishment. But the new lesson learned by the child's organism is that to follow the Pang can lead not to life and survival but to the equivalent of death. The small child's body-mind ecosystem is exquisitely sensitive, and in its earliest years it experiences everything on the level of life or death. In order to continue to survive, the organism will learn, sometimes immediately, how to deploy a secondary set of neurophysiological impulses that bypass the primary ones. Communication is still the goal because communication is still necessary for survival, but instinctively the organism now knows that the Pang must be bypassed. The Pang and its primary impulse route have proved ineffective, even dangerous. Communicate the Pang and you might die.

Perhaps it is as soon as the next day that the little boy or girl is playing in the late afternoon and again feels a life-or-death *need* for a chocolate-chip cookie. The child is quick to recall the previous day's lesson. The Pang is suppressed; breath is detached from the Pang-center. The *need*, together with some breath found in the upper part of the lungs well away from the dangerous Pang-center, is rerouted to a set of muscles above the throat. A little smile emerges, lips and tongue and jaw pick up the *need*, the voice no longer resonates throughout the body with the reverberation of a fight for life but flows nicely and inoffensively up into the cheeks and head. The child walks carefully into the kitchen and says in light, high tones of beguiling sweetness, "If I'm a very, very good little boy or girl and say pretty please with sugar on it, can I have a chocolate-chip cookie, dear Mommy or Daddy or caregiver? Please, pretty please?" And Mommy or Daddy or caregiver says, "What a good little boy or girl you are. You've learned how to speak nicely. Here are two chocolate-chip cookies!"

The child's organism has learned the next major lesson in communication: follow secondary neurophysiological impulse routes in order to survive.

This crude outline shows in almost allegorical form "why the voice does not work." *How* we learn to unhook from the brilliance of how the voice works to the less direct and consequently less truthful mechanisms of a voice running on secondary impulse pathways is particular to each person and is infinitely varied, but the skeleton of "The Chocolate-Chip Cookie Story" may be faintly discernible behind the psychophysical biography of a majority of those who seek to improve their relationship with their voices.

Secondary impulse conditioning continues throughout the formative years and results in a habitual mode of communication that may seem to be fine for the person one becomes.

In Step 1 of How the Voice Works, I give an example illustrating "the need to communicate," but even that need cannot be taken for granted. By adulthood the ability to receive a stimulus may be impaired to the point that an exchange of greetings is a one-way trade. Assuming it does occur, however, responding to "good morning" may be subject to secondary impulses such as "Why is he talking to me? He doesn't usually say a word." Or "What's that funny bruise on her forehead?" Or "I know, you're going to ask me to sign a petition," etc. This interrupts the voyage of electrical impulse to breathing and laryngeal musculature, and sends a second electrical impulse that tells the breathing muscles to hold tight so that they will not react spontaneously. The breathing muscles fail to deliver the natural fuel of breath to the vocal folds, but the necessity of replying remains, so a little breath is found under the collarbone, just enough to activate vibration, while the muscles of the throat, jaw, lips, and tongue work twice as hard to compensate for the lack of breath power. The resultant tone is thin, and the message it carries is noncommittal. That is one way, out of a thousand more subtle ones, of avoiding a spontaneous response, and acts as an illustration of how Steps 2, 3, and 4 in How the Voice Works can be subverted by secondary impulses.

It is not that spontaneity is right and calculation is wrong, but that spontaneity should be possible and seldom is. Defensive neuromuscular programming develops habits of mind and muscle that cut us off from the instinctual connection between emotion and breath. The voice cannot work to its true potential if its basic energy is not free breath. As long as we are emotionally protective our breathing cannot be free. As long as breath is not free the voice will depend on compensating strength in the throat and mouth muscles. When these muscles try to convey strong feelings, a number of possible results can occur: they find a safe, musical way to describe emotion; they drive sound monotonously up into the head; or they tense, contract, push, and squeeze with so much effort that the vocal folds rub together. Then the folds become inflamed, lose their resilience, become unable to produce regular vibrations, and, finally, grow little lumps on them as they grind together without the lubrication of breath. Then all that is heard is a gritty, hoarse sound and, ultimately, nothing.

The same inhibitory messages that confuse Steps 1 to 4 also interfere with Step 5 in which "the vibrations are amplified by resonators."

There are some constructive interferences that create harmonics and enrich the sound with complexities, but before these can be relied on, the interferences that restrict range and resonance must be removed. Usually these interferences occur when breathing is restricted. If the throat is tense with effort, it constricts the channel through which sound travels. Most commonly this constriction prevents the vibrations from traveling freely down into the lower resonating chambers of the pharynx and chest, diverting amplification to the middle and upper resonators. The result is a light, high, or strident tone. Sometimes throat tension, coupled with an unconscious need to sound manly or in control, can push the larynx down so that the sound only resonates in the lower cavities, and a monotonously rich, deep voice is developed that cannot find nuance and varied inflection from the upper part of the range. If the soft palate and back of the tongue have joined the battalion of substitutes for breath, they may bunch together with muscular effort and drive the voice up into the nose rather than allow it free passage between them into the mouth. The nasal resonator is powerful, dominating, and unsubtle. If the voice settles in the nose, the speaker will be heard, but what is heard may not be what is intended. Nuance is ironed out, and a variety of thought cannot find free play through a corresponding variety of resonating qualities. Content is distorted by the one resonating form available.

These are three of the most obvious distorted reactions in the resonators that can occur when the voice is inhibited by habitual tensions. More subtly, the whole tuning apparatus is subject to any inhibitory messages sent from the mind that tighten the body. If the breathing muscles tense, so does the muscle tissue lining the pharynx. As those tiny muscles tighten in response to inhibitory messages, they can no longer perform their subtle movements, tightening and releasing in response to the constantly changing pitches of thought inflection, regulating the aperture through which sound flows and amplifying its changing pitches. Such muscle tension diminishes the ability of the voice to be inflected directly by thought. Voice inflections can also be manipulated by what one hears and with conscious muscular control, but as one's manipulative skill increases, so does the distance from the truth.

By the time we look at Step 6, "The resultant sound is articulated by the lips and tongue to form words," it may seem that everything has gone so far wrong that true communication is impossible. The breath and resonators have fallen victim to tension, and the compensating lips and tongue are being asked to compensate for so many duties that their simple articulative ability is buried under this newfound burden. If the tongue is not relaxed while basic sound is being formed, it cannot easily perform its natural function, which is to mold that sound. The tongue is attached to the larynx (by the hyoid bone), and the larynx communicates directly with the diaphragm through the trachea. Tension in one of these three areas causes tension in the other two. As long as there is tension in the tongue it will articulate with more effort than necessary, thereby diminishing its sensitivity of response to motor impulses from the speech cortex.

The tongue is intimately connected with the inner workings of the vocal apparatus, while the lips reflect a slightly different aspect of those inhibitions. They are part of the complex facial musculature that responds to inhibitory messages from the mind by drawing a curtain across the window of the face. The face can be the most or the least revealing part of the body. Some faces harden into impassive masks behind which their owners can calculate, plan, and maintain invulnerability; others assume the mask of appeasement—the muscles of a cajoling smile gradually programming a permanent upward slant; others have fallen into such heavy dejection that a moment of optimism can hardly lift the corners of the mouth. It is perfectly normal for facial posture to reveal the emphatic parts of a personality formed in the course of forty or fifty years. But in the early years those muscles can be prevented from prematurely setting by allowing them to pick up the complexities of changing moods and responses. Muscles of the face, like all the muscles of the body, become flaccid or stiff without exercise. For this natural exercise to happen, though, people must want to reveal themselves, be unafraid of such openness of countenance, and believe that vulnerability in communication is strength.

The lips, as guardians of the mouth, can either develop into heavily armed portcullises or into well-oiled doors that open easily. The stiff upper lip is no mere symbol of British phlegm; it exists and seems to stiffen in response to a determined need not to show fear or doubt. It can also stiffen to hide bad teeth or a smile that its owner thought unattractive in formative years. The freedom of the top lip is essential to lively articulation. Articulating responsibility should be equally divided between the top lip and the bottom lip to achieve maximum efficiency. If the top lip is stiff, the bottom lip will be doing at least eighty-five percent of the work and will probably enlist the jaw as extra support. The jaw is clumsy compared to a lip, and articulation will not be economical in such a situation.

It would take a whole book to chart the deviations the voice can take to prevent its owner from being known. There are voices that have grown expert in proclaiming a hard, aggressive go-getter in order to shield a frightened, insecure little boy; voices that sigh out wispily to disguise the strength of a woman who unconsciously knows that in a man's world she must pretend weakness to achieve; voices that are rich and relaxed and deep, signaling confidence and accomplishment where there are none; voices that ring with a haughtiness that hides panic. The false voice can be tuned to exquisite duplicity.

This introductory description, however, is intended only as a preamble to a positive book, dedicated to the voice that will transparently reveal the truth about its owner, if the owner so wishes.

In case you feel that I have presented a daunting prospect of work, I would like to emphasize, now and continually, that clear thinking and free emotional expression help tremendously in solving the problems. A psycho-physical approach is a perfect example of the conundrum, "Which came first, the chicken or the egg?" but the following two maxims should underlie all work on the voice:

- Blocked emotions are the fundamental obstacle to a free voice.

- Muddy thinking is the fundamental obstacle to clear articulation.

Preparation for the Work

You are embarking on quite a lengthy journey of voice discovery that will appeal to all your senses and heighten your consciousness of who you are and how you function.

Work on the voice is initially subjective, self-examining, and somewhat introverted. I recommend that you keep a journal in which you record your reactions to the exercises you experience. You may be working alone with this book, with a friend, in a group, in private with a teacher, or in a class with a teacher. In every case you are searching for your own free voice that will easily express your true thoughts and feelings or those of the character you are playing.

Get into the habit of writing down your impressions of breath, voice, and body.

Expand your vocabulary of voice to include physical, emotional, and sensual reactions of all your senses, not just your hearing.

You may be depending consciously or unconsciously on hearing to judge the effectiveness of your voice. In order to open your voice up to the assessment of one of your other senses, I initially suggest that you try to see your voice imaginatively before beginning the technical work.

Get a set of crayons and some drawing paper.

(1.)   Draw a picture entitled,
       "My Voice As It Is Now."
       (Before you put crayon to paper, close your eyes and take a minute to invite the picture into your mind's eye).
(2.)   Now draw another picture entitled,
       "My Voice As I Would Like It To Be."

(3.) Draw the outline of a doughboy or gingerbread man. Inside the body, color, impressionistically or figuratively, whatever you see as the problems that prevent your voice from being the voice you would like it to be.

Look at the pictures and make lists of words that are suggested by each picture. The words that occur may come from the language of form and shape, or color, or texture, or emotions, or psychology.

From these words quickly write, without much thought, a poem entitled, "A Poem To My Voice."

Let the feelings that came as you wrote your poem and the language that sprang out of the pictures expand the way you relate to your voice as you begin to work on it.

To a certain degree you have, with these pictures, become your own authority on the state of your voice, what is wrong with it and what you need to work on to allow its full potential to emerge.

Now—you can start a detailed examination of your voice as your own authority. Maintain your journal with your expanded vocabulary and with any other pictures, colors, or abstract shapes that help develop your connection of imagination with voice.

With each new phase of work I will suggest both the amount of time it might take to learn an exercise and the length of time you should practice and absorb it before moving on to the next one. For example: one hour to learn an exercise followed by one week to practice it.

These times are offered as a guide and will undoubtedly need to be adapted to each person.

In my plan, each new phase will begin on a new workday and the full progression of exercises will take from twenty to thirty days to learn. When you add the practice weeks to the learning hours you will find that it takes between six months and a year to acquire the information and absorb the experience before you begin to own and understand this method of work. Your voice will develop according to how disciplined you are.

Part One

The Touch of Sound

The First Four Weeks of Work
Physical Awareness, Relaxation, and Freeing

The exercises throughout are presented with a timetable that suggests the length of time necessary to learn each new exercise, the amount of time it takes to practice the exercise, and the amount of time it may take to cover all the exercises. These are suggestions only. Each student or teacher will work at his or her own pace. The serious student may expect permanent vocal improvement after six months to a year of work.

Audio examples for many of the voice exercises throughout this book can be heard online at: www.kristinlinklater.com.

Click on AUDIO.

1

Workday One

Physical Awareness: The spine
The support of natural breathing . . . a tree

■ Prepare to work for:
ONE HOUR

The first step toward freeing the natural voice is to develop an ability to perceive habits and register new experiences. Such an ability must be both mental and physical, and the perception must eventually be refined to extreme subtlety in order to observe the minutiae of neuromuscular behavior that serve the need to communicate. It is fruitless to expect such subtlety when you begin to work, since few people have an immediate capacity for fine psychophysical awareness: you must take carefully graded steps to arrive at a state that you can trust to feed back reliable information. We will begin with relatively large, simple images and exercises before progressing toward the subtle economy with which the natural voice works best.

The first exercise will be useless if you read quickly though the instructions and realize that the resultant movements are to stretch and drop the spine down. It is a familiar exercise, and can be done quite mechanically, achieving some superficial release through the large external muscles of the body. But it is the process by which the stretching and dropping down are arrived at that constitutes the exercise. It is generally true in all the exercises that follow, that it is not what you are doing that is important, but how you are doing it. The conscious mind has an alarming capacity for subverting new experiences, either confusing them with things that are familiar and safe, or leaping ahead to the result and by-passing the process. For instance, to greet the sense of deep relaxation with the comment, "This is how I feel just before I go to sleep at night," reinforces the familiar equation of sleep and relaxation, successfully precluding a new possibility: that of relaxation generating energy. The overall aim of the work on the spine is to develop physical awareness through specific relaxation. As knots of tension undo, they release trapped energy into the body, creating a lively state of awareness and potential mobility.

More specifically, you will find that the efficiency of the vocal apparatus depends on the alignment of the body and the economy with which it functions. When the spine is out of alignment, its ability to support the body is diminished and muscles intended for other uses must provide that support. If the lower spine is weak, the abdominal muscles supply substitute strength for the torso; if the abdominal muscles are employed in holding up the body, they are not free to respond to breathing needs. Similarly, if the upper part of the spine abandons its job of carrying the rib cage and shoulder girdle, the rib muscles may take on the responsibility of holding the chest high, in which case they are unavailable for intercostal breathing. Finally, when the vertebrae of the neck are not well aligned, the whole channel through which the voice travels is distorted. With a weak neck, the jaw muscles, tongue muscles, laryngeal muscles, even lips and eyebrows become supporters of the head, leaving little chance for a free passage for sound. A strong, flexible, and well-aligned spine, then, is the essential starting-point for free breathing and a free voice.

Moshe Feldenkrais, whose work on psychophysical reeducation has become part of many actor-training programs, says in his invaluable book *Awareness Through Movement*:

> Any posture is acceptable in itself as long as it does not conflict with the law of nature, which is that the skeletal structure should counteract the pull of gravity, leaving the muscles free for movement. The nervous system and the frame develop together under the influence of gravity in such a way that the skeleton will hold up the body without expending energy despite the pull of gravity. If, on the other hand, the muscles have to carry out the job of the skeleton, not only do they use energy needlessly, but they are prevented from carrying out their main function of changing the position of the body, that is, of movement.

The first step, then, in freeing the voice, is *getting acquainted with your spine* and with your skeleton. The more you can imagine the following movements in terms of the skeleton, the more economically the muscles will work. Talk to your bones.

Much of this work asks you to close your eyes as you clarify the picture of the inner workings of your body. When this is the case I suggest that you tape the instructions and play them as your guide. Otherwise, read ahead and memorize the instructions.

STEP 1   Stand easily with your feet six to eight inches apart. Be aware of your weight evenly distributed over both feet; be aware that the weight of your body is balanced equally between the balls of your feet and your heels.

- In your mind's eye, picture the bones of your feet.

- Picture the shinbones growing up from your ankle joints.

- Picture your thighbones growing up from your knee joints.

- Picture your hip joints and the pelvic girdle.

- See the sacrum—the large bone in the middle of the back of the pelvis—at the base of your spine.

- Picture your spine growing up from the sacrum, through the small of your back, then on up between your shoulder blades, with the rib cage floating around it and the shoulder girdle on top.

- Feel your arms hanging from the shoulder sockets.

- Picture your upper arm bones, elbow joints, forearms, wrist joints, and bones of your hands and fingers.

- Let your mind's eye flow back up through your arms and into your neck.

- Picture your neck vertebrae going up into the skull.

- Picture the topmost vertebra on a level with your ears and your nose.

- Picture your skull floating, like a balloon, off the top of the spine.

STEP 2   Focus your attention into your elbow joints; rotate them forward and let them float gently up in front of your body toward the ceiling. This should involve your upper arms only, the shoulder muscles stay relaxed, the forearm muscles are relaxed, the hands hang loosely.

Focus your attention on your wrists, and let them float toward the ceiling. Leave your hands hanging.

Focus your attention on your fingertips and let them float to the ceiling.

- Imagine that someone is pulling you up a little by your fingertips, and allow your ribs to be stretched from above, up out of your waist; leave your pelvic girdle, legs, and feet out of the stretch.

Now do one thing and one thing only: allow your hands to relax until they hang from your wrists.

relaxation

←tension

- Register the contrasting sensations in your hands and in your arms. Label the sensation in your hands "relaxation," and the sensation in your arms "tension."

Now let your forearms relax until they hang loose from your elbows.

- Register the contrasting sensations in your forearms and hands, and in your upper arms and shoulders. Label the sensation in your forearms and hands as "relaxation," and the sensation in your upper arms as "tension."

Now let your upper arms drop heavily and hang loosely from your shoulders.

- Register the weight of your arms, the blood running back into your hands, and the change in temperature. Label the sensation in your arms "relaxation." Feel the force of gravity adding weight to your arms.

Now let the weight of your head drop heavily forward so that your head and neck hang off the top of your torso.

Feel the weight of your head dragging on the big vertebra that connects the neck-spine to the body-spine—sometimes called the "bull" vertebra. Gradually give in to the weight of your head, allowing the bull vertebra to drag the shoulder girdle with it. Then let the weight of your head, shoulders, and arms draw the spine slowly down toward the ground, giving in to gravity, vertebra by vertebra, through the rib cage to the small of your back. Try to picture the vertebrae one by one.

- Let your knees relax so that your weight remains over the middle of your feet. Check that you do not rock back on your heels or forward on your toes. Check that your knees do not lock. When the weight is too much to support, release the lower spine quickly and hang upside down.

- Picture your torso hanging from your tailbone, giving in to the force of gravity.

- Breathe easily. You are doing this to relax all the torso muscles, shoulder muscles, neck muscles, head and arms.

  If your legs begin to hurt in this unaccustomed position, run your hands up the backs of your calves and thighs several times from ankles to buttocks, stroking away excess tension.

Now focus your attention on your tailbone and, from there, begin to build your spine up again, vertebra by vertebra, as though building a castle of nursery blocks one on top of the other.

  Talk to your bones. See your skeleton.

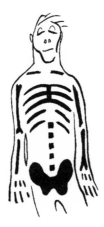

- Do not use your stomach muscles; leave them hanging loose; breathe. Relax your shoulder muscles.

- Do not suddenly straighten your knees; let them gradually straighten without stiffening as your balance shifts.

- Find the vertebrae that carry your rib cage and build them up from the small of your back to the bull vertebra.

  You are now an upright, headless torso. Picture your neck spine hanging forward at a right angle to your body spine.

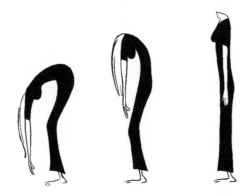

- Focus on the top seven vertebrae that make up the neck and gradually bring them back up until they are in alignment with the rest of your spine. Be aware that your head is floating up as a result of your neck coming up. You do not need to lift your head.

STEP 3   With your eyes closed, run your mind's eye down from your head to your feet and then let it travel up from your feet, up through your legs, to your torso. Consciously relax any muscles that begin to tighten in the stomach, buttocks, shoulders, or neck. You are actively transferring the energy needed to remain upright from the large, external muscles of the body, to an internal picture of the spine constantly growing upward against the force of gravity. Think of the spine as a stream of upward-moving energy that is fueled by the mind. It is as though the spine were a tree, growing up from roots in the sacrum, the legs, and the feet, with its branches springing out to become the rib cage.

Be aware of the shape your body cuts in the air.

Be aware of the feeling of air touching your skin.

Open your eyes and walk around the room, noticing that it is your skeleton that is walking.

Stand still again and, closing your eyes, turn your attention inward and become aware of your body from the inside. Spread the relaxation from outside muscles to inside muscles. With your body-mind's eye, look at your face from inside and relax the face muscles; look down through your throat seeing it as an empty, open column; look down through the lungs inside your rib cage; see the diaphragm as the floor to the lungs and the ceiling to the stomach; look down from the diaphragm to the pelvic floor, and on down through your legs to where your feet are planted on the floor.

Let your body-mind's eye travel once more from the bones of your feet up through the skeleton to your skull and then back to your spine.

Stand quietly for one or two minutes being aware of your spine supporting the skeleton that floats between your skull and the bones of your feet while the muscles and flesh of your body hang loosely on your bones.

Stretch, yawn, open your eyes, and shake your body all over.

This exercise is the first in a long series designed to transfer the message systems that run from brain to body, from large external muscles to fine internal ones. The natural voice is run on the involuntary nervous system through involuntary musculature. Taking a simplified look at the muscle systems of the body, we can see them organized into two to five layers ranging from the large outside muscles that we can consciously control to the innermost layer of muscles contiguous with the skeleton, which are under the control of the involuntary nervous system. The innermost layer of muscles may be pictured closest to the bones and the organs. These muscles are not under voluntary control. They are "proprioceptive" muscles: they "see themselves," and they operate under their own perception. They can, however, be influenced through imagery and emotion.

■ **COMMENTARY**

The best actors, and perhaps this can be said for the best performing artists in general (musicians, dancers, singers), are relaxed in performance. That is, they have no extraneous tension. Their muscles are ready to receive the impulses necessary to fulfill action and will ripple with energies in the service of particular stimuli. When the impulse has been expressed, the muscles release and ready themselves for the next job. Tense, muscular performances may generate external excitement but seldom arouse profound emotional response in an audience. "Maximum effect with minimum effort" is the hallmark of great art. Great art is rooted in truth. Minimum effort demands a commitment to inner processes of imagination and emotion that stimulate the body and voice to truthful expression from the inside out. The body and voice will reveal large and small truths most authentically with a certain effortless ease, even in extremity.

In order to develop a voice that will create maximum effect with minimum effort and therefore be truthful, actors must exercise the vocal musculature in a way that conditions the voice to respond to imaginative and emotional stimulus. In the preceding and subsequent exercises we are beginning to do just that. Very simply, we are beginning to replace an unconscious and inaccurate picture of how the voice works with a conscious one that is both anatomically more accurate and economical, and is trained to respond to thought-feeling impulses.

STEP 4   In this step you will be asked to reenter the experience of Step 3 but to make new observations. It is good to do this sequence with your eyes closed, so if you are working on your own, read or record the following instructions before starting.

> Standing easily, with a sense of your spine moving up to support your torso, close your eyes again. With the purpose of relaxing the inner muscles of your body, allow your body-mind's eye to travel from inside the top of your skull down the inside of your face, relaxing the outer mask that your face muscles present to the world, down through your throat, down through your chest. Notice the tiny, inevitable movements of your breathing as you move your mind down into your stomach, down through your intestines and lower stomach into the pelvic floor. Undo any tension you are holding inside. Maintain a clear image of your spine moving upward as you relax the muscles around it or you will collapse.

Allow the whole of the inside of the torso to be available to the movement of your breath.

- Observe the reaction of the inside of your body to the involuntary movements of your breathing apparatus.

- Then, deep inside, feel the need to yawn and stretch; slowly and luxuriously yield to that need.

- Yawn, stretch, and shake out your body as though you just got up in the morning or as a dog yawns, stretches, and shakes its skin back into place.

- Register how your body feels; register how you feel.

In the course of these initial exercises you will have made conscious decisions about how your physical energy is to be deployed. If you have followed the process in detail, both mentally and physically, you will have momentarily dislodged a few habitual muscle responses. You should have experienced the contrasting sensations of relaxation and tension in the parts of your body that are relatively easy to contact. This experience is the basis for developing the ability to notice tensions in more inaccessible parts of the body (such as the back of the tongue, the center of the diaphragm, and the upper lip) and to be able to release them.

The ability to relax must be cultivated slowly and with specific intent, otherwise it can degenerate into the state of general collapse that Jerzy Grotowski rightly disparaged: "One cannot be completely relaxed as is taught in many theatre schools, for he who is totally relaxed is nothing more than a wet rag." There is, however, a vital difference between relaxing for the sake of relaxation, which inevitably includes mental collapse, and relaxing in order to accomplish something. Our aim is to remove unnecessary habitual tensions so that the muscles are free to respond to impulse without the short-circuiting created by habit.

PRACTICE

Stretch and relax your spine every morning for the next two or three days. Be aware of the preceding details and become aware of your skeletal behavior and the contrasting tension and relaxation you feel throughout the day.

2

Workday Two

Breathing Awareness: Freeing the breath,
the source of sound . . . the air

■ Prepare to work for:
45 MINUTES TO ONE HOUR

You cannot live without breathing—without air. Your breath is the source of your life as well as the source of your vocal sound. Your breathing habits have developed as you developed into the character you are now. The profound goal of the serious actor is to transform into other characters in performance. This entails transforming ways of behaving, ways of thinking, ways of feeling, ways of breathing that are true to the behavior, thoughts, feelings, and breathing of the character you are creating. As long as the actor's breathing patterns are inflexibly held in habitual muscle usage, the hoped-for transformation will only be skin deep. To enter and live the life of a different character, one must be able to let go of deeply ingrained breathing patterns and temporarily allow new behavior from the psyche of the character one is playing to govern the breathing musculature. The events that happen to the dramatic character must be experienced in the breathing process if that character is to be believed and his or her voice is to be authentic.

What follows is a guide to the psychophysical geography of breathing. You will not find rules for correct breathing. There is no one way to breathe that is correct for all purposes. Breathing can be organized to support differing demands: the demands made on a swimmer's lungs are different from those made on the lungs of an opera singer or a Yoga devotee. The breathing processes developed by swimmers, opera singers, and Yoga practitioners are of no use to the actor. I realize that this may initially seem a controversial idea, but you do not have to believe me in order to continue. I would like you, however, to think about purpose as you explore your breathing. The purposes of opera singing, professional swimming, or serious Yoga practice demand the development of breathing control, partly so that random impulses, particularly random emotional impulses, do not upset the necessary breathing rhythms determined by the activity at hand. The purpose of acting requires the consciously crafted pursuit of spontaneity. The actor's breathing musculature must be able to pick up rapidly shifting thoughts and feelings engendered by an imaginatively created state of being. For the actor who values truthful expression, breathing control must be diverted from muscle to impulse. The ultimate controls are imagination and emotion.

The next steps should be undertaken in an open-minded state of pleasurable expectation. Take each step slowly, for its own sake, and allow yourself to be entertained by your experience. Do not be goal oriented.

Having reached a state of some awareness and relaxation through an initial exploration of the spine, you are now ready to begin to explore the breathing process. The complexities of the breathing machinery are such that it is wise not to jump to any conclusions about how it works at this juncture. Instead, begin to develop the ability to *observe without controlling*. The aim is to remove habitual muscular controls and allow your involuntary processes to take over. It is quite possible for the conscious mind to become aware of the function of the involuntary nervous system without interfering, but it may be an unfamiliar activity. The tendency may be to observe, correctly, that when you breathe in, your stomach moves out, and when you breathe out your stomach goes in, and to use that observation to start controlling your breath with your stomach muscles. You might start to pull your stomach in, which blows the breath out, and to push your stomach out, which draws the breath in. This is a misuse of perception.

The involuntary breathing muscles are subtle, complex, powerful, and deep inside your body. Any voluntary controls that you apply will involve muscles that are large, clumsy, external, and at several removes from the lungs. Conscious control of the breath will destroy its sensitivity to changing inner states and severely curtail the reflex connection between breathing and emotional impulse. It is worth repeating here the warning that you cannot imitate a reflex action. Natural breathing is reflexive, and to restore its reflexive potential, the only work you can do is to remove restrictive tensions and provide a diversity of stimuli. These stimuli can provoke subtler, deeper, and eventually stronger reflex actions than are normally exercised in habit-run daily lives. Your breathing muscles will soon become responsive instruments of the art of speaking.

It is a good idea to start the observation of your breathing in a standing position so that later you may benefit by contrasting this observation with that of sitting or lying down.

STEP 1   Repeat the physical awareness spine exercises. Rediscover the tree that supports you, its roots and branches.

STEP 2   Stand easily with a long spine and relaxed muscles and allow your awareness to move inward and down so that your focus rests deep inside the center of your body.

■ Tune in to the small movements that are happening as breath enters and leaves your body.

■ Allow your involuntary breathing rhythm to tell you what it is.

■ Let your breath tell you what it wants from you.

The breaths that keep you alive from one moment to the next— in, out, in, out—are small.

■ Consciously, all you can do is keep releasing tension from your stomach area, your shoulders, and lower belly; be aware of the breath moving your body, rather than your body moving the breath. Remember that your natural breathing rhythm may not be your familiar breathing rhythm.

Explore the following description of the breathing process:

■ The outgoing breath is complete inner relaxation.

■ The incoming breath will happen automatically if you wait.

STEP 3

■ Let the breath release out of you.

- Wait—but don't hold your muscles—until you feel the need for a new breath.

- Yield to the need.

Let the breath be replaced—do not actively "breathe in."

- Let the breath release again.

- Relax into a small internal pause.

- As soon as you feel, deep inside, the tiny impulse of need, give in to it, and allow the new breath in.

- Repeat the mental processes of Step 3, observing, but not controlling, the reflex actions deep inside your body:

- Let the breath release out

     Wait, without holding your breath

- Allow the breath in

- Immediately let the breath out

     Wait with your muscles completely relaxed

- Allow the breath in

- Immediately release the breath out

     Wait

- Allow the breath in . . . etc.

- Continue with this observation for two or three minutes.

■ COMMENTARY

On a tiny scale, these breaths are very central and are sufficient to keep you alive from one moment to the next. The more relaxed you are, the smaller the exchange of oxygen necessary to sustain you. It is worth noting that in deep meditation, breathing slows down radically and sometimes is barely perceptible. Anxiety and tension either speed up the breathing rate or slow it down laboriously, or dictate a longer, heavier exchange.

Everyday, relaxed, normal breathing has a more or less universal rhythm and universal pace. That is, everyone breathes in almost the same rhythm as everyone else once habitual tensions have dissolved and involuntary processes are re-established. One outgoing breath to the next takes about four seconds. Of course the basic rhythm is there only to be disturbed by changing needs, so that you will probably find that after observing your natural rhythm of breathing for a minute or two you will be taken by an irresistible need to sigh or yawn, which will radically alter the rhythm. But it is extremely important to be able to return at will to your relaxed natural breathing rhythm in full awareness. (The rhythms of breathing when we are asleep are not a reliable guide to relaxed breathing. Not only are the breathing muscles responding to a slowed down metabolism, but if you observe the breathing of an adult asleep you will probably notice irregular rhythms that reflect the stress we often process when we sleep. A baby's breathing, on the other hand, can teach us a lot.)

STEP 4

■ Continue the breathing awareness from Step 3, adding an awareness of whether you are breathing through your mouth or your nose. If through the latter, let your mouth drop open so that you are breathing through your mouth, not through your nose. Don't open wide, just open enough to allow the breath to pass through.

If your mouth is relaxed, the outgoing breath should automatically arrive in a small "fff" somewhere between the top teeth and the lower lip or directly between the two lips.

- Lick your lips and feel the cool incoming air passing over them and then feel the warmth of the outgoing air. The warm outgoing breath will pass through your wet lips forming a loose "fff."

Don't make a "fff" sound; let the sound be the natural by-product of the release of breath and the relaxed position of the mouth.

Depending on the individual mouth, the "fff" may occur between the two lips or the top teeth and the lower lip; the important point is that with the small "fff" you begin to program your breath to release from the center of your body to pass through the front of the mouth, which is what happens with a free sound. All breathing awareness exercises are blueprints for sound; it is essential therefore that all breathing exercises should be done with the mouth open as it is when speaking. In repose, or when walking in the street, it is aesthetically and hygienically practical to breathe through the nose, which serves to clean, filter, and moisten the air on its long, relatively slow passage to the lungs. For speaking, the breath must be able to respond quickly to fast-changing impulses, and a direct, open passage through the mouth is clearly needed. If you open your mouth too wide, however, the breath will make its impact most obviously in your throat rather than the front of your mouth, and you will hear "hhhhh" rather than "fffff." By opening your mouth too wide you are programming a route for sound that emphasizes the throat and will not be free. Let me say that, for actors, nasal breathing is utterly counterproductive to truthful speaking.

In practicing the breathing awareness exercises, it is necessary to realize the difference between saying "the breath should be in the front of the mouth, so I will put it there," and "the breath will arrive in the front of the mouth if it is released freely from inside and there is no tension on the way out that holds it back." It is necessary to condition the mind to be primarily interested in the causal, release point and merely observe the resultant, arrival point.

STEP 5

- Continue the awareness of your natural breathing rhythm. Now picture the diaphragm moving upward as the breath releases out and falling downward as the breath drops in. Your diaphragm is a large, domed muscle that forms the floor to your lungs and the ceiling to your stomach and intestines. Its edges are attached to the bottom of your rib cage. You cannot tell the diaphragm how it should move—it is not an active muscle under the control of your conscious mind. But you can influence it by picturing its movements accurately.

- With your mouth just open, allow small "fff"s on each outgoing breath. Feel that your breath and your observing mind are both in the same place—the center of your body. Make sure that you are not split in two, with part of you sitting up in your head, commenting on or controlling what is happening from there. You and your breathing are one and the same thing. When your breath releases, you release. When you and your breath release out, your diaphragm releases upward through your rib cage; when you and your breath are renewed, the diaphragm drops downward, opening the lungs. Both the movement up and the movement down can be experienced as release in the diaphragm.

- Let each outgoing breath contain a feeling of "willing escape." You escape from inside yourself to the outside world. Each incoming breath should be a feeling of welcome renewal. Expiration and inspiration live in the continuous cycle of a natural rhythm of breathing.

- Now feed into your middle the impulse for a gentle "sigh of relief."

  No sound—just breath.

- Observe how your breathing reacts to the stimulus of a simple easy feeling of relief.

- You will find that more breath comes in in response to the impulse and that more breath releases out on a longer "fffffff" as the relief pours out—keep your mouth relaxed.

- Again consciously decide to feel a sigh of relief. Observe the reaction in the involuntary breathing musculature and in the movement of the diaphragm.

Picture your mind (the impulse-dispatcher), your feelings (impulse-receiver), and your breath all in the center of your body.

- Again feed in the impulse for a sigh of relief.

- Feel the relief go deeper inside your body—perhaps as far down as the pelvic floor.

- Release the relief and the breath as one.

- Relax inside. Allow the breath to be replaced.

The pelvic floor is an elastic web of muscles that lies within the ellipse of the pelvic girdle. (There is a connection from the diaphragm to the pelvic floor that will be explained more specifically later.) For now, begin to picture the floor of your torso within your pelvis, about twelve inches below the diaphragm and responsive to breath.

You can affect the breathing musculature, provoke it to greater effort, but do not confuse the consciousness of emotional control through the application of visual and emotional impulses, with conscious muscular control.

■ **THE SIGH OF RELIEF**

Sighing and yawning are organic animal activities that the body initiates when it needs an extra charge of oxygen. Babies, dogs, and cats yawn copiously and without embarrassment many times a day. They also sigh soundlessly when their bodies need more oxygen. Adult humans have largely been educated out of these natural functions. Yawning in public is held to be rude, and sighing tends to serve an emotive purpose. Both can cause embarrassment.

>

If, however, you can now begin to enter the pleasures of yawning and sighing for their own sake, you will revitalize your body and your mind. The life of your body and your mind depends on the circulation of oxygen; they may well have been undersupplied in this essential nutrition and their life underenergized because of habitual tension and inhibition.

In establishing the breathing groundwork for freeing your natural voice, you must be able to differentiate between a "sigh of relief" and a "big breath." A big breath engages the muscle machinery of the body without any feeling content, while a sigh of relief is triggered by a thought-feeling impulse. For the actor who wants a voice that will reveal thoughts and feelings rather than merely describing them, exercising the sigh of relief means exercising the connection between thinking and feeling, breath and voice. The ability to create and re-create causal impulse is part of the actor's art. Creating and re-creating a genuinely felt sigh of relief as the underlying energy for breathing and voice reeducates connection. The repetition of exercises means exercising the ability to create imaginative cause.

Actors are often urged to "let go," to "release" in their work. If, as is most often the case, they have grown up conditioned to "control," it may be impossible to accept the invitation to "release." Deep in their mental processes lies the protective counter-command: "don't let go, don't reveal what you're thinking and feeling—it's dangerous." The primary neural pathways have long since ceded their expressive knowledge to secondary impulses of defense and control.

The sigh of relief is the first key to unlocking the doors to those primal impulse centers and reopening the primary neuro-physiological routes between brain and body. The key is mental but it can be turned by physical means. We cannot assume that when we give ourselves the message "let go" or "release" we can do it. We first have to experience in very simple and incontrovertible ways what "letting go" is really like. The force of gravity is one of the best allies we have for finding out what "letting go" is.

STEP 6 Here is a simple game you can play with your mind, your body, and gravity that may clarify and develop your understanding of the sigh of relief.

- Stand at ease and float one arm up from your side until it makes a straight line out from your shoulder, parallel to the ground, and at right angles to your body.

- Ask yourself the question "What keeps my arm up in the air against the pull of gravity?"

I often spend a long time with my students at this point as they suggest "My muscles," "Nothing," "It just stays there," or "God," but eventually I can convince them that it is the mind that is telling the arm to stay up in the air.

- Now tell yourself, "I'm going to take my mind out of my arm."

Again, after much philosophizing and trial and error in my classes, it becomes apparent that when the mind "lets go" of the arm, the arm drops because of gravity. (Body-mind consciousness keeps us standing upright against the pull of gravity. Unconscious, we fall.)

- Now carefully observe the attributes of that drop. The drop will be sudden, uncontrolled, and the arm will hit the side of your body with some force.

The observation shows that when the mind "lets go" and gravity takes over, energy is released. Your job is now to transfer that experience to the sigh of relief.

- Feed in an impulse for a deep, pleasurable sigh of relief (without sound) that seems to hold in it as much potential energy as your arm floating up against the pull of gravity. If you find a sigh of relief elusive, imagine a situation in which something bad was about to happen, but was averted. Feed the resultant relief deep into your breathing area and feel breath being drawn in.

- Now take your mind out of the breathing area. Breath will release with an equivalent energy to that released when your arm dropped to your side. The sigh HAPPENS as a result of letting go. Its energy sends the diaphragm flying UP through your rib cage.

The energy of the sigh's release depends on the size of the entering impulse. Although gravity is not giving a helping hand to the outgoing sigh, the mental experience gained from your arm's dropping to gravity should directly influence the sigh experience. Gravity can teach your mind how to let go.

- Now float your arm just halfway up toward your shoulder (about fifteen inches, or at a forty-five degree angle).

- Ask yourself the question, "What is keeping my arm up against the force of gravity?"

- The answer is the same: "My mind."

- Take your mind out of your arm.

Your arm will drop suddenly, giving in to gravity; it will hit your side but with only half the force experienced when it dropped from your shouder.

- Transfer this experience to a sigh of relief (no sound, just breath) that is now medium size.

A medium-size impulse of relief enters the body-mind bringing with it a medium-size amount of air, and when it lets go it releases a medium-size gust of air. But it is still a "letting-go." The energy release is still sudden and not controlled by conscious musculature. The diaphragm still flies up—but not so far.

- Finally, float your hand up off your wrist, leaving your arm by your side.

- Ask yourself the question, "What is keeping my hand up against the force of gravity?"

- The answer is the same: "My mind."

- Take your mind out of your hand.

Your hand will drop from your wrist, suddenly, giving in to gravity. It will tap the side of your body with a delicate energy that is free of conscious control.

Transfer this experience to a tiny, central sigh of relief.

However small and interior this breath is, it goes out with the release, relief, or letting go. The energy that is released may be minuscule but it is free. The diaphragm releases upward in a tiny movement from its central point.

The natural rhythm of breathing is free, uncontrolled, and infinitely subtle. This exercise begins reconditioning the body-mind to experience communication as release and communication as a by-product of a need to speak that has the freedom to do so. We begin with a sigh of pleasurable relief—eventually it will be relief even when we are releasing large or painful feelings.

Let gravity be your teacher.

STEP 7 This will all be made easier now by lying flat on your back on the floor and observing the breathing processes in a position where no energy is expended on standing upright. All your attention can go into noticing how breathing works when the body is fully relaxed.

The following exercise clearly needs to be heard rather than read. Tape the guided visualization or have a friend read the instructions —slowly.

■ Lying on your back, let your whole body give in to gravity.

■ Send your mind into the soles of your feet and think of relaxing your toes and feet so that they appear to drop away from your ankles.

- Imagine your ankle joints are filled with air.

- Let your calf muscles relax so that the flesh, skin, and muscle seem to dissolve off the shinbones.

- Imagine your knee joints filled with air.

- Let your thigh muscles relax so that the flesh, skin, and muscle seem to dissolve off the thighbones. Imagine your hip joints and thigh sockets filled with air so that your legs do not seem to be attached to your torso.

- Let your buttock muscles, pelvic muscles, groin, and lower belly muscles dissolve and melt.

- Be aware of your spine giving in to gravity from the tailbone to the skull.

- Let the small of your back relax, but realize that there is a natural curve there—don't try to flatten it out.

- Let the whole stomach area melt, dissolve, relax.

- Picture the area between your shoulder blades spreading away from your spine to either side.

- Imagine the rib bones as soft as the belly: let them give in to gravity and release into breath.

- Picture the torso releasing along and across the floor.

- Imagine your shoulder sockets filled with air, so that your arms seem hardly to be attached to your torso.

- Be aware of the weight of your arms and hands, heavy and abandoned on the floor.

- Be aware of your fingers.

- Let your attention travel back up your arms, through your shoulders, and into your neck.

- Let your neck-spine give in to gravity, but realize there is a natural curve in these top seven vertebrae—don't try to flatten it.

- Let your throat relax.

- Feel the weight of your head on the floor.

- Let the jaw muscles relax right beside your ears so that your teeth are not clenched.

- Let the tongue relax inside the mouth so that it is not clamped to the roof of the mouth.

- Be aware of your face muscles and let them melt so that the skin of your face feels heavy on the bones.

- Let the cheeks relax, and the lips, the forehead, the eyelids.

- Let the scalp muscles relax.

- Now let your attention sweep back down through your whole body, abandoned on the floor.

- Imagine you could melt down through the floor.

- Take a little time to enjoy this sensation.

Now become aware that in the middle of the stillness of your completely relaxed body, there is an inevitable involuntary movement as your breath enters and leaves you.

- Let your mouth drop open. Lick your lips. Feel the cool air being drawn in from outside, traveling down to the center of your torso, and then feel it being released from there, warm, to escape again to the outside.

- Flop a hand onto your breathing area so that you can feel from outside a reflection of what is happening inside. (For the moment I will designate "the breathing area" as the section below the front ribs and above the navel. The part your hand rests on is called the abdominal wall.)

- Notice that on the outgoing breath, the area under your hand falls toward the ground as the abdominal wall drops.

- Now feed a huge, deep sigh of relief (without sound) far down into your body—imagine the relief moving down into your groin, moving the pelvic floor—and then let the feeling and your breath fall out of you with abandon.

- The breathing area now extends below the navel; the lower belly, as well as the abdominal wall, seems to move in response to the sigh.

■ **COMMENTARY**

Here, you are enlisting the aid of gravity to increase the possibility of complete muscular release on the outgoing breath. The whole belly area should be able to drop suddenly, without controls, with much the same quality of release that happens if you lift your arm off the floor and then let it relax completely, giving in suddenly to gravity. You can test your body-mind's willingness to relinquish physical control of breathing by asking it to hand the process over to the pull of gravity. Until you can remove all controls, there is no way of choosing controls when necessary; you are still prey to unconscious habitual controls.

The exercise, therefore, is to:

- Feed in a feeling of relief (causal impulse).

- Let it fly out of you uncensored by controls (resultant communication).

- Observe that a larger, deeper impulse of relief triggers a larger breath experience.

- Now that you're on the floor, observe the movement of the diaphragm in all these impulses as it releases toward your pelvis as the breath enters and as it "whooshes" through the rib cage as the breath releases out.

Observe that the impulse moves the breath and the breath moves the body.

If you think along these lines you are less likely to add extra effort to the economical work performed by the involuntary nervous system.

- Explore varying degrees of strength in the causal impulse feeding into the breathing center—first, the natural breathing rhythm exchanges to a small, contented sigh, then to a larger, grateful sigh, and finally to a huge, deep sigh of relief. Use your imagination to create situations to stimulate appropriately the differing intensities of the sighs.

- Relax back to natural breathing.

STEP 8

- Slowly, with complete physical awareness of your skeletal activity and muscular relaxation, rise from the floor to a standing position. Let your head be the last part of your body to rise.

As you stand upright, see how much you can retain of the physical sensations you experienced while on the floor, for instance:

- Imagine that the floor is still supporting your back.

- Leave your stomach muscles as sloppy as they were when you were lying down.

- Imagine the force of gravity is behind you and let the abdominal wall fall toward it on the outgoing breath.

- Observe the natural rhythm of your breathing.

- Observe any differences between breathing lying down and standing up.

- Observe that the diaphragm now moves vertically rather than horizontally.

- Observe any differences there may be between your breathing now and the last time you were aware of it while standing.

Understand what you are experiencing in terms of change, rather than in terms of right and wrong:

Where, specifically, in your body do you feel movement in response to breath? In your ribs? Back? Sides? Belly? Groin? Internally? Externally?

What feels better than before? What feels worse? How do you feel?

From where is the breath releasing? Where is it going?

Can you feel or picture the diaphragm dropping when the breath enters and then "whooshing" up through the rib cage when the breath releases out?

Do you feel more awake? Do you feel sleepy? Do you feel confused?

Have you found anything new?

I do not have answers to these questions—you do. It is important that each of you keeps asking such questions and keeps answering with a growing knowledge of what is true in your individual, organic experience.

The difficulty in working on oneself is to admit new experiences. Most of us have considerable investment in our conditioning because it has brought us this far and is reasonably reliable and safe. If you ask yourself questions about the new sensations you have experienced and make it an exercise to articulate your answers out loud, you will learn and change twice as fast. As has been pointed out before, the mind is reluctant to embrace deep change, and will play devious games to maintain the status quo. We are dealing with functions that should be automatic, and it takes great determination to change habits programmed at this level. In these exercises the new experiences are on a deeper level of consciousness and when you verbalize the experience, you bring it up to a more familiar level of consciousness, and the new experience becomes reinforced, making a firmer imprint.

Here is a scene often enacted, with variations, in the course of voice classes I have taught; it illustrates some of the ways in which the mind manages to escape change. The pupil has been taken through the work described in this and the previous lesson, and it is visibly evident that the breathing is deeper in the body, freer, and less labored.

ME: How do you feel?
PUPIL: Fine. Good.
ME: What do you feel?
PUPIL: I don't know exactly.
ME: Do you feel any differences?
PUPIL: Not really. I feel dizzy, and a bit nauseous.
ME: What about your breathing? (Silence). Do you notice it affecting any new parts of your body?
PUPIL: Oh, yes. It's much easier.
ME: Where?
PUPIL: Wait a minute; I'll have to think back. Mmmmm-yes- well, I've never felt it in my lower back before. (Or stomach, or legs, it doesn't matter.)
ME: What do you feel happens there now?
PUPIL: Well, it's sort of as though I breathe into my buttocks (Or pelvis, or knees, etc.).
ME: OK, fine.
PUPIL: Is that right?
ME: If that's how you felt it, that's fine for the time being.
PUPIL: But are you supposed to breathe in your ass?

We might then go on to discuss the fact that the lungs only go down as far as the diaphragm, which cuts the body in two horizontally, and that when breath goes in, the diaphragm moves down, pushing the stomach down, which in turn pushes the lower intestines down, so that there are graphic movements in the lower torso in response to breath. These movements are not confined to the front of the body; therefore, the lower spine must be free of tension to allow full use of the breathing apparatus. It lengthens in response to large breathing demands, helping to create the greatest space possible inside the torso into which the lungs can expand and shorten on release. These spine movements are almost imperceptible when standing, but can easily be observed when lying face down.

The important thing in badgering the pupil about what had happened in the course of the exercise was to find even one specific point in the general experience that could be articulated and therefore learned, both organically and consciously. The diversionary tactics employed by the pupil's mind to avoid coping with something new were, roughly, as follows: The first answer, "Fine—good," indicates that he thinks I will be flattered by the success of the exercise and leave him alone. The second response, "I don't know," can be interpreted as "Let me enjoy my subjective experience which is private, personal, and will be spoiled if I talk about it;" this is generally resistant. The third response, which translates to, "I will not admit change for the better; I will concentrate on this rather unpleasant, disoriented, dizzy feeling" is avoidance.

■ COMMENTARY

If you can learn to accept nausea or dizziness when they occur you will find you can embrace the state as a useful disorientation out of which you can explore a new use of yourself. If, however, you are frightened by the experience, you may throw up or faint and, by so doing, you will have successfully escaped a new experience. The release of tension in some extremely nervous people, and the consequent submission of the lungs to the powerful involuntary nervous system, can be such a turnover in the whole state of being that dizziness is a way of life for a time. Once such people have fainted a couple of times, they become familiar with the process and find the moment when they can choose to go with it and pass out or focus on something more interesting such as the exercise at hand. This may sound callous but without such confrontation, significant change and growth can be postponed forever. It should also be emphasized that it is not necessary to faint or throw up in order to liberate your breathing.

It is very natural to feel a bit dizzy on standing up after lying on the floor for some time because of the alteration in the balance mechanism and because, with deep relaxation, more oxygen enters and leaves the body, stimulating circulation and pumping more blood to the heart and the brain, thereby altering the glandular and chemical status quo. Dizziness in this work is nearly always healthy because it demonstrates that something has changed.

In soliciting feedback from my students I try to teach a way of learning that recognizes and tackles a persistent tendency many of us have to be self-denigrating, self-judging, and ultimately more ready to fail than to succeed.

Here are some other common responses to the question "How do you feel?": "I was really cold lying on the floor;" "My back hurt when I stood up;" "My legs started shaking;" "I didn't like looking at my bones like that;" "I missed it all because I went to sleep;" "I tensed up all over again when I stood up."

Each of these experiences may well seem preeminent to the student but none of them relates to the exercise, which had to do with breathing. I will then ask the next question, "Was that the *most interesting* thing that happened in the course of that long exercise in breathing awareness?" As I prod and provoke, the student will eventually say, "Well, I felt much more breath go in than I ever have," or "I saw all sorts of colors when I started really sighing," or "I thought I was going to cry."

The lesson I try to teach here is that *first* one must articulate anything, however small, that is *fresh, new,* or *interesting.* After that, one can talk about the problems and the pains. Any new experience must be acknowledged if it is to become an agent of conscious change. Otherwise the new experience will disappear and old habits will settle back in. A most persistent old habit may be a silent, negative litany almost unconsciously beating inside the head: "You didn't get it;" "You'll never make it;" "You're not clever enough;" "You haven't got what it takes;" "You probably didn't understand the instructions;" or some other phrase once delivered long ago by a parent or teacher who suggested you would not succeed, and was imprinted on your hypersensitive young heart and made indelible by every subsequent small failure. In order to protect yourself from the possibility of failure on the exercise in question, you evade the issue by reporting in on irrelevant "problems."

If you cultivate the habit of looking for the *fresh, new,* or *interesting* experiences and articulating them, you will gradually erase the negative litany and replace it with your own positive litany. Celebrate whatever you experienced in the exercise that was of fresh interest instead of flagellating yourself with unpleasant or unsuccessful things. The slogan is "Celebrate—Don't flagellate!" This does not mean you have to have a wonderful or revelatory or profoundly meaningful experience—just that transformation comes in small, incremental steps and each step should be positively acknowledged.

Thus I encourage you to celebrate whatever you experienced in the previous exercises that was *fresh* (an experience that was somewhat familiar but suddenly caught your interest afresh, or something you had known before that appeared in a new light), *new* (never before experienced), or *interesting* (piqued your curiosity or made you think twice about it) as you explored some initial awareness of your natural breathing process. Consider the alternative: what you have just done was stale, old, or boring.

In this exploration it has been suggested that the involuntary nervous system does things best. That if you allow your breathing to tell you what it wants, you will not have to waste energy controlling or sustaining it consciously. That the ultimate controls for the breath are thoughts and feelings. That instead of sending active messages to yourself, such as "breathe in," "breathe out," "take a breath," "inhale," "exhale," you send passive messages such as "allow the breath in," "let the breath out," "let the breath enter," "let the breath fly out." The nouns attached to breathing are no longer "inhalation," "exhalation," but are "incoming breath" and "outgoing breath." If you do not change the language attached to the breathing process, you will not change the behavior. It takes longer in the beginning, but once reprogrammed, you will find the newly found natural way much more efficient than anything you could consciously devise.

PRACTICE

Do your spine and breathing exercises for two or three days. Be aware of any tensions, and make the decision to relax; notice how your breathing responds to the events of your day; notice moments when your breathing holds and why; notice how you feel when you relax and breathe naturally; make use of your friend, the sigh of relief.

Make notes of your observations.

3
Workday Three

The Touch of Sound:
Initial vibrations . . . pool of water

■ Prepare to work for:
ONE HOUR OR MORE

My insistent endeavor, in this and subsequent chapters, will be to shift the job of judging sound from the aural sense to the tactile and visual senses. As long as work on the voice includes listening to sounds to check their quality, there will be a conditioned split between the head and the heart, and emotion will be censored by intellect rather than shaped by it. By the *touch* of sound I mean the feeling of vibrations in the body. We will initially explore sound as another inhabitant of that central part of the body housing breath, feelings, and impulses. The impetus for sound is impulse, and the raw material is breath; in order to remove effort from the throat, it helps to imagine that sound, as well as breath, starts from the middle of the body. Be prepared for a powerful application of your imagination in this. People tend to be conditioned to an unconscious physical sense that they communicate from just behind the face, with an unconscious visualization of the passageway for the voice going from the throat through the jaw. Here you will be challenged to find a communicating center a good eighteen inches lower than expected and a passageway some four to six inches higher.

Thus far I have led you through a preliminary exploration of your body and your breathing, one which required you to expand your sense of self. We shall now branch out, and imagery will now come more and more into play. I shall again refer to Antonio Damasio (see Preface and Introduction), a neuro-scientist who sheds light on the interactions of body and emotion in the creation of consciousness and often suggests a fresh articulation of specific stages in the actor's journey. In his book *The Feeling of What Happens* he uses the term *core consciousness.*

> (Core consciousness) provides the organism with a sense of self about one moment—now—and about one place—here. The scope of core consciousness is the here and now. Core consciousness does not illuminate the future, and the only past it vaguely lets us glimpse is that which occurred in the instant just before. There is no elsewhere, there is no before, there is no after.
>
> (p. 16)

Though I generally use the word *awareness* in teaching, I think that Damasio's term *core consciousness* is the state of being alive, alert, and aware that the actor seeks as a launching pad to creativity. It is the foundation for "extended consciousness" (Damasio) and the exercise of imagination. The touch of sound is an exercise of the imagination rooted in the here and now.

In the following exercises I will be asking you to use the power of imagery to help stimulate your voice to become free. Imagery is the language of the body. Imagination is the language of acting. When you regularly employ imagery to exercise the experience of voice, you program a mind/body connection that brings imagination out of the head and into the realm of the body. Images arouse feelings that trigger impulse and action. Imagination in the head is not of much use to the actor (I would call it "invention"), but embodied imagination is the stuff of acting. Embodied imagination can be exercised and developed as muscles can. Only when imagination is embodied in the actor's organism will the actor perform as a unified entity. The way you train your body and your voice will determine the way your body and voice serve you on stage. I would emphasize that imagery is not confined to the visual. All the other senses contribute "imagery" to the body-mind and the sense of smell and the sense of touch are particularly powerful in provoking memory and emotion. Here is Antonio Damasio again:

> I regard the problem of consciousness as a combination of two intimately related problems. The first is the problem of understanding how the brain inside the human organism engenders the mental patterns that we call, for lack of a better term, the images of an object. By object I mean entities as diverse as a person, a place, a melody, a toothache, a state of bliss; by image I mean a mental pattern in any of the sensory modalities, e.g. a sound image, a tactile image, the image of a state of well-being. Such images convey aspects of the physical characteristics of the object

and they may also convey the reaction of like or dislike one may have for an object, the plans one may formulate for it, or the web or relationships of that object among other objects. Quite candidly, this first problem of consciousness is the problem of how we get "the movie in the brain," provided we realize that in this rough metaphor the movie has many sensory portals—sight, sound, taste and olfaction, touch, inner senses, and so on.

(From *The Feeling of What Happens*, p. 9)

Images are constructed either when we engage objects, from persons and places to toothaches, from the outside of the brain toward its inside; or when we reconstruct objects from memory, from the inside out, as it were. The business of making images never stops while we are awake and it even continues during part of our sleep, when we dream. One might argue that images are the currency of our minds.

(*Ibid.*, pp. 318-19)

Steps 1 and 2 rely on a lengthy physical awareness and visualization process and are best done with eyes closed. If you are working alone you should record the instructions for the first two steps. Steps 3 through 8 follow later.

STEP 1

- Stand easily, being aware of your long spine moving up the middle of the back, carrying the weight of your torso off your legs.

- Let your stomach muscles relax.

You must sacrifice your vanity for a little while in the interest of inner relaxation. Let your stomach sag, without becoming swaybacked or locking your knees.

Keep sending two messages:

- Lengthen the spine.
  Let the muscles go.

- Tune in to the natural, everyday breathing that is deep inside your body.

- Induce a deep sigh of relief.

- Be aware of the breath responding and releasing through your mouth on an easy and loose "fff."

- Feel that the breath is relief and the relief is breath. See if you can induce a large enough feeling of relief for the ingoing breath to open you all the way down into the lower half of your torso, from the diaphragm down to the pelvic floor.

- Picture the billowing movement of the diaphragm as it drops to receive breath and whooshes up through the rib cage to release it.

From the pelvic floor let your body-mind's eye travel down through your legs to your feet, and then continue on down from your feet to the ground below and deeper still to the electro-magnetic currents that run below the surface of the earth.

- Picture those electro-magnetic currents flowing back up from beneath the earth through your feet, legs, and torso to your breathing area.

- Let your mind rest with the easy in-and-out of your breath.

Now introduce a picture that can take over the inside of your body from the diaphragm downward.

- *Picture*:
  A deep, calm forest pool with a surface roughly level with your diaphragm and its depths in your pelvic region. The pool is fed by underground streams that come from below the earth through your legs.

- *Picture*:
  Your spine as if it were a great tree rooted at the edge of the forest pool.

■ *Picture*:
The surface of the pool suffused with sunlight.

■ *Picture*:
A small image of yourself standing at the edge of the pool, leaning against the tree looking at your reflection in the sunlit surface of the pool.

■ *Picture*:
The surface of the pool reflecting an enlarged image of your face looking up to your real face with a slight smile. Your lips are open.

STEP 2   When the image is clear, transform the picture from a pool of water to a pool of the vibrations of sound. The pool is now the pool of your voice.

■ With your body-mind's eye, look at the image of your face on the surface of the pool. Focus on your mouth, lips open, perhaps smiling slightly.

Allow a bubble of vibration to break the surface of the pool, escaping through the image of your lips and through your actual lips:

■ Huh

As the mouth is only a little bit open and quite relaxed, the resultant sound of this sigh from the pool of vibrations will be a bubble, a rather formless "huh." (It is similar to an English *her* or the American *her* before the R changes the vowel or some American pronunciations of the vowel sound in *hut*. I shall be spelling it "huh.") If the mouth opens wider, the sound becomes more like "haa-aah" in *father*; if the mouth is not relaxed enough to drop open easily, three-quarters of the sound will go into the nose. The sound should be the primal, unformed, neutral one that happens when there is no tension in the throat or mouth to distort it and no vowel demand to mold it.

- And now a double bubble comes up from deep down below, breaking the surface of the pool:

- Huh-huh

- Leave the mouth loosely open.

Feed in the impulse for a sigh of relief deep into the pool of vibrations.

- Sigh the relief out on a long fountain of vibrations that rises up from the underground springs and out through your mouth.

- Hu-u-u-u-uh

- Relax inside, and allow the breath to replace itself.

Yawn, stretch, open your eyes, and shake the vibrations out from the pool through your whole torso and all your limbs.

Explore the possibility of sighing relief out on the vibrations of sound. Picture the source of feeling and vibration deep inside your body, with nothing impeding the "hu-u-u-uh" sound as it sighs through your mouth to the outside. The pool is a pool filled with relief.

Make sure that the relief connects with one hundred percent vibrations, not fifty percent breath and fifty percent vibrations.

This is general work to focus your mind toward a causal energy source for your voice that involves image and feeling and to begin to experience a tangible connection between sound vibrations and feeling. The imagination has been invoked, and at the same time the anatomy of breathing has been accurately engaged.

In Step 3 you will be looking for a more precise and sensitive touch of sound. The more economically the breath and vocal folds interact, the better, both for the sake of vocal health and in pursuit of a faithful communication of thought. Paradoxically, an inaccurate picture of vocal anatomy most successfully achieves the economy of function between breath and vocal folds. The voice works best when the starting points for breath and vibration are fused in one picture, which is at some distance below the larynx.

To begin, we will zero in on the center of the diaphragm as the fuse-point. In the interests of economy this involves a specific picture of the diaphragm as the most central and initial point of connection between the breath and the sound. The picture includes, consciously or unconsciously, the powerful plexus of nerves known as the solar plexus. Although emotions and feelings are registered throughout the body in differing degrees of vividness, feelings of sadness, joy, anger, shock, and grief are commonly registered with tangible sharpness in the solar plexus/diaphragm area. For those of us who wish our voices to convey the emotions we feel, the fuse-point of breath, sound, solar plexus, and diaphragm becomes palpable with the repeated exercise of imagination. The experience of voice originating in and coming out from that fuse-point becomes habitual. This experience becomes the touchstone of truth and, eventually, the natural way to speak. You might argue that most of your communication is unemotional, but it is a fact of the human organism that we exist in an emotional flux that cannot be stopped and is part of the essence of life.

Here again is Antonio Damasio, to whom I referred at the beginning of this section:

> Normal human behavior exhibits a continuity of emotions induced by a continuity of thoughts. The contents of those thoughts, and there are usually parallel and simultaneous contents, include objects with which the organism is actually engaged or objects recalled from memory as well as feelings of the emotions that have just occurred. In turn, many of these "streams" of thought—of actual objects, of recalled objects, and of feelings—can induce emotions, from background to secondary, with or without our cognizance. The continuous exhibition of emotion derives from this overabundance of inducers, known and not known, simple and not so simple.
>
> The continuity of the melodic line of background emotion is an important fact to consider in our observation of normal human behavior.
>
> (From *The Feeling of What Happens*, p. 93)

Taken out of context, this seems like a good note for a book about acting.

Given that the actor must observe and understand his or her own human behavior before s/he can know how to take on the behavior of a character in a play, let us return now to further exploration of the behavioral connection between emotion, breath, and voice.

Your exploration will focus not just on the diaphragm, but the center point of the diaphragm. You cannot feel the diaphragm, but by picturing it, you can influence its action and sharpen and sensitize the mind's connection with sound. The more accurately you can visualize the diaphragm and its movements, the more you can restore and enhance its function.

In repose, the diaphragm is dome shaped. The largest single muscle in the body, it is attached at its circumference to the bottom of the rib cage from the breast-bone and abdominal wall in front, to the spine in the back. It cuts the whole body in two, horizontally.

When breath comes in, the diaphragm moves down, flattening. When breath goes out, the diaphragm moves up, the dome becoming more cone-shaped. The downward movement is contraction, and the upward one expansion, but this is one of the scientific facts that only serves to confuse the lay practitioner and is best translated by subjective perception. Subjectively the sensory picture is of expansion. As breath comes in, the lungs expand and the feeling in the diaphragm area is of expansion downward, a small expansion for everyday breathing and a larger one for larger expression such as sighing. The outgoing sensory breath picture is of the diaphragm releasing up through the rib cage. As long as the external abdominal muscles dominate this experience, all interior life is diminished.

You will find in the following three illustrations an idea of how the diaphragm moves as breath goes in and out.

Before moving to Step 3, feed in several sighs of relief with the picture of your diaphragm as a thin, elastic, rubbery dome being blown down by the incoming breath, and up by the outgoing breath. The picture applies to the large effect of a sigh impulse; the movements are infinitely subtler for ordinary breathing. For the ultimate outgoing sigh release, the dome of the diaphragm can be pictured softening, softening, softening in the release until it almost becomes cone shaped with the tip of the cone almost reaching the collarbone. Then you can induce a sudden drop of the diaphragm to the floor of the lungs. Don't squeeze the breath out—soften it with release.

STEP 3   Visualize a point at the very center of the dome of the diaphragm that responds to the tiny in and out of everyday breathing. With your mouth open, observe the in and out of small "fff"s in the rhythm of natural breathing. Use the picture of the center of the dome of the diaphragm as the starting point of breathing.

■   Now let the thought of an unformed neutral sound enter the center of the dome of the diaphragm on the incoming breath and be realized in vibration on the outgoing breath. The sound that results will be "huh."

This is the "bubble" that emerged from the "pool of vibrations" in Step 2.

Stay within the rate and rhythm of your natural breathing.

Instead of "fff" on the outgoing breath, there is now a small "huh" sound.

■   As soon as the "huh" has released on the escaping breath, relax in the center of the diaphragm, and breath will replace itself.

Let the picture of the pool of vibrations and the release of the bubble "huh" merge with this exploration

Release the "huh" vibrations lightly and let them go. (They last no longer than the small outgoing "fff.")

Breath will automatically drop back in.

Don't listen to the sound—picture it and, if possible, feel it. (Eventually you will actually feel vibration in the center of your diaphragm but don't worry if you can't feel it now. If you keep introducing the picture, the tangible sensation will come.)

The sound touches the center of the diaphragm as a result of the picture and the thought. You do not make the sound—the sound happens as a result of causal thought/impulse.

This is "The Touch of Sound."

- Let the "huh" thought enter again and again be realized in the touch of sound: "huh." Relax, and the breath will drop back in.

- Repeat this within the ordinary rhythm of your natural breathing.

It is a small sound, and a small exchange of breath.

- Now let there be a double-release bounce of vibrations, "huh-huh," still in the rhythm of natural breathing. This is the double bubble from the center of the pool of vibrations. You can induce a bubble but you can't make one.

The touch of sound is in the center of the diaphragm.

- Huh-huh

- Wait for the breath to want to replace, then yield to that need.

- Breath goes in:

($\triangle$ will be the symbol for a new breath.)

Stay with the touch of sound sequence:

- Huh-huh

- Relax inside.

- Breath goes in. $\triangle$

- The touch of sound

- Huh-huh

- Relax

- The breath replaces. $\triangle$

- Huh-huh

■ Huh-huh △ huh-huh △ huh-huh △

Now exercise this touch of sound following semitones down from a middle C and back up to middle C again. Then speak "huh-huh" once more.

■ Repeat the "huh-huh" on ascending pitches as you drop your spine down and on descending pitches as you build it back up to standing.

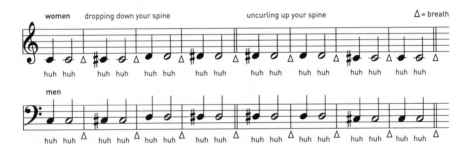

Throughout Step 3 explore the physical sensation of sound in the center of your body. The physical sensation of breathing should remain as close as possible to the sensation there is when you are breathing naturally without sound. Try not to make the sound; try to let sound be the by-product of the "touch" picture in the same way that you do not produce light in an electric bulb: you press a switch or put a plug in a socket, and light happens. The analogy is exact—let sound happen. You are practicing dealing with cause and letting effect follow.

You should take a break at this point. In the next phase of the initial exploration of breath, sound, and image, I will lead you through a lengthy pictorial journey lying on your back on the floor. You must set aside twenty to thirty minutes for the work and, if possible, tape the instructions rather than try to read them as you go. If you can have with someone else read the instructions, that would be best.

STEP 4   Gravity and breath: there are some physical positions that are wonderfully conducive to experiencing the connection of breath, voice, and impulse. The positions themselves are not so important as the images of the positions that you create and maintain. The positions we will experience now are beholden to the force of gravity for their effectiveness.

I will ask you to play with two counteractive pictures. The first is the picture of *gravity*, an active magnetic force that lives in the center of the earth. Gravity loves to feed off your excess tensions. When you lie on the floor, gravity will happily suck tension out of you. When you stand up, gravity will happily play games with you to see how you can compete with his pull. Gravity is constantly challenging us in the game of life.

The second picture is more imaginative. Create a picture, vague or clear, of a Grand Marionettist in the sky who has strings attached to every joint and bone of your body and who is playfully engaged in an ongoing contest with gravity.

This imaginative exercise is designed to induce the most economical of relationships between mind and body. You will exercise the power of mind over matter by asking the bones of your body to respond to your imagination as if the muscles were out of the picture altogether.

This is a deliberately long, slow, contemplative process.

Do not hurry.

Do not aim for a result.

Be lazy. "Waste your time." (Moshe Feldenkrais, *Awareness Through Movement*)

Lie down on the floor on your back with your legs released into their full length.

- Close your eyes in order to deepen your familiarity with the inner geography of your body.

- Let your arms slide out from your sides and align with your shoulders so that your arms are at right angles to your torso.

- Introduce a picture of Gravity. Allow every part of your body to give in to the pull of Gravity. Allow all your tensions to be drained out of you by Gravity's hunger.

- Picture the bones of your body lying on the ground free of muscular constriction.

Now picture the Grand Marionettist in the Sky.

- Picture the string he has attached to your right knee joint. Let him pull on the right knee string so that your right knee moves up toward the sky, dragging your heel along the floor until your foot is flat on the floor.

Don't use any muscles. Picture the bones.

Notice that the small of your back on the right side has fallen closer to the floor.

- Now picture the string the Grand Marionettist in the Sky has attached to your left knee joint. Let him pull on this string so that your left knee moves up toward the sky, dragging your heel along the floor until your foot is flat.

Notice that the small of your back on both sides of your torso has fallen closer to the floor.

- Now the Grand Marionettist pulls on the right knee string so that your knee and thighbone swing up and float over your belly.

- Picture the smooth round top of the thighbone as it rocks in the cradle of your hip socket.

- Now the Grand Marionettist pulls on the left knee string so that your left knee and thighbone swing up and float over your belly.

- Picture the smooth round tops of both thighbones as they balance in the cradles of your hip sockets.

- Then the Marionettist swings both knees over to the right and lets the strings go so that your knees fall to the floor, left knee on top of right knee, comfortably close to your chest.

- At this point let your head drop to the left.

Your torso is now experiencing
a diagonal stretch.

- Let your legs, thighs, and hips relax completely to gravity to your right while your head and left shoulder blade and arm relax completely to your left. Don't do anything. Let gravity take your torso into as long and elastic a diagonal stretch as possible.

- Breathe. Sigh into any tight or painful places.

- Stay in this position as long as you can tolerate it allowing the force of gravity to undo tensions and open the torso.

Picture the right hip socket.

- Imagine that your lungs go all the way down to your hip socket. Enlarge the size of the picture of your hip socket, increasing in your imagination the space available for your lungs.

- Feed the impulse for a deep sigh of relief all the way down to the hip socket. Picture the sigh-breath releasing without sound along a wide diagonal breathing channel that travels from the right hip socket to the left shoulder socket, out through your mouth and also through an imaginary mouth in your left shoulder.

■ As the sigh releases, picture the horizontal release of the diaphragm through the rib cage.

Bring back the picture of the Marionettist.

■ He pulls on the string attached to your left knee and swings it up over your belly bringing your foot off the floor. As your back falls into the floor your right knee will inevitably be drawn up off the floor to hang over your belly. Both feet are off the floor.

■ For a moment the knees and legs are suspended over the torso, then the strings draw them to the left, and as the Marionettist releases the strings, your knees fall heavily to the floor on your left, comfortably close to your chest. Your head drops to the right.

Repeat the pictorial exercises now for the left hip socket and a diagonal channel going from that space all along the inside of the torso and out through your right shoulder.

■ Sigh—without sound—from your left hip socket along the diagonal channel. Bring back the picture of the Marionettist.

■ He pulls on the string attached to your right knee and swings it up over your belly, your foot off the floor. As your back falls into the floor, your left knee will inevitably be drawn up off the floor to hang over your belly, and both your feet will be off the floor.

■ For a moment your knees and legs are suspended over the torso, then the strings are released and both your feet fall straight to the floor.

You are now on your back with your knees up and your feet flat on the floor.

Picture the two hip sockets and the space between them that encompasses the whole pelvic basin.

■ Now feed in a huge impulse for a sigh of relief that is big enough to fill the great cavity of the pelvic basin and the hip sockets.

As this great sigh-breath escapes (without sound), it will flow out through the length and breadth of your torso from the pelvic floor to the shoulder girdle and the mouth, and your diaphragm will flow up through your rib cage.

Adding Sound

In the next exploration, repeat all the stages of the diagonal stretch exercise with careful reconstruction of the images.

STEP 5 Having arrived in the diagonal stretch with your knees over to the right and your head to the left, look with your mind's eye down into the right hip socket space, and picture, if you can, the vibrations of sound preexisting in that space. You might visualize the vibrations as water gathered in the rock-pool of your hip socket.

- Now feed the impulse for a deep, long sigh of pleasurable relief way down into the rock-pool hip socket, galvanizing the vibrations into life. Let the vibrations be a river of relief flowing out along the wide, diagonal channel that leads from your right hip socket and out through your left shoulder and your mouth.

- Hu-u-u-uh

- Feed in two or three new impulses, each time picturing sound vibrations as a broad flowing river of relief that flows unimpeded through the diagonal river channel with no boulders, no dams, everything open.

- Hu-u-u-u-uh

- Float your legs over to the other diagonal stretch and repeat the visualization with the sensation of the river of relief and vibration flowing from your left rock-pool hip socket through your torso river-channel and out into the air in front of your face.

- Hu-u-u-u-uh

- Now float your knees into the middle, up over your belly, and drop your feet to the floor.

Picture that a great reservoir of the vibrations of sound preexist in the pelvic basin from hip socket to hip socket.

- Feed in a huge impulse for a sigh of relief big enough to draw breath down and fill the whole pelvic region. Let the sigh impulse enter the reservoir of sound and release a long, broad river of vibration and relief that flows out through the whole torso and into the air in front of your face.

- Hu-u-u-u-uh

- Now induce an enormous yawn that starts in the middle of your body and stretches you out to your fingers and toes.

- Yawn with sound and see the vibrations traveling down through your legs, out through your arms, up and out through your head until the whole of the inside of your body seems to be flooding with the vibrations of sound.

STEP 6 Slowly roll over on to your side, then onto your hands and knees; tuck your toes into the floor, float your tailbone up into the air while leaving your head hanging heavily down, then shift your weight off your hands and on to your feet. Slowly uncurl your spine with your head coming up last.

Shake your whole body loosely, as if you were trying to shake your skin and flesh off your bones—or like a dog shaking water off its back.

- Shake the vibrations of sound out from your whole body.

Walk around. Check your state of body and state of mind. Note the details of things that are fresh, new, or interesting. Say what those things are out loud. Describe out loud anything that was fresh, new, or interesting about your voice, anything that struck you in the course of the previous exercise.

It may be hard to prevent your muscles from helping make the sound at this point. It may seem that the sound still centers in your throat however much you try to visualize it lower down. As you relax more and more, you should find that your abdominal wall can give in to gravity, and that both your picture and the sensation of sound happening deeper in your body will become clearer.

STEP 7   Lie down on the floor again.

- Sigh with relief with sound. As you sigh out, jiggle your loose belly with your hands so that the sound gets shaken manually.

- Hu-u-u-u-uh
  (Let this sound go on as long as possible.)

  Imagine you are massaging the actual vibrations inside your belly,
  so that you become more and more familiar with the feeling
  of the vibrations being there rather than in your throat or mouth.

Then, reintroduce the central, sensitive touch of sound that happens in the very center of the dome of the diaphragm.

- Huh-huh △

Huh-huh △

With the same sensitivity and clear picture of the central connection with sound:

- Count one to five.
  Say your name.
  Describe how you feel.
  Speak a poem.
  Do all of this with the awareness of the physical sensation of sound in the center of your body.

It's as though the inside of the whole of your torso from the pelvic floor to the shoulder girdle is available to breath and vibration. You choose to have the thought-impulse make economical and sensitive contact with the solar plexus, the emotional receiving and transmitting center.

STEP 8 Roll over to your hands and knees, tuck your toes under, release your tailbone to the ceiling, shift the weight off your hands to your feet, slowly build up your spine and repeat the whole process standing.

- Emit a sigh of relief on sound.

Hu-u-u-u-uh △

- Jiggle the sound with your hands on your belly.

Hu-u-u-u-uh △

  Then:

- Huh △ huh △ huh △

- Each new breath (△) is a tiny central sigh of relief.

- Repeat with pitches, dropping *down* your spine as you go *up* through the pitches and coming *up* your spine as you go *down* in pitch.

- Huh-huh △ huh-huh △ huh-huh.

The sounds should be gradually getting easier, freer, deeper in the body—more pleasurable.

Remember that we are only dealing here with the source of sound, so do not be alarmed if it all seems very deep and introverted and self-indulgent. It should be. The depth of the sound, in terms of pitch, is a result at this stage of both the breathing muscles' and the laryngeal muscles' relaxing. You are feeding in very low energy because the first steps are concerned with undoing tension. Relaxed vocal folds produce a low frequency of vibrations and low sound.

It is vital that you cultivate a familiarity with the state of relaxation. If that state is practiced and easily available when you are making little demand on your voice, there is a chance you will be able to maintain a balance between necessary tensions and unnecessary ones when demand is increased. This is the road to achieving maximum effect with minimum effort. You haven't a chance of singing a high C or delivering a speech charged with emotional intensity without undue strain if you have not mastered relaxation while exploring deep, easy, low-energy sound.

I have placed a deliberate emphasis on turning attention inward at this stage. This is to condition you to work causally, which, in the case of the voice, means feeding the source of sound, building the need to communicate, and accumulating inner energy so that speaking will be a release. There is no advantage in developing a vocal instrument that performs dutifully, but has nothing it must say. I would like to point out that this inner energy and connection is also the key to truthful acting for the camera.

Here are some typical observations made by my students after doing the previous floor exercises:

"The more clearly I could see the Grand Marionettist in the Sky and play with that image, the less I used my muscles."

"I began to feel how much farther down in my body my breath can go. The inside of my body became huge."

"Every once in a while I could feel sound starting in my hip socket or pelvic area, and I was surprised at how powerful it was. It was quite scary. It didn't seem like my voice."

"I felt vibrations in my bones and along the floor."

"Even after I stood up I could still feel sound vibrations coming up from down below."

"My voice seemed to be more in my body and my mouth and less in my throat where it usually is."

Having articulated the things—however small—that were fresh, new, or interesting, you should now write them down in the journal that accompanies your ongoing work. Perhaps redo the gingerbread man with a rendition of how you would *like* your voice to live and move in your body—without blocks.

You may now pay attention to the things that seemed problematic. You may write them down or draw pictures of them.

■ COMMENTARY

This has been a long and, I hope, relaxing session. As you go about your day, pay attention to what is happening in your breathing. Notice the moments when you seem to hold your breath and register what it is that makes you stop breathing. Is it a moment of fear? of boredom? of indecision? of feeling inadequate? (You are, of course, continuing to breathe, but minimally, just under your collarbone).

Once you have noticed when you are not breathing, you have the opportunity to breathe consciously in a situation when you may unconsciously be protecting yourself by holding your breath. I can assure you that as you renew your breathing deep in your body, the oxygen that is released into your blood and your brain will enhance your ability to function.

I have a personal experience in this kind of daily observation that you might find helpful. It often happens that when I am in the presence of people who intimidate me—intellectually or socially—I feel stupid and can't think of anything to say. At the same I may notice that I am hardly breathing, that my stomach muscles are tense and that my buttock muscles have tightened. When I relax my buttocks I immediately become more intelligent and find all sorts of things to talk about. The buttock muscles connect with deep breathing musculature that is woven into the pelvic floor and when all these muscles relax, more oxygen is released into the circulation. I assume the livelier blood chemistry affects the brain because I am no longer stupid. Try it!

PRACTICE

Practice the spine, breathing, and touch of sound exercises for a week.

4

Workday Four

Freeing Vibrations:
Lips, head, body . . . rivers of sound

■ Prepare to work for:
ONE HOUR AND A HALF

Having established a working picture of the vibrations of sound originating in the middle and lower depths of the body, we are now going to explore how those vibrations can be amplified and encouraged to grow. The next few exercises are based on three general ideas:

(1.) Vibrations are murdered by tension.
(2.) Vibrations thrive and multiply in an atmosphere of relaxation.
(3.) Vibrations love to have attention paid to them.

To deal with (1.), we will isolate and eliminate pockets of muscle tension that trap and stifle vibrations. After having eliminated tension, we will consciously encourage relaxation for (2.). And for (3.), we must recognize vibrations when and where they occur, welcome them, indulge them, and nurture them.

Given the opportunity, vibrations' nature is to multiply: to re-sound or resound. They reverberate off a variety of sounding boards. The first of the sounding boards we shall work with is formed when you close your lips on sound. Vibrations, originating centrally, will re-sound on them.

Each new exercise you do should grow out of the previous one. Before entering this exploration of vibration, prepare with the previous exercises: the pool of vibrations, the diagonal stretch, the sighing, and the images and pictures of sound releasing from deep inside the body.

If you are standing, the sound releases upward like a fountain
of relief.
If you are lying down, the sound flows like a river.
If you are hanging head downward, the sound is like a waterfall.

Freeing the Vibrations: Lips

STEP 1

- Stand fully aware of your skeletal support and loose muscles, sigh the
  vibrations of sound up from the pelvic floor, and shake your belly
  with your hands.

- Hu-u-u-u-u-uh △

- Re-create the sigh impulse and, on the next long sighing "hu-u-u-u-uh,"
  slide your hands from your belly up to your chest as though you are
  drawing the vibrations into your chest.

- Hu-u-u-u-uh △

- Bring your hands back down to your belly, re-create the sigh impulse
  and on the next long sighing "hu-u-u-u-uh" slide your hands from
  your belly to your chest and then onto your face. *As your hands touch
  your face, close your lips on the sound.*

Let your hands awaken your awareness to the tactile, physicalized sensation
of your voice. See and feel it traveling from the originating source deep
down in your body to the arrival place in your face. You should be able to
feel clearly the buzz of vibrations between the skin of your hands and the
skin of your face. Don't lose connection with the starting point in your
pelvic floor.

- Repeat

- When the next long sigh of sound arrives on your lips and hands, let
  it continue as you *open your lips, and your hands move forward off
  your face.* Your hands seem to draw the vibrations off your face and
  out into the air in front of you.

- ■ △

You will notice that when your lips close on the vibrations, the sound that occurs is "mmmmmm."

These "mmmmmm" vibrations strengthen the voice by contributing extra sound—the lips re-sound the initial touch of sound vibrations.

The long sigh is now a "hu-u-u-u-ummmmmmmmm-uh."

- ■ Repeat several times using your hands as a guide to your awareness of the vibrations.

- ■ Then repeat the exercise without your hands. Your awareness of the buzz of vibrations and their movement outward will substitute for your hands.

A fountain of vibrations flows vertically upward and onto your lips and then escapes horizontally into the air.

- ■ Using your hands again: establish a flow of sound vibrations that releases up from the pelvic floor and that you can shake from your belly with your hands.

- ■ Hu-u-u-u-u-uh △

- ■ Now think the word *I*—personalize it. Let that thought be an impulse that goes down to your source of breath and sound and then releases on a long drawn-out expression of who you are. Use your hands to draw the "I-I-I-I" from your belly through your chest and out through your open mouth.

- ■ I-I-I-I △

- ■ Feed in the deep sighing *I* thought-impulse, but this time as your hands touch your chest, bring in the word *am*.

- ■ Am △

It is as though the sense of who you are starts deep in the pelvic floor and then spreads into the region of your heart and lungs with a physical awareness of your state of being in the vibrations.

- Repeat, and then as your hands feel the vibrations on your face and lips and move forward into the air, the word *me* releases out of your body.

- Me △

- On one long sigh of relief, place your hands on your belly on "I"; on your chest on "am"; then on your face and out to the air on "me."

This will make a very clear personal connection between you and your voice. As you continue with sounds that are not formed into words and may seem more abstract, search for ways to create and re-create a personal connection so that it is always *you* being released through your voice, not just the sound of a musical instrument.

Continue to move your hands over your body as you develop the previous experience into a more formal exercise that can be repeated.

If possible, you should use a piano to confirm pitches.

- Establish your connection with the central starting point of sound on the double-bubble release "huh huh."

- Then, finding a pitch that is close to the sound that has just happened, let the sound now happen on pitch.

- Huh-huh △

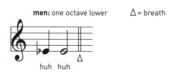

Now, let the sound continue as though on a long sigh, still on pitch, but this time close your lips on the sound.

huh huh mmm

- Register the feeling of vibrations on your lips.

- As you hum, massage your face with your hands.

- △

- Re-create the sigh impulse, but this time open your lips while continuing the sigh sound.

huh huh mmm uh

- Huh-hummmm-u-u-uh

- Stop.

- Relax inside, and let the breath replace △

- Repeat the impulse and the thought.

huh huh mmm uh

huh huh mmm uh

- Huh-hummmm-u-u-uh

- As your lips close, place a finger on them to feel the vibrations and then, as your lips open and the sound escapes, move your finger forward to lead the vibrations out.

Try to carry out this exercise purely through the physical steps, letting the sound be a by-product. Don't try to figure out what the resultant sound will be because you will merely be repeating an old and familiar sound, rather than discovering a new set of physical sensations in which the "sound" of the sound is relatively unimportant. It is the feeling and the picture of the sound that matters.

Now let the pitch drop—just a semitone.

■ Sigh out "huh-hu-u-u-u-uh" on pitch, picturing the vibrations streaming up from the middle of your body and through your mouth.

■ Close your lips gently on the vibrations.

■ Feel the vibrations on your lips as though they were gathering reinforcements there.

■ Allow your lips to open and the sound will stream out, reinforced by the extra vibrations found on the sounding board of your lips.

■ Relax inside, let the breath drop back in.

■ △

Repeat the process on several more pitches, going down in semitones to a comfortably low note, then up again to the easy mid-register pitch you started on.

The sound that happens when you close your lips on the vibrations is commonly known as humming. Keep working with it, however, in terms of physical awareness. When I take a short cut and ask you to hum, try not to respond mechanically with familiar humming, but let the vibrations flow from the middle of your body, through your mouth: close your lips and let the vibrations gather reinforcements from the sounding board of those lips. Think of the vibrations on your lips as though they were strawberries and cream—delicious!

There is nearly always some tension in the lips, either through undue effort or habit. Since one of our underlying premises in exploring how to increase vibrations in the voice is that tension murders vibration, the next step will be to see whether the lips can relax more and thereby deliver more reverberation for sound.

STEP 2   Blow air out through your lips so that they flutter. This is sometimes called a "lip trill."

This is rather difficult to describe on paper, but horses do it in a relaxing way, babies do it, and small children do it with sound when they are pretending to be trucks and motorcars. It is not essential as an exercise, but it relaxes and stimulates the whole lip area; it wakens dormant vibrations; it helps energize the sound in the very front of the mouth; it is also fun to do. So it is worth working out the movement, with and without sound. Here are a few introductory ideas and different ways of describing it if you are still in doubt.

■   (1.) Put your fingers in the corners of your mouth and stretch your lips sideways into a wide grimace. Let go suddenly and blow out through your lips, vibrating them with the air.

- (2.) Put your index finger against your front teeth between your lips as though you were miming brushing your teeth. Let your lips relax completely so that they fall on your finger. As though you were going to hum, let vibrations flow through your mouth.

- Imagine the vibrations are toothpaste, your finger a toothbrush, and brush your teeth up and down leaving the lips quite relaxed. Revert to a childlike state of playing with sounds between your finger, your lips, and your teeth.

- Retain the relaxation of the lips, remove your finger, and blow out through your lips with the vibrations. The resultant sound will start with a loose sort of *b* and then sputter or flutter into a vibration that lazily imitates that of a motor. Let this happen very loosely, as though your lips started in your cheeks, and feel the vibrations spread as far as possible over your face. It will probably tickle. Look in a mirror to make sure the corners of your lips are loose, not tucked in.

STEP 3

- Blow out through the lips on vibration, this time on pitch (start with an easy, mid-register pitch); on the same breath, bring the lips together in a hum, then open the lips and let the vibrations escape. Here now, are the physical steps and physical awareness for this exercise.

- Loosen up extra vibrations on your lips by blowing through them, gather those vibrations together on your lips where they touch each other, let the vibrations escape as your lips open.

- Sustain the exercise with a long drawn-out sigh of relief under it.

- Then relax inside and let the breath drop in to replace what has been used.

- Repeat on descending and ascending pitches. (The symbol ∼ will be used to represent "blowing out through the lips on vibration.")

- 〰 mmmmu-u-uh

Take your time; don't hurry the ingoing breath; let the sequence of actions find their own pace and rhythm while you explore and become familiar with the vibrations.

STEP 4

- Repeat Step 1, observing any changes that you experience. You may, for instance, find that there are more vibrations naturally happening in the very front of the mouth. Move your lips around on the humming, as though savoring the taste of the vibrations before letting them escape.

Vibrations thrive on having attention paid them.

- Become a connoisseur of vibrations:
  Taste them.
  Spread them around your face.
  Luxuriate in them.
  Indulge them.

- Really bring your mind into your lips as they touch—imagine your two lips as two slices of bread making your favorite sandwich. Imagine the vibrations as your favorite sandwich filling: peanut butter and jelly, mozzarella, honey, tuna. Focus on the taste of the filling of your sandwich as you hum.

Now that sound is being prolonged through three phases (touch of sound, vibrations gathering on the lips, and escape of sound from the lips), you are naturally making more demands on your breathing. You have begun, in effect, to use longer sentences. They are primitive sentences, and the earlier exercises, "huh-hummmmmuh" or "um-mmmm-uh," can be regarded as three-word sentences. With an impulse to communicate, the faster thought/speech impulses in the brain can be conditioned into spontaneous integration with breath / sound responses in the body. Be sure, therefore, in dealing with longer "sentences," however primitive, to sustain the thought, which will automatically make the breath last. You need never try to sustain the breath as such; the breath will serve a sustained thought.

It is very important never to continue the sound until you run out of breath. Let each set of sounds have an easy, rhythmic pattern that stimulates the breath but does not punish it. The breath serves the thought, and each thought has an intrinsic length. Each new thought has a new breath: short thoughts have short breaths, medium thoughts have medium breaths, and long thoughts have long breaths. Seldom does an organic thought drive the breath through to the last gasp. No purpose whatsoever is served by learning to sustain a breath over a longer and longer span of time; all that happens is that the natural elasticity of the breathing muscles is impaired, and capacity is reduced because the effort involved creates tension, and tension contracts. Everyone has a natural breathing capacity, which when free from inhibitory tension is fully capable of serving the individual emotional and imaginative capacity. The assumption here is that work on the voice is in the interest of the human truth it expresses.

I shall use the suggestions "sigh out on a hum," "sigh the sound into your head," and so on in the early exercises. This is to condition a combined muscular and emotional release at the beginning of every sound. The responsibility for sustaining the breath throughout a sentence is thus relegated to mental activity.

There is basic mental conditioning contained in the treatment of "huh-hummmmmuh" as a sentence with a beginning, a middle, and an end. The touch of sound, "huh huh," is the beginning; the gathering of vibrations on the lips, "mmmmmm," is the middle; the escape of vibrations from the lips, "uh," is the end. Through the application of awareness, your mind should be contained in each of the "words" that make up this sentence; this will program the unification of thought and sound. When you "sigh with relief" through each sentence, you involve yourself on a feeling level as well as a mental and physiological one. A sigh of relief is a very easy feeling to induce, and if you commit yourself to that feeling as an integral component of these early exercises, you will be practicing the synthesis of feeling, thought, body, and voice in simple ways that will make it that much easier for you to freely attack, "Once more into the breach, dear friends, once more/Or close the wall up with our English dead . . ." or "Brave warriors, Clifford and

Northumberland, come, make him stand upon this molehill here . . ." when playing, respectively, Henry V or Queen Margaret in *Henry VI*, Part 3.

■ COMMENTARY

It is necessary to explain such phrases as "sigh out the sound on pitch," "let the sound happen on pitch," and "let the sound continue on pitch." These phrases are used to avoid a conditioned response to the word "sing." The immediate response to the idea of pitch for some people is "I can't sing" or "I'm tone deaf," while others respond by producing sound quite differently from the way in which they would produce a speaking sound because they have been trained to sing. The word "sing" is too loaded to be used casually in the present basic work. At this stage there is no difference in the physical procedures necessary for speaking or singing other than that, in singing, a pitch is sustained, while in speaking, you come off the pitch immediately. Speaking spontaneously engages half tones, quartertones, eighth tones, even sixteenth tones in inflection and intonation while in conventional singing, whole, half, and quarter-tones are predetermined and sustained. The speaking voice can, however, benefit from music, and the use of ascending and descending pitches introduces new notes and a fresh range of tonal possibilities that will automatically liven up your speaking voice in ways you could not con-sciously plan. At this point the whole emphasis in the work is on physical awareness, and it helps to have variety in range and pitch while practic-ing the physical processes. If you repeat an exercise only in your habitual speaking voice, you will tend to remain within your customary range and habitual patterns of inflection and never expand into unknown areas.

Freeing the Vibrations: Head

At this stage we will be freeing and amplifying the vibrations of the voice mainly while humming; the effective hum means that there is an open chan-nel from the breathing area directly onto the lips. As we move from the awareness of a small vibration surface, the lips, to larger re-sounding surfaces, first the head and subsequently the whole body, make sure that the hum remains free of the tongue.

■ COMMENTARY

Humming is the sound that happens when the passageway through the
mouth is blocked and sounds can only exit by way of the nose.
But it is not enough to say "the mouth" is closed for a hum because the
passageway through the mouth can be closed off by the lips or by the
front of the tongue touching the front of the hard palate (the upper gum
ridge) or by the back of the tongue touching the back of the hard palate
or the whole of the tongue being clamped to the roof of the mouth or
any combination of these positions.

It is quite likely that your tongue is leading a secret, traitorous life and
that when you say to yourself "close your lips on the sound so that a
hum occurs" some part of your tongue is also picking up the message
and adding an "nnn" or an "ng" to the "mmm."

To test this, look in a mirror:
Sigh a hum onto your lips and then open your lips letting the sound
release forward "aaa" Now put the back of your tongue up to touch the
back of your hard palate (and probably the soft palate as well) in an
"ng" sound—really feel the touch between the tongue and the palate—
drop the back of your tongue and let the sound escape on an "aaah"

ng

aaah

>

Now put the front of your tongue up to touch the upper gum ridge (just behind your top teeth) in an "nnn" sound—really feel the touch between the front of the tongue and the gum ridge—and drop the front of your tongue and let the sound escape on an "aaah."

Now play a mouth awareness game, looking in the mirror to see that the part of your mouth you have sent the message to is actually doing the job:

On a pitch put the
(1) Back of your tongue to the back of your hard palate "ng." Now open—"aaah."
(2) Front of your tongue to your upper gum ridge "nnn." Now open— "aaah."
(3) Lips together "mmm." Now open— "aaah."
(4) Lips together "mmm," then *add* the back of tongue to the back of the hard palate "ng." *Then* open the lips—back of tongue / hard palate remaining closed "ng." THEN open—"aaah."
(5) Back of your tongue to the back of your hard palate "ng." Then *add* the front of the tongue to the upper gum ridge "nnn." *Then* drop the back of your tongue while the front of your tongue/upper gum ridge remains closed. *Then* open from the "nnn" to "aaah."
(6) Lips together "mmm" and *add* the back of the tongue to the back of the hard palate "ng." Keep the lips together and open and close the back of tongue and back of hard palate behind the closed lips.

>

Register where the vibrations predominate when the back of the tongue is up and when it is down.

Clearly the vibrations gather more into the nose when the back of the tongue is up and touching the soft palate and focus much more into the lips when it is down.

This final experience of the hum—when only the lips are closed and there is a clear space behind them—can be called the effective hum.

The other hums are not wrong or illegal in any way; they just don't deliver vibrations as effectively into the front of the mouth. The effective hum is the one that heals and nourishes and strengthens the voice.

Remembering that no vibrations can exist freely unless the breath is free, (that is, be sure to continue to create and re-create a sigh to fuel each new sound) let us return to the vibrations that amplify sound, with an exploration of what happens when the whole head and neck area starts to relax.

Tension, to a greater or lesser degree, is common in the back of the neck, the jaw, and throat. As long as such tension exists in such a vital part of the vocal channel, vibrations are trapped in contracted muscles. The job will be to release those vibrations by undoing the tension. The aim in the following exercises will be to relax the muscles of the neck and throat and, in a sense, to get rid of your head. Physiologically you will be rolling your neck and head around in a loose circle; psychologically you will be transferring yourself from your head to your middle, so that the controlling center is not in the shopping list part of the brain, but deep inside the body.

We are going to be focusing attention on the back of the neck and picturing the top seven vertebrae of the spine that comprise the neck. The topmost vertebra is just up inside the skull, roughly on a level with your ears and nose. The vertebra that is the bridge between neck and body-spine is the big one that sticks out at shoulder level called the bull vertebra. It is very visible in Spanish fighting bulls and combines a picture of strength and vulnerability. There is a nerve plexus centered in this vertebra that spreads its corolla up through the neck, out into the shoulders and down between the shoulder blades. These nerves seem particularly sensitive to messages of anxiety, fear, and doubt from the brain and they tell the surrounding muscles to tense up in protective mode. The protective stance of hunched shoulders, short, stiff neck, and rigid jaw then gives a message back to the brain of determination, belligerence, responsibility, and confidence. (It is, I think, pure coincidence that the word *shoulder* contains the word *should*. A great deal of shoulder tension is holding all the things we know we *should* do; our responsibilities, goals, and ambitions.)

With a triangle of tension going from the base of the skull, down the neck and out to the end-points of the shoulders it is hard for messages to flow freely from the brain through the spinal cord into the rest of the body. For a free and expressive voice we want impulses to be able to travel unimpeded back and forth between the solar plexus/diaphragm region and the brain.

For the actor this neck and shoulder tension can be a kind of Bermuda Triangle where creative impulses sink without a trace. Annihilated by tension, the impulses never reach their creative destination.

With all this in mind to add motivation and interest to the next activity, here it is.

STEP 5

■ Stand easily with your feet just apart, your spine long, and your stomach muscles relaxed. Let the whole neck drop forward, giving in to gravity.

- Feel the weight of your head pulling on the bull vertebra

- Picture the seven vertebrae of the neck and roll them to the right, until they hang over your right shoulder with the head heavy and your right ear directly over your shoulder.

- Register the stretch on the muscles and tendons in the left side of your neck as the head drops heavily to the right and the left shoulder drops toward the floor. (Check in a mirror to see whether you are facing straight forward—facing straight forward will give the optimum stretch to the muscles and tendons on the left side of the neck.)

- Let the neck fall forward again with the head dropping heavily to gravity, and then let the neck and head roll over to your left shoulder.

- Register the stretch in the right side of your neck—right shoulder dropped, head dropped in the opposite direction, side neck muscles stretching between the two.

- Now, maintaining the picture of the right side of your neck as very long, float the neck up until it is in alignment with the rest of your spine with your head balanced on top.

- Drop the neck heavily forward and roll it to the right shoulder— feel the stretch and then, maintaining the picture of the left side of your neck as very long, float the neck up until it is in alignment with the rest of your spine with your head balanced on top.

- Picture the very long sides of your neck.

- Keep your upper spine long—don't collapse.

- Slowly now, keeping the sides of your neck long, lengthen your neck backward. (*Do not let the neck collapse.*)

- Let your jaw relax and your mouth drop open. Picture your throat stretched, making the front of your neck very long.

- Now roll your long neck up over one shoulder, let it drop forward while noticing the length of the back of the neck and then continue rolling on to the other shoulder.

- Maintaining a picture of the sides, front, and back of your neck lengthening and shortening as they move from shoulder to shoulder and forward and then back, roll your very long neck around in a big circle, first in one direction, then in the other.

You roll your neck, and your head goes with it.

- Roll your neck (and head) loosely from right to left, and then from left to right, on to your shoulders. Feel the stretch in the opposite muscles and tendons when it is on the shoulder. When the neck is back, let your mouth and throat drop open. When it is up on the shoulder, feel the stretch, and when it is forward, feel how heavy it is.

Let the neck be active and the head passive.

If you think about rolling the head you will tend to twist the neck and involve only the top three or four vertebrae. The neck should be moving from the bull vertebra that sits at the bottom of the neck and the top of the body-spine. You can check to see whether you are involving the neck as fully as possible by noticing where your face is in relation to your shoulder as you roll over the side. You should, if you are really releasing the neck from its base, be looking straight ahead as you go over the shoulder. If your head is the activator, you will tend to be looking at the shoulder or at the floor as you go over the sides. Your earlobe should be directly above the shoulder in the side position—another checkpoint.

- Roll the neck and head slowly, heavily, in a big loose circle from right to left several times.

- Roll from left to right several times.

- Then roll a little faster, allowing gravity and momentum to take over.

Remember that the objective in rolling the neck and head is to relax the muscles at the back of the neck and to begin to release the throat, tongue, larynx, and jaw; that is, to free the channel through which sound travels.

STEP 6 Leave the head dropped forward for a moment.

- Focus your mind firmly on the back of your neck and bring it back and up through the neck vertebrae until the neck is in alignment with the rest of the spine and the head is balanced easily on the top vertebra.

Tune into the breathing center and sigh a hum on a sustained pitch from there onto your lips.

- Mmmmmmmmmmmmmmmmmmm (Sigh of relief underneath.)

- As soon as you feel the vibrations on your lips, drop your neck and head forward and roll them around in a loose circle as explored in Step 5.

- Remind your throat to drop open behind your closed lips as your neck rolls round.

- When you get to the end of the sigh and an easy neck/head roll, relax in your middle and let the breath drop back in.

- △

- Again sigh a hum onto your lips and picture it reverberating through your whole head.

- Drop your neck and head forward and roll around the other way.

- Relax for the new breath.

- ■ △

- ■ Hum again (on pitch) and roll in the other direction.

- ■ △

Don't go too long on each breath. Let your breath have its own life without pushing till you are empty.

- ■ Find a new pitch for each new head roll, going up three or four notes, then down three or four notes.

Despite the fact that your lips are now closed to form a hum, let your throat and jaw relax open behind them as your head rolls over backward. Your lips are elastic enough to cover the gap, and the effect is similar to stifling a yawn in polite company, keeping the lips together, but yawning somewhere in the recesses of your throat.

STEP 7

- ■ Bring your neck up into alignment with the rest of your spine.

- ■ Sigh a hum on pitch into your head and feel with your fingers all the different places that are vibrating with sound.

- ■ Touch your lips, cheeks, nose, forehead, top of the skull, back of your neck, throat, and chest.

- ■ Take enough time to explore fully, both with your fingertips and your awareness, how the vibrations feel in the different places.

You will notice that the vibrations are much stronger in some places than in others, but don't be prejudiced in favor of the strong ones. Get to know the quality of the lighter, weaker vibrations as well as the rich, strong ones.

With the added awareness of all the places you have explored tactilely:

- ■ Again, roll your head and neck on a hum. Sigh the hum out.

- Mmmmmmmmmmmmmmm

- Remind your throat to stay open.

- Let awareness replace the touch of your fingers, and with awareness register the vibration in your lips, your face, your skull, your throat, and your chest.

- △

- Roll your head in the other direction humming on a new pitch. Notice the emphasis of vibration shifting according to whether your head is dropped forward or backward.

- Picture the vibrations like ball bearings inside a big ball, shifting and rolling as the ball rolls.

- △

- Repeat several times in alternating directions.

STEP 8

- Then, standing, with an awareness of your head balanced lightly on top of your neck, repeat the "huh-hummmmmuhs" as practiced in Step 3, with the physical awareness of all the vibrations that you felt in your head now pouring into your speaking voice.

Indulge the feeling of sound and realize that this is your voice.

- Feel and picture the vibrations flowing out from all sides of your head.

Keep reminding yourself that you are not just doing vocal exercises; you are aiming to free your natural speaking voice. Beyond that, the aim is to free yourself through your voice. Although I can give clues as to how to achieve those aims physiologically, only you know what they might mean for you psychologically. After each exercise, find a perfectly simple, personal thing to say and say it out loud, with an awareness of what you have just been doing "technically."

Sigh with relief through the touch of sound "huh-huh."

- Wallow in vibration on "mmmmmmmm." Let the vibrations escape into the air on "uh."

- Let the breath replace and then:

Sigh out "that feels good" with the same physical awareness that you had on "huh-hummmmmmuh."

- Or sigh out "I wish I knew what I was doing" or "I'm hungry and I want my dinner" or anything that expresses the feeling you have at this moment.

- Relax, shake yourself, move about, jump up and down, and stop concentrating.

You have loosened the lips in order to free vibrations from them; you have loosened your head and neck in order to free vibrations from them; you have been checking to see that there are no tension-murdering vibrations in the area of your lips and neck and head.

Freeing the Vibrations: Body

In Step 9 you will be loosening the whole body to free more vibrations from an even larger area. The progression of exercises from lips to head to body moves logically from small awarenesses to larger to large. Vibrations thrive and multiply as attention is paid them. As specific tensions are noticed and removed the conditions are enhanced for releasing vibrations that can amplify basic sound.

STEP 9

- Stand easily with your spine long and your head floating up off the topmost vertebra.

- Relax your stomach muscles so that the natural rhythm of breathing takes over.

- Choose an easy, mid-register pitch and sigh a big, easy hum on to your lips.

- As you hum let your head and neck drop heavily forward and immediately give in to the weight of your head and drop down through the spine.

- Hang from your tailbone with your head down.

- Let your breath replace.

- △

- Breathe naturally as you hang upside down.

Make sure your neck is relaxed and your knees are bent, so that you are comfortably balanced.

- Sigh a new hum as you hang upside down and notice how the vibrations behave in this position.

- △

- Hum again as you hang there and gently shake your body loose.

Where do the vibrations predominate?

- Let the breath replace.

- Sigh a new hum (on another note) and build up your spine to a standing position as you hum.

Register the shifting emphasis of the vibrations as you come up to standing.

■ △

Where do the vibrations predominate when you are upside down?

Where do they arrive when you are upright again?

Do not take too long building up the spine. If the breath does not last easily, let a new breath in. If you build slowly, you should allow yourself two or three breaths; if you go faster, you can do it on one.

Do not hang upside down for too long or you will become unnecessarily dizzy. Take it easy; explore the sensations.

■ Repeat the process (dropping down the spine on a hum, and building it up again) on different pitches within a low register.

■ Next—drop down the spine on a hum.

■ Let an easy breath come in.

■ △

■ Sigh out on a new hum. Uncurl your spine quickly, and when you reach the top let your mouth drop open so that the sound can escape.

Mmmmmmm-u-u-uh

Imagine, that in the course of dropping down your spine—which was established as a relaxation exercise for the whole body—you are freeing vibrations from your whole torso. Imagine that when you reach the upright position again, all those free, loose vibrations are thriving inside your body but are trapped by your lips and longing to be free of you. When you open your lips you allow all the vibrations that were imprisoned inside you to escape into the air.

■ Play with the whole process again, dropping down your spine on the hum, relaxing for a new breath, coming up on the hum, and releasing the vibrations through open lips when you are upright.

Develop an interest in the vibrations and what they feel like, as though they had a life of their own that you can encourage with relaxation or diminish with effort and tension.

- Personalize the vibrations so that you may be pleasurably involved with them—let them warm you up, or cool you down; let them tickle you in surprising parts of your body; give them colors; let them pick up your moods, thus producing a feeling that can underlie the exercise. From this simple game of connection between imagination and vibration, you can practice freeing your feelings through your voice.

The introduction of the word "feelings" into a supposedly technical exercise for vibrations leads me to underline the premise that this voice technique uses the imagination to unify in one place within the body, mind, feeling, breath, and sound. It is an economical way of looking at the process of communication. Feelings are an integral part of the technique.

■ COMMENTARY ON VIBRATIONS, CONNECTION, AND THE INNER ABDOMINAL BREATHING MUSCLES

I suggest that vibrations can travel through all the bones of your body— if you want them to. Cartilage and bone are made of perfect material for conducting vibrations. If you imagine vibrations flowing through the bones of your body you open your mind to a sensory and imagistic connection that can then automatically translate the content of a text into the experience of that text in physical, emotional, and sensory terms. These psychophysical voice experiences form a vibrant foundation for the actor's craft.

I am now going to invite you to connect the humming exercises to the diagonal stretch experiences introduced in Workday Three.

The involuntary breathing mechanisms of the body are comprised of three distinct muscle behaviors: diaphragmatic, intercostal, and inner abdominal. The inner abdominal muscles are knit into the under floor of the diaphragm and run diagonally down into the lower spine and then

>

---

connect with the muscles of the pelvic floor. Part of the structure of these inner abdominal breathing muscles is formed by tendon/muscles called crura. "There are crura in various parts of the body: for example, a crura of the diaphragm; crura cerebri, crura of corpora cavernosa, crura fornicis, etc. In the respiratory system the diaphragm is connected to the spine by two pillars or crura—tendonous musculature that connects the diaphragm to the lumbar vertebrae. They can be subdivided into the right and left crus. Their major function is to connect the diaphragm to the spine. The right crus has a more extensive origin than the left. This is because the liver is right sided and a key action of the right crus is to aid the descent of the liver with inspiration."

Now the thing that is of deep interest in the experiential wisdom of how the voice works is that the diaphragm houses the great nerve center of the solar plexus and that the inner abdominal muscles weave themselves around the smaller but arguably even more powerful nerve center whose home is in the beautiful triangular bone at the base of the spine called the "sacrum."

Solar means "of the sun." *Sacrum* means "holy place." Western empiricism tells us that our emotions are palpably registered in the solar plexus—suggesting that our emotions are to us the equivalent of the life-giving force of the sun to the earth. It is also an inescapably experiential fact that the creative force of sexual energies emerges from the sacral nerve center. The sacrum houses many of our deepest, most instinctive urges. The sacral nerve center is the practical, autonomic home of instinct, intuition, and creativity. It seems clear that both sexual and the deepest artistic impulses spring from the sacral nerve center. Creativity is procreative however expressed.

The breathing muscles that are connected to the sacrum relay instinctive, intuitive, creative messages from brain to body to voice. These are the inner abdominal breathing muscles, which include the crura. The breathing muscle that is connected to the solar plexus relays emotional messages from brain to body to voice. This is the diaphragm breathing muscle. The breathing muscles connected most directly and extensively to the lungs provide capacity and power that serve the larger needs

>

of the instincts and the emotions. These are the intercostal breathing muscles. Experientially, one or another of the areas may predominate according to the nature of the communication, and the responses in the volume of breath will be larger or smaller according to the stimulus. But free, impulse-connected breathing involves all these muscle-groups in simultaneous reflexive responses. This dissection of function is too neat to describe the complexities of the breathing process but will perhaps contribute to a partial road map of the geography of mind, body, and voice.

While external abdominal muscles can control breathing, either consciously or through habitual tension, our goal in this work is to stimulate and connect with the inner involuntary systems.

I would now like to lead you through some mental-physical exercises that are particularly aimed at a reconditioned connection between you and your sacral breathing, which means between you and your instinctive life.

Floor work: Connecting Voice
With the Inner Abdominal Breathing Muscles

My students enjoy these exercises as much for sheer pleasure and sensuality as for the vocal results. To begin with, the aim is to connect the experience of vibrations on the lips with the visualizations of the diagonal stretch, hip sockets, and the pelvic floor. The lips are the portal to the outside world. They lead to extroversion. The mind must be able to hold in awareness, the internal source point, and the externalizing arrival point to achieve the maximum power of communication.

Preparation:

- Lie down on the floor.

- Use the picture of the Marionettist in the Sky to achieve the most economical execution of the diagonal stretch: knees to the right, head to the left.

- Then let the thought of a long sigh of vibrationary relief spark sound in the right hip-socket and flow through the long, broad river channel from hip socket to shoulder socket. As the vibrations reach the mouth—close the lips and feel the vibrations on the lips and in the head, and then open the lips and let the vibrations escape.

- Hu-u-u-hummmmmmm-u-u-uh

- △

- Let the sigh impulse reconnect down to the hip socket.

- Repeat this several times on different pitches (still in a low register).

- Let the Marionettist bring you over to the other diagonal stretch.

Re-create the experience of sound starting in the hip socket and sighing through on to the lips and out.

- Hu-u-u-hummmmmmm-u-u-uh

- Try it on different pitches.

- Float the knees to the middle (over the belly, feet off the floor) and drop the feet to the floor.

- Float the right knee up over the belly.

- Clasp your hands over the front of the knee, fingers laced.

- Picture clearly the place where the top of your thighbone goes into your hip socket.

- Feed a sigh of relief—*without sound*—down into the hip socket and as it releases shake your knee with your hands so that the top of your thighbone shakes the breath from the hip socket out through your mouth.

If your hands directly influence your knee and thighbone, the breath will loosely shudder throughout the length of the body and out into the air in the front of your face.

The movement in your hands is more a vibration than a violent shake. The shoulders must stay loose and uninvolved.

As you do this you are committing your mind to a causal impulse that starts deep in the inner abdominal breathing musculature and meets no blockage on the way out through the length of the body.

- Drop the right foot to the floor.

- Float the left knee up over the belly. Hands clasped over the front of the knee, repeat the sighing, vibrating breath experience.

- Drop the left foot to the floor.

- Again float the right knee up over the belly and drop the clasped hands over the knee.

- Feed in the sigh to the hip socket and find the vibrations of *sound*. With your hands, shake/vibrate the sound from the hip socket all the way out through the long inner channels of the torso—onto the lips—and out.

- Hu-hummmmm-u-u-uh

This exercise shakes the "hum" from your hip socket to your lips and then out into the space beyond your lips.

This ensures that there are no blockages anywhere to be encountered between hip socket and lips because the vibrations jiggle, wobble, shudder, or shake as they escape under the influence of the shuddering thighbone.

- Drop the right foot to the floor and repeat with the left knee, thighbone, and hip socket.

- Repeat several times on each side going down on pitch, then up, then down again as you change legs.

- Then drop both feet to the floor.

Then focus into a picture of your whole bony pelvic structure.

- With your feet flat on the floor, knees up, float your pelvis two inches up off the floor. Picture your pelvis as if it were an old-fashioned garden swing, hanging from the supporting struts of your thigh-bones. Gently bounce the pelvic swing up and down.

- Lay the pelvic swing back down on the ground.

- Let the sigh impulse go all the way down into the pelvic floor where it turns into the vibrations of sound

- Hu-u-u-uh

- Close your lips on a hum that floats the pelvic garden-swing up two inches off the floor and gently bounce the pelvic swing up and down, bouncing the vibrations as pleasurably as one might bounce small children on a swing

- Mmmmmmmmmmmmmmmmmm—u-uh

- Then, as you return the pelvic swing to the ground, a new breath impulse enters with a new pitch, and the sound is again bounced gently from the pelvic swing onto the lips and out.

Repeat several times with new pitches every time.

- Relax back onto the floor, retaining a clear picture of sound-impulse penetrating down to the pelvic floor and release a sighing

- Huhummmmuh

- Feel the resultant vibrationary flow of voice arriving clearly on the lips and moving from there out into the air.

Slowly roll over onto your hands and knees, and from there find your way back to standing with as economical a use of muscular effort as possible, your head coming up last.

- Keeping your sense of self and impulse source as deep in the body as possible, repeat the touch of sound and the amplification of vibrations standing:

- Hu-u-hummmm-uh

- Try it on several different pitches.

- Shake the vibrations out through your whole body, bouncing your knees and then your shoulders.

- Notice what fresh, new, or different experiences of sound have occurred.

- Speak them.

- Speak a few lines of text.

- Write down in your journal the new physical experiences of your voice.

- Draw a new picture of your voice.

PRACTICE

A combination of all the exercises learned on Days One through Four for a week. You may make use of the Intermission Warm-Up outlined next.

I will now arrange a short warm-up comprised of the exercises explored up to this point. This will be a suggested pattern of work combining the movements and sounds that must be repeated regularly if they are to reprogram the communicative channels, with accompanying reminders as to where the attention should focus at any particular moment.

Workout for Relaxation, the Spine, the Head, Breathing, Touch of Sound, Humming:

Lie on your back on the floor.

- Choose, from your memory, a place that gives you a particularly good sense of peace, tranquility, and relaxation: lying on a beach, in a green meadow in the sun, on a boat, but not in your bed. Imagine you are lying in that place and can give your limbs up and let your muscles relax. It helps to have the sun or a warm fire in your picture.

Take time to let your mind move slowly through your body from your toes to the top of your head undoing any tiny pockets of tension that you find in the course of the journey. If you do this in the context of a clearly visualized and remembered place that you like, the process of specific relaxation will probably be accompanied by feelings of pleasure.

- Allow these feelings to color as much of the subsequent work as possible.

- Turn your attention to the tiny involuntary rise and fall of natural, relaxed breathing deep in the center of your body. Let your lips fall apart and feel the outgoing breath escape over the front of your mouth making a small "fff" as it leaves your body. Wait for the breath to replace in its own time. Continue your awareness of the natural breathing rhythm until it seems genuinely to have found its own pace and place deep inside.

- Introduce the picture of the Marionettist in the Sky and let him float your knees up over your belly and over to the right in a comfortable diagonal stretch. Feel and picture a sigh impulse going deep down into the right hip socket and release the sigh on breath (no sound).

- Let the next sigh impulse connect the feeling of relief with the vibrations of sound, starting in the hip socket and flowing through the long diagonal river channel through the torso and out through the mouth.

- Hu-u-u-u-uh

- Repeat in the left diagonal stretch.

- Float the legs back over to the right diagonal and let the thought of a long sigh of vibrationary relief start in the right hip socket and flow through the long, broad river channel from hip socket to shoulder socket and as the vibrations reach the mouth, close the lips and feel the vibrations on the lips and in the head, and then open the lips and let the vibrations escape.

- Hu-u-u-hummmmmmm-u-u-uh

- △

- Then let the sigh impulse reconnect down to the hip socket.

- Repeat this experience several times on different pitches (in a low register).

- Let the Marionettist bring you over to the other diagonal stretch.

- Re-create the experience of sound starting in the hip socket and sighing on to the lips and out.

- Hu-u-u-hummmmmmm-u-u-uh

- Try it on different pitches.

- Float the knees to the middle (over the belly, feet off the floor) and drop the feet to the floor.

- Float the right knee up over the belly.

- Clasp your hands over the front of the knee, fingers laced.

- Feed a sigh of relief—*without sound*—down into the hip socket and as it releases, shake your knee with your hands so that the top of your thighbone shakes the breath from the hip socket out through your mouth.

- Drop your right foot to the floor.

- Float the left knee up over the belly. Hands clasped over the front of the knee, repeat the sighing, vibrating breath experience.

- Drop the left foot to the floor.

- Again float the right knee up over the belly and drop your clasped hands over the knee.

- Feed in the sigh to the hip socket and find the vibrations of *sound*. With your hands, shake/vibrate the *sound* from the hip socket all the way out through the long inner channels of the torso—onto the lips—and out.

- Hu-hummmmm-u-u-uh

Repeat.

- Then drop the right foot to the floor and repeat with the left knee, thighbone, and hip socket.

- Repeat several times on each side.

- Then drop both feet to the floor.

- Next focus into a picture of your whole bony pelvic structure.

- Feet flat on the floor, knees up, let the sigh impulse go all the way down into the pelvic floor where it turns to the vibrations of sound

- Hu-u-u-uh

- Close your lips on a hum that floats the pelvic garden-swing up two inches off the floor and gently bounce the pelvic swing up and down, bouncing the vibrations out

- Mmmmmmmmmmmmmmmmmmm—u-uh

- Then, as you return the pelvic swing to the ground, a new breath impulse enters with a new pitch, and the sound is again bounced gently from the pelvic swing onto the lips and out.

- Repeat several times with new pitches every time.

- Relax the pelvis down onto the floor.

- Now move your mind's eye from the pelvic floor to the center of the diaphragm. Be aware of the tiny movement of the natural rhythm of breathing in that center. Notice that the movement of the diaphragm is horizontal within the body and that it is reflected in an up and down movement on the external abdominal wall.

- Now let the thought-impulse of an unformed, neutral sound enter the breathing center so that the outgoing breath is turned into vibration.

- Huh-huh

- △

- Repeat the thought-impulse on each outgoing breath in the rhythm of your natural breathing.

- Huh-huh △ huh-huh △ huh-huh △

- Alternate "huh-huh" and "fff" to see how close you can stay to the sensation of just breathing when you add sound.

Make sure the "huh-huh" is a pure sound, and the "fff" is a pure breath. It sometimes helps to think of sound as black, breath as white, and a breathy, mixed sound as gray. All that is needed to achieve a "black" sound while releasing the breath is a really clear thought. If your sounds are "gray," you are probably concentrating too much on relaxation for its own sake and not enough on what you want to do through that relaxation.

- Now introduce the thought of descending pitches. Start on a comfortable mid-register note and gradually drop down, if possible, semitone by semitone, or tone by tone and so on, until the sound is so low and loose that it almost gargles.

See how low you can go without pushing down. Relax deeper and deeper inside your body for the deeper sounds; as soon as you feel you have to strain at all, start moving up in pitch again. Stay within the natural breathing rhythm.

- Speak the sound again.

- Huh-huh.

- Then slowly begin to get up from the floor, economically, rolling first onto your hands and knees and uncurling up the spine, maintaining as much relaxation as possible and leaving your head till last.

Stand, feet just apart.

- Yawn and stretch throughout your body.

- Stretch up to the ceiling—elbows, wrists, and hands.

- Then let your hands drop till they hang from your wrists; wrists and forearms drop till they hang from your elbows; upper arms drop till they hang from your shoulders; your head drops; the top of the spine gives in to the weight of the shoulders; and the head drags on the spine, vertebra by vertebra, until the whole torso drops, hanging head downward from the tailbone.

- Feed a deep sigh into your back, then let your diaphragm give in to gravity as the breath releases.

- Then build your spine up, vertebra by vertebra.

- Head floats up on top.

- Stomach muscles stay loose.

- Knees are free.

- Spine is long.

- Breathe easily, giving into the involuntary rhythm.

Induce small "fff"s.

Introduce the touch of sound

- Huh-huh

- △

- Huh-hummmmmuh.

- Blow out through the lips without sound to loosen them.

- Move all the face muscles around.

- Blow out through the lips on sound

- ∿ mmmmmmmuh.

- △

- Repeat on descending pitches.

- Now, *speak* it

- Huh-hummmmmuh

- Do it with the same physical awareness as when you sustained the pitch.

- Relax for a new breath.

- △

- Now speak it again

- Huh-hummmmmmuh

Do it with conversational inflection.

- △

Ask a question through:

- Huh-hummmmmuh

- △

- As if a friend had asked, "How was your day today?" describe your day entirely on "huh-hummuh"s with a new breath impulse for each new thought impulse.

- Once again

- Huh-hummmmmuh

- △

  As soon as you think about "speaking," your focus tends to move up into your face. Clearly send the "question" impulse down to the feeling/breathing center, and let the question/breath/vibration response flow up and out through the torso, throat, and mouth. Add surprise, urgency, doubt, or amusement to the question, and the central connection will be pinpointed by the feeling content.

- Drop your neck and head heavily forward, and then roll them loosely around in a wide circle to relax the neck and throat muscles.

- Circle your neck and head in the other direction.

- Sigh a hum on an easy pitch as you roll your head and neck.

- △

- With a new note, a new breath impulse, and a new hum, roll your neck and head in the other direction.

- Repeat four or five hums on different pitches, with your head rolling in alternating directions.

■ **MEMO**

Check that you are humming on a pure "Mmmmmmm."

Only the lips should be touching to form the hum. The tongue should not be touching the roof of the mouth in the middle, the sides, or the back. There should be space behind the lips, clear down to the breathing center.

- Roll your head and hum a few more times on different pitches to be aware of the above.

■ **MEMO**

Don't squeeze the breath out to the last drop; stop before getting tight inside. Induce a genuine sigh impulse under each new breath so that the exercise does not become mechanical. Have the courage to let your head really drop at the front. If you are saving your head, you are probably also tightening your jaw or throat or tongue.

- Bring your neck up so that your head finds its balance point.

Describe out loud how you feel, and what you feel—spontaneously and immediately, without censoring it. Release the sound of how you feel into your voice.

- Now again sigh the hum from your middle and this time let your head drop forward as the hum continues. Let the weight of your head take you all the way down your spine until you are hanging head downward humming.

Feel the vibrations dropping out through the top of your head.

Register whatever sensations occur.

Make sure your knees are slightly bent, weight balanced between the heels and the balls of the feet, stomach muscles relaxed.

- Let the breath replace

△

Notice that in this position your back can respond to your breathing needs more freely than the front of your body can—take advantage of this awareness.

- Sigh a new hum onto your lips, and build your spine up again to standing, and when upright let your lips open to allow the sound to escape.

- Relax inside to let your breath replace

△

Then on a slightly higher pitch, repeat the exercise.

- Drop down through the spine on a hum:

    A new breath at the bottom
    Induce a new hum.

- Come up the spine humming.
  At the top let the mouth drop easily open, releasing the sound.

Let what is happening to your body affect the sound. You may wish to pre-serve the sound in a straight, unwavering line, but that is a false sense of control. Whatever the body does should affect the sound, so let the vibrations get moved around and shaken as your body drops down.

- Alternate the humming-and-head-rolling, and the humming-and-dropping-down-through-the-spine on changing pitches. Begin to explore slightly higher notes in the context of this exercise.

- As you open at the top:
  Bounce your knees.
  Bounce your shoulders.
  Jump up and down.
  Release more and more free energy.

Use your awareness in speaking again.

- Huh-hummmmmuh.

Finally speak a poem, a speech, or some dialogue from a play while:

(1.) On the floor in the diagonal stretch
(2.) Bouncing the pelvis
(3.) Feeling the connection with the diaphragm center, hand on the abdominal wall, feeling the drop with each outgoing thought
(4.) Bringing the connective picture into the upright, standing position
(5.) Bouncing the knees as you speak the text
(6.) Bouncing the shoulders as you speak the text
(7.) Jumping up and down as you speak the text

The aim should be to find the freedom physically to express the freedom of your imagination Your body may provide new ideas and inspiration of which your brain may not have been aware—if you give it the opportunity.

When you come back to a text, you should focus all your interest in the content and meaning of that text, and be prepared to judge whether your voice has been freed at all by the subjective criterion of your enjoyment of your work.

The Second Four Weeks of Work
Freeing the Channel. What is the Channel?

Work on the voice must fluctuate between freeing the breathing muscles that deal with the source of sound and freeing the throat, tongue, and jaw muscles that are part of the channel through which the sound travels.

We have dealt, to a certain extent, with how to release the breath more fully, thereby providing essential support for sound. There are, however, many muscles that wrongly consider their help vital as voice makes its journey through the body. As long as the muscles of the jaw, tongue, and throat provide support for sound, the breath will remain lazy in the performance of its duties. It is important, but sometimes difficult, to become aware of such false support in order to remove it and focus the work where it belongs. Work on the channel is in a sense passive; work on the source, active. Passive and active messages must be sent simultaneously: relax the channel; stimulate the source. Gradually, as the source support (the breath) becomes surer, the channel muscles can take a much-needed rest and become available for their true functions. Generally speaking, the jaw's true functions are: (a) to hold teeth and chew food, and (b) to widen the exit when some powerful emotional/vocal content needs to escape. The tongue's true function in speaking is to articulate vowels and consonants. The throat is composed of many elements that will become familiar as we progress. We will start with the jaw.

5
Workday Five

Freeing the Channel: Jaw awareness and relaxation
Getting rid of tension . . . prison gate or open door

■ Prepare to work for:
ONE HOUR

Our first step will be to break down the general picture of the head and neck. The skull is split into two large bony structures joined by a hinge. As both these structures have teeth, and as the words "head" and "skull" are too general, I shall call one the top jaw and the other the bottom jaw for the time being.

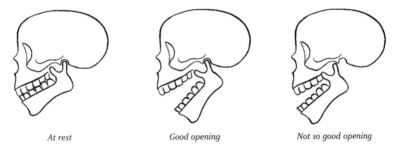

| At rest | Good opening | Not so good opening |

It is helpful to imagine the bottom jaw as being hooked onto the top jaw, rather like a false beard, right beside the ears. The actual connection fits a small bone at the back of the lower jaw into an inverted horseshoe indentation in the upper jaw. There is plenty of play in the hook mechanism, or hinge, and the most effective space between the top and bottom jaws is created when the bottom jaw drops down and back. It is much more common to find that it goes down and forward when the mouth opens wide, despite the fact that it has to be pushed to get there, making a very inelastic passageway that allows too slow a response to changing demands of communication.

The natural—but not necessarily familiar—drop for the bottom jaw is toward the back of the neck. This happens when the muscles in the hinge are fully relaxed. Yet tension in the jaw is so common that ligaments shorten, muscles contract, effort is needed to open the mouth and the effort can push the jawbone forward. Messages to the jaw are complicated by the knowledge that opening your mouth involves the jaw, and "open your mouth wider" is the careless advice given by choirmasters, singing teachers, and frustrated directors who can't hear a word the actor is saying. The unconscious image evoked by that admonition deals with the front of the face and yet the essential space needed is at the back of the mouth, not the front. Indeed trying to open wide in front can mean closing more at the back through sheer effort, thus defeating the main objective, which is to give the voice more room in the throat.

The muscles joining the top jaw and the bottom jaw are complexly interwoven with those spreading through the face and the back of the neck. They run vertically, horizontally, diagonally, internally, and externally. To get maximum response in this top part of the voice channel it helps to think of the bottom jaw as dropping and the top jaw as lifting from as far back as possible. The top jaw action takes some of the burden off the bottom jaw as far as supplying space is concerned, diminishes the danger of pressing the tongue and larynx down, which can cause strain, and suggests spaces in the upper pharynx as added passages for sound.

The movement, up and back as well as down and back, when taken to an extreme, resembles instinctual reflex movement in response to large emotional impulses of fear, anger, grief, and joy. This can easily be seen in animals: a lion roaring, a dog attacking, a cat spitting in self-defense. It can also be seen in the extremes of human emotion that are expressed in screaming or howling. The faces of people screaming with hysterical joy at a rock concert or with hysterical fear and pain in battle move into similar muscle configurations whatever the specific emotional content.

In a small child it is possible to see how the face reveals the nuance of intensifying feelings through a gradual opening of the face, but as we mature our guarded defenses condition our faces, throats, and jaws against moving in those directions except in uncontrolled response to violent stimulus. It is almost impossible to express subtle and median feelings accurately and openly because the muscles have learned to behave in ways that disguise rather than reveal. To disguise the rictus of fear, the upper lip learns to stiffen bravely; to disguise the pleasure felt when one is complimented, the corners of the lips turn deprecatingly downward rather than up in a smile. To preserve the impression that one knows what is going on under any circumstance, the middle of the face immobilizes into impassivity, quelling the ripples of anxiety, questioning, or naive response that might give one away in a hostile world. Sometimes a fixed smile of eternal appeasement imprints itself on the face of one who fears the strength of his and others' anger to kill and be killed.

One of the strongest and most universal muscular defense systems is in the jaw hinges. Clenching the teeth is a sure way to avoid opening the throat wide enough for a scream of fear to escape, so a bulging jaw muscle comes to represent bravery and strength. Rage is nailed down in the muscles of the jaw. When the camera zooms in for a closeup of a set jaw, you know that the battle will commence and the strong man will win. If the jaw muscle twitches, however, you must infer some conflicting emotion and inner struggle, even a little neurosis. "He bit back the anger that rose in him." "She bit her handkerchief to stifle her sobs." A piece of wood or a bullet ("bite the bullet") was put between the teeth of those about to be operated on before the days of anesthetics, partly to prevent the patients from biting their tongues, partly to keep them from screaming. We have been conditioned, subtly and not so subtly, to use the jaw more as an iron gate to be slammed shut against the onslaught of emotions than as a wide-flung portal through which imprisoned feelings can leap to freedom.

Few of us after the age of six or seven have the opportunity to scream daily, in joy or anger, or indeed to howl with laughter more than once or twice a week if lucky. Natural exercise for the jaw muscles is hard to come by, and, stretching so seldom, they lose their elasticity and length.

We do yawn, which is a help, but even that superbly therapeutic action is apt to be curtailed so as not to offend others. As you begin to work to free the jaw, the tongue, and the throat, you will probably start to yawn a great deal. Indulge your yawns, encourage them, expand them: they stimulate circulation by increasing oxygen intake and they provide a spontaneous, natural stretch for important channel muscles more discreetly than by screaming regularly.

More than yawning is going to be necessary if the actor is to recondition the response of the jaw muscles to the impulse of feeling. Such reconditioning must happen because that which helps one to cope emotionally in terms of society can block one disastrously in terms of the theater.

The first things to do are to learn how to relax the jaw muscles and to learn to recognize tension when it occurs in that somewhat hidden area.

Clench your back teeth and bite hard. Bite and relax several times and with your fingers feel the jaw muscles as they bunch and release below the ear.

Now yawn and put your fingers in your ears as your jaw opens. You will feel the bony hinge movement both inside and just outside your ears. This is where to put your mind when you are asked to "let the jaw relax."

STEP 1

- For jaw awareness and relaxation put the heel of your hands on the jaw hinge area on either side of your face. With a small circular motion, massage your jaw muscles.

- Next, pressing quite heavily into the cheeks, smooth the bottom jaw down away from the top jaw until the mouth hangs loosely open.

- Imagine that your bottom jaw has no muscles of its own and depends solely on your hand for movement.

- Put the back of your hand under the bottom jaw and with your hand lift the jaw up until the back teeth touch lightly.

Leave your jaw heavy and slack.

(If your front teeth touch, you may be pushing the jaw forward. It is relatively rare for the jaw to be set far enough forward for the front teeth to meet in a natural bite.)

Let it be the back teeth that touch, not the lips.

If you take your hand away the jaw must drop, given the imaginary circumstances of having no muscles of its own.

- Take your hand away. Your jaw will drop.

- Imagine little lead weights being attached to the back angle of the jawbone, below the ears, so that it relaxes down farther.

- With the back of the hand lift the jaw back up.

- Take the hand away so that the jaw drops.

- With the hand lift the jaw up.

Repeat several times.

Your mind should be observing the result of this process in the jaw hinges. Without having to push the jaw down actively, the ligaments and muscles within the hinge mechanism should be getting gently stretched by the weight of the bone dragging at them. If you attempt this stretch by actively exercising the jaw, you will impair the muscular elasticity and increase the muscular control.

We are looking for an opening that does not take the jawbone out of its inverted horseshoe groove in the bottom of the skull.

STEP 2

- With your neck long and your head floating, put your thumbs under your jawbone and your fingers on top of it so that you have a firm grip on the jawbone on either side of your chin. Your hands are again providing the muscles for the bottom jaw.

- Start with the teeth closed lightly.

Throughout this exercise the actual jaw muscles are acted upon; they do not perform the movements.

- Without moving the bottom jaw at all, lift the top jaw up and off the bottom jaw until your mouth is open.

- Using your hands, lift the bottom jaw up to meet the top jaw so that the teeth touch at the back.

- Without moving the bottom jaw again, lift the top jaw up and off the bottom jaw until the mouth is open.

- Once more, with your hands, lift the bottom jaw up to the top jaw.

At this point your head should be as far back as it can go.

- With your hands, bring your bottom jaw down.

Your head will now be back, your mouth wide open, and your jaw still in the grip of your hands.

- Keep your bottom jaw where it is: bring your top jaw up and over onto the bottom jaw.

■ **QUESTION**

Where are the muscles that move the top jaw? Try the exercise again and try to find out through your own observation before going on. This whole exercise is more mental than physical because it asks the mind to reroute its messages and relabel the destinations of those messages. It cannot, therefore, be performed mechanically.

Having redone the preceding top-jaw, bottom-jaw exercise steps, perhaps you have found that the muscles moving the top jaw are in the back of the neck. There may be some sense also of muscle activity just under the cheekbones as part of the top-jaw movement.

- Repeat the whole process, clearly sending the messages first to the hands and then to the back of the neck.

To the hands.
To the back of the neck.
And so on.

As the back of the neck takes on more responsibility for supporting the top jaw (the skull), the actual jaw muscles will be able to release more.

STEP 3

- Think of lengthening the back of the neck to provide a strong support for the whole head.

- Take hold of the bottom jaw with both hands and find a gentle swing that takes it down and back and then up again. Be aware that you are loosening the jaw muscles inside the grooved hinge that connects the jaw to the skull.

■ MEMO

Don't waste time moving it from side to side; we do not use that movement in speaking, and it is too forceful and dislocating to be helpful in relaxing. Don't move the jaw up and down with its own muscles during this exercise; you will only make them more efficient in controlling and defending your communication.

Now is the moment to reconnect with your breathing and with the source of sound so that you may persuade the jaw that it has nothing to do with the basic formation of sound. In the story of the chocolate-chip cookie it was the wonderfully adaptable, eager-to-help muscles of the jaw, tongue, and throat that intervened between the Pang and the wail and saved the small child from the danger of emotional expression. They did well to do so. But now you have a choice: you can continue to be forever protected or you can enter the complex, sometimes chaotic realm of your emotional world and learn to navigate within it. Within emotional turmoil lie the seeds of creation.

- Take hold of the bottom jaw with both hands and gently discover a way to swing it that takes it down and back and then up again. Slowly loosen and shake the jaw freely.

Be aware of the space between the upper jaw and the lower jaw.

- Picture the roof of your mouth belonging to your upper jaw and your tongue belonging to your lower jaw.

- Picture the space between the two jaws and sigh breath—no sound— through the space. Shake the jaw loose as you sigh the breath through.

  > Picture the breath sighing over the roof of the mouth. Do not let it get caught in the jaw movement. The breath goes through the space above the jaw.

Once the picture of the space through the upper part of the channel is clear, let the sigh impulse find the vibrations of sound.

- Sigh a river of vibrations through the spaces of the mouth and shake the jaw loose *in order to prove you are not using it for the basic formation of sound.*

Look straight ahead—let the sound sigh out horizontally to the world.

- Repeat the sigh and the jaw-shaking several times, sighing on pitches that gradually go higher.

Let your hands drop. Leave the jaw hanging heavily:

- Huh-hu-u-uh

- Hu-hummmmu-uh

You may find that the vibrations are richer, farther forward in the mouth, more palpably connected from the source of breath to the front of the mouth because the jaw is not eating up vibrations on the way.

You can try this hanging head downward, sighing the vibrations from your tailbone to the roof of your mouth, shaking the jaw loose with your hands. And then, maintaining the release as you slowly come back up the spine, sigh the sound through the roof of the mouth, shaking the jaw as you build up to standing.

As the jaw begins to yield its support for the voice, you will notice a clearer connection with your breathing impulse center. Take advantage of this by speaking a piece of text or a poem or singing a song. Follow the thought-feeling impulses that lie behind the words.

PRACTICE

Two days

6

Workday Six

Freeing the Channel: Tongue awareness
Stretching, loosening, releasing . . . story-teller

■ Prepare to work for:
TWO HOURS

The next area for work in freeing the channel for sound is the tongue. As a teacher of voice production who sometimes borders on the fanatical, I am at my most technically obsessed when it comes to the tongue. My obsession is ultimately futile because once the speaker is emotionally connected to the truth the tongue is going to behave as it ought—articulating emotional content into words that convey the specific intelligence of that emotion.

However, on the road to that ideal goal, the tongue can construct a myriad of exquisitely fabricated simulations of truthful story telling. We must first be able to persuade the tongue that nothing it has to say is as convincing as the story told by breath and emotionally connected vibration. The voice and the breath are the servants of emotion while the tongue serves the intellect. Eventually there is no hierarchy in this division of labor—emotion and intellect, voice and speech must be equally balanced in communication, but to begin with we have to be sure that the tongue is not hijacking impulses that should be traveling directly to the diaphragm.

The tongue is all flesh and muscle from the tip to the roots. Any part of the tongue can pick up and deflect impulses from their path to the breathing/solar plexus area. But the back of the tongue is particularly adept at this kind of intervention.

COMMENTARY

The role tongue tension plays in subverting the freedom of the voice is
so powerful it is worth invoking mythology to illustrate its behavior.
If we play with the relationship of the Greek gods to earthly mortals in
terms of the human mind and body, Mount Olympus, the home of the
gods, would be situated in the head and mortal existence in the body.
The thoughts in our heads may sometimes seem as dysfunctional as
the family of the gods and our earthly garden given to weeds as well as
flowers. We could connect many of the gods to many different aspects
of our behavior, but I am particularly interested in assigning Hermes,
the messenger between Olympus and Earth, to the tongue. Hermes was
known to be a liar, a trickster, as our tongues have learned to be; but
also, under Roman guise, Mercury, the silver-tongued, the eloquent.
Neither Hermes nor Mercury is always reliable—Mercury was the god of
merchants who hoped to make a quick buck if their salesmanship was
slippery-tongued enough. The messenger I would much rather employ is
Iris, the goddess who also had the job of carrying messages from heaven
to earth but whose medium was the rainbow: many-colored, evanescent,
a pot of gold at its base, or so we were told when we were children.
I picture the pot of gold as the truth we find in the sacral source at the
bottom of our spines. I picture the many-colored rainbow representing
the many colors of our emotional lives. I can see that if we commit to
Iris, then Hermes and Mercury will become perfect servants of her
truth. How would they dare to flick their feathered heels at her glory?

Think, as we progress, of breath and sound as Iris's rainbow carrying
truthful feelings that will be articulated by an obedient tongue into
words faithful to their origin.

Now we will examine the tongue itself. The roots of the tongue are attached
by means of the hyoid bone to the larynx. If you examine your tongue both
with the help of a mirror and with your mind's eye, you will perhaps realize that, although the tip is relatively familiar to you, there is a large area
inside the mouth going down into your throat that you do not know much
about and that seems to have a life of its own. Watch your tongue for a

minute or two, with your mouth open wide enough for you to see through to the back where the tongue thickens. Observe whether it moves involuntarily, whether it is humped up in the middle or hollowed, whether it lies thick and relaxed with the tip touching the lower teeth, or thin and retracted. Within the thickness of the tongue lie muscles that are highly sensitive to the psychological condition. Nobody says, "I am so nervous my tongue's all tight inside my mouth," though one might say in similar circumstances "my stomach's tight" or neck or shoulders. Yet any nervous tension, or habitual difficulty in communication, creates contractions in the tongue that pull it back, flatten it, or bunch it up in the throat. Such contractions change the shape of the throat-mouth cavity, distorting the resonating response and the subsequent vocal quality. Since the tongue is joined to the larynx, the state of one area must affect the other. Either tension in the tongue spreads to the larynx, affecting the free play of the vocal folds, or tension beginning in the larynx spreads to the tongue affecting articulation. Tension in the larynx also contributes tension to the diaphragm and vice-versa. When your mouth goes dry with stage fright, your tongue muscles have tightened so that your salivary glands have stopped functioning.

For working purposes it is enough to regard the tongue as one of the compensating "helpful" muscles that assumes responsibility for sound when the breath is not free. If the tongue is persuaded to take a rest, the breath may start to take on its true function again, but the only argument for transferring all the support the voice needs to the breath is the desire for expression and a sensitive pickup of emotion. The tongue can support sound without necessarily contributing to vocal strain. A chest voice, belted out in a high register, is largely dependent on muscular support from the back of the tongue; and some fascinating personality voices develop by virtue of a gradual takeover by the tongue muscles producing gravelly or hoarse two-note tones. Many ethnic singing styles from Bulgarian to Korean rely heavily on the tongue muscle, as do overtone and reinforced harmonic singing.

But the tongue has no function in the economical and organic formation of sound, and all the notes throughout the range of the voice can be produced without any tightening in the back of the tongue. For emotion to be expressed freely through the voice, the tongue must be relaxed.

Hermes must give way to Iris.

Awareness of the tongue and its behavior is developed initially by learning to stretch it fully and relax it consciously. You cannot stretch the tongue adequately by sticking it straight out of the mouth, as it is attached to the floor of the mouth in such a way that only a small section is affected with a straight stretch. In order to stretch the tongue right down to its roots, follow the exercises described next.

I will be asking you to distinguish between five different parts of the tongue:

(1.) The tip (which, at rest, touches the back of the bottom teeth)
(2.) The blade (the flat front of the tongue that is not attached to the floor of the mouth)
(3.) The middle (right under the central dome of the hard palate)
(4.) The back (lying under the back of the hard palate and under the soft palate)
(5.) The roots (you can only see them with your mind's eye, attached to the larynx by the hyoid bone).

STEP 1

■ For tongue stretching, place the tip of the tongue deep down behind the bottom teeth—the very tip of the tongue should be touching the lower gum ridge behind the bottom teeth, the blade of the tongue is against the back of the bottom teeth.

■ Think into the middle of the tongue and roll it forward and out of the mouth like a big wave breaking over the bottom teeth, until you feel the back of the tongue coming up out of your throat and the whole tongue is stretched from tip to roots.

■ Then let the middle of the tongue relax back onto the floor of the mouth while the tip of the tongue remains in contact with the bottom teeth.

The active muscles should be in the middle of the tongue. As they roll forward they pull the back of the tongue up and out of the throat.

■ Repeat the stretching and relaxing movements several times and observe the following points, adjusting where necessary:

If you press too hard into the bottom teeth you will either push the jaw forward, creating tension in the jaw hinge or you will push it down creating tension in the larynx. Try to let the jaw drop down and back. Think of lifting the top jaw up to create space in the upper part of the mouth channel, through which the tongue can move freely.

Make sure that the upper lip and teeth lift well away from the tongue and that the throat releases wide behind the tongue so that you are creating large spaces as the tongue stretches. At first the throat has a tendency to close during this exercise; to check whether this is happening, hold your nose and see if you can breathe. If you are breathing through your mouth while stretching the tongue, your throat is open.

Once the top and bottom jaws are open wide enough to let the tongue stretch out fully—leave them open. After the first stretch the only movement should be in the tongue; the jaws remain wide. If you smile slightly during the exercise you will find the upper-jaw lift is easier and the tongue movements are freer. This position is similar to the facial posture of a lion roaring or a cat yawning. The top and bottom teeth are exposed, the cheek muscles are lifted up and the throat is open for the roar or the yawn. We have been civilized out of the extremity of this animal-roar opening and, as a consequence our average mouth opening is diminished. When you next see a cat yawning or a lion roaring (a photograph will do), notice that the tongue is forward in the mouth; sometimes it sticks right out of the mouth. Our tongue-stretching exercise is designed to help restore some of our animal impulse behavior in the interest of clearing an open channel for the voice to travel through.

- Keep the blade and tip of the tongue attached to the back of the bottom teeth both while rolling the tongue forward and when it relaxes back into the mouth. Continue to use a mirror to see whether what you feel is actually happening. Your physical awareness cannot be trusted yet to feed you accurate information.

In the course of the exercise, whenever the tongue relaxes flat you should be able to see clear through to the back wall of your throat, but be sure the tongue relaxes flat, don't pull it down.

STEP 2

- Induce a yawn and at the same time stretch the middle of your tongue forward out of your mouth and hold it in the stretch.

- Breathe in and out with the middle of the tongue stretched forward for about thirty seconds. Then relax the tongue back into the floor of your mouth.

Observe the obstacles to this activity that may occur.

There are so many individual patterns of tension possible in the tongue, the lips, and the jaw that it is impossible to cover here all the things you may find happening in your mouth. A common difficulty is in isolating the tongue from the jaw. One may think one is stretching the tongue but in fact the jaw is moving up and down cleverly intercepting the message to the tongue and denying the tongue the experience of a real stretch. Sometimes the top lip wants to come down to meet the tongue as it moves forward, muscling in on an act that is intended solely for the tongue. Sometimes it is the whole face that stretches wide and then collapses, making its owner believe that the tongue is working really hard.

Only the diligent use of a mirror will ensure that your message is getting directly through to your tongue and that its movements are completely isolated from all the other would-be collaborators. You must encourage them to stay out of the exercise, which is for the benefit of the tongue.

Another common problem is the inability to relax the tongue flat after the stretch. If there is habitual contraction in the tongue muscles, then the stretching, rolling-forward movement is in direct opposition to the habitual state and it may take some persuasion to reverse the tendency to pull the tongue back.

STEP 3

- Feed in a deep sighing yawn that opens the throat, and release from the diaphragm-pelvic region a long "haa-aah" that pours out through the channel. As the sound releases, stretch and relax your tongue three times.

- Haah-yaah-yaah-yaah-yaah

Do not try to *make* that sound. Follow the physical instructions: feed in an impulse for a sigh—"haa-ah"—then roll the middle of the tongue forward and back three times in order to prove you are not using the tongue for the basic formation of sound.

Having sighed the sound out, stretching and relaxing the tongue several times, stop, relax, and check the way your mouth and throat feel. They may feel a bit larger, with more open spaces visible to your mind's eye. Take advantage of this awareness to find the touch of sound.

■ Huh-huh

Then feed in an impulse for a deep sigh of relief and, as it releases, feel the vibrations pouring onto your lips

■ Huh-hummmmuh

Notice whether there are any different sensations or impressions of the channel through which the sound flows, and whether the vibrations feel different in any way.

STEP 4

■ To loosen the tongue allow it to lie relaxed in the floor of the mouth with the tip lightly touching the back of the bottom teeth—this is home position for a relaxed tongue. To be very precise, the tip of a relaxed tongue touches the place where the bottom teeth grow out of the lower gum ridge.

■ Now focus your attention on the middle of the tongue. Gently move the middle of the tongue forward and back in a small-scale version of the previous exercise, but this time without opening your mouth any wider than its normal opening. The jaw will remain relaxed with the teeth not more than half an inch apart. Think of this as a loosening of the tongue.

■ *The tongue moves inside your mouth. Put the tip of your little finger between your side teeth and loosen the tongue to make sure you are not opening too wide.*

- Now gradually speed up the forward, back, forward, back movements of the middle tongue until you feel you are lightly shaking the tongue loose throughout its length.

You are loosening the tongue, not exercising it, no longer stretching it.

- Sigh—with breath only, no sound—as you loosen your tongue. Picture the sigh-breath traveling along the roof of your mouth—do not let it fall into the tongue.

Separate the breath from the tongue.

Your next objective will be to use your consciousness of tongue loosening to see whether the tongue can remain loose when sound is added. The exercise will be to release sound from the breathing center while loosening the tongue at the same time, thereby proving that the tongue has no function in the basic sound-making process.

STEP 5

- Feed a sigh of relief deep down into your breathing area and release it on vibration—a sustained "hu-u-u-h"—on pitch.

- As the sigh-sound flows out along the roof of the mouth, loosen your tongue.

- You are loosening your tongue in order to get rid of any tension, any help it may want to give to the sound-making process.

- Picture a solid stream of vibrations flowing from your middle up and out through your mouth; then loosen your tongue, rolling it gently forward and back several times as the sound streams out above it.

- To check that your jaw is not moving, again place the tip of your little finger between your side-teeth as you sigh the sound vibrations along the roof of your mouth and loosen your tongue.

This exercise works when you give really clear physical messages. Try not to be distracted by what your ear tells you. For the moment explore the physical sensations arrived at by the application of clear mental pictures and clear physical instructions. If you had no tongue, the sound could flow with complete freedom through a wide, unblocked channel. Imagine the ease with which you could do voice exercises if your tongue were detachable and you could put it on the table at the beginning of a vocal workout; only when you came to articulation would you put it back in. Your aim in the following exercises should be to get rid of the tongue as nearly as possible and to observe what happens to the sound as a result.

Practice Step 5, applying the following points of awareness:

■ Feed a deep impulse for a sigh of relief into your feeling/breathing center and free it out on a pitch

■ Hu-u-u-uh

hu - u - u - u - uh

■ Loosen the middle tongue, rolling it quickly and lightly forward and back under the flow of vibrations. Creating and re-creating a new sigh-impulse for each new pitch-thought, continue up the register as far as you can comfortably go without pushing.

Observe, meanwhile, that (1) the jaw stays loose, (2) the belly relaxes for each ingoing breath, (3) the sighs become more full as you go higher, (4) the sound sighs forward on a horizontal line out of your mouth and into the air rather than dropping onto the tongue and being pulled back into the throat.

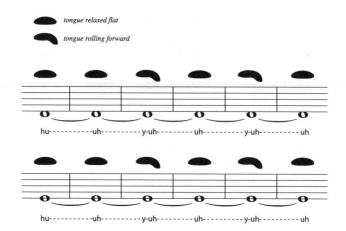

- Now expand your awareness to take in the changing sounds that occur as your tongue moves. The vibrations no longer arrive in a straight "hu-uh-uh-uh" but are molded by the tongue movements into new shapes. Notice what sound occurs first when the tongue rolls forward and then when the tongue relaxes. You will perhaps discover that as the tongue rolls forward the sound resembles a loose *Y*. So that what is happening is this:

- Hu-yuh-yuh-yuh-yuh

- Repeat the tongue-loosening exercise with the awareness that the physical movements are causal and that the *Y* sound is the result.

The physical awareness is the working area; you can expand that awareness to take in the resultant sound aurally but if you merely repeat the sound you heard, if you merely say "hu-yuh-yuh," you will achieve the opposite of the desired result. You are using the tongue as an articulator and exercising its muscular ability. The desired result of these exercises is to remove the tongue from the basic sound-making process. This is a very important point.

Be more interested in the genuine feeling of the sigh of relief than in the sound.

STEP 6   To reprogram the impulse route, repeat Step 5—tongue loosening with sound—applying the following pictures:

- Visualize the stream of vibrations springing from its source in the breathing center and flowing out through the mouth above the tongue, which is relaxed, loose, and out of the way beneath the sound.

The stream of vibrations is active, releasing energy. The tongue loosening is passive.

- Picture an alignment running from the center of the dome of the diaphragm, through the dome of the roof of the mouth, and into the dome of the top of the skull. Picture the vibrations of sound streaming up through these domes while the tongue loosens.

- Repeat the whole process on ascending pitches while you drop your spine down so your head hangs down. Sigh the vibrations through the center of the three domes to gravity.

- Slowly build your spine back up to standing as the pitches descend.

Do not strain to go higher in pitch but use the consciousness of a relaxed tongue to begin to explore your upper range.

STEP 7

- Let your tongue lie relaxed on the floor of your mouth, tip touching the back of the bottom teeth. Find the touch of sound in the center of the diaphragm and speak "huh-huh."

- △ Huh-hummmuh

- △ ᨑ ᨑ Mmmmuh

- △

- Roll your head on a hum; repeat two or three times in alternating directions.

- Drop your spine down on a hum, △, come up and release the sound at the top; repeat two or three times on ascending and descending pitches.

- Questions:
  Do you notice any change in the feeling of the vibrations from the last time you did this exercise?
  How does your mouth feel?
  Has your breathing altered in any way? Or has your perception of it altered?
  How do you feel? What do you feel?

The next step continues the reprogramming process with the same basic tongue movements as before but with a more specific aim and thinking process. The premise on which the next exercise is based is that if the tongue is free, the sound will be released forward and will arrive unimpeded in the front of the mouth. In order to encourage this possibility the specific thought process will now emphasize the forward part of the tongue loosening, asking the tongue to roll the sound forward into the teeth.

STEP 8

- Roll the middle tongue forward (tip of the tongue down behind the bottom teeth) as described in Step 4 for tongue loosening, and leave it in the forward position.

Notice that in this position there is a very narrow space left between the surface of the tongue and the upper gum ridge.

- Release sound from the breathing center through that space. The vibrations, molded by the narrow space, will naturally form a "heee" sound. Play with the tongue position until you feel the vibrations against the top teeth.

- Now whisper "hee" aiming the breath over the tongue into the top teeth; then voice it.

- Let the tongue relax flat on the floor of the mouth. The space between the surface of the tongue and the upper gum ridge is now larger, and the only sound that can happen without altering the space is "huh."

- Play with the two tongue positions and repeat the forward rolled vibrations "hee-hee-hee," and then repeat the tongue-relaxed vibrations, "huh-huh-huh."

As you move from "hee-hee-hee" (tongue rolled forward) to "huh-huh-huh" (tongue flat), use a mental image of the tongue actually rolling the vibrations forward into the teeth on the "hee." Then, as the tongue drops into the floor of the mouth, picture the vibrations moving on forward and out of the mouth on the "huh"s.

Let the breath replace between each set of sounds. Do not lose connection with the central starting point of the sigh of relief.

- Practice on ascending and descending pitches.

hee

huh

- Now alternate the "hee" and "huh" three times with a new breath for each sound.

- Sigh out the "hee," rolling the tongue forward, and on one long breath drop the tongue flat letting the sound change to "huh." Repeat twice more.

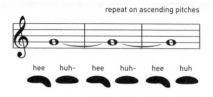

- Do the same thing taking out the connecting h's.

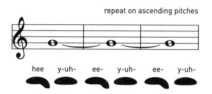

Remember! Create and re-create the impulse for a sigh of relief to spark the new breath for each new pitch.

There is hardly any difference between this exercise and the basic tongue-loosening exercise. What has changed is the mental use of the tongue loosening. The mind is now focusing on the arrival of the vibrations in the front of the mouth as the tongue releases up and out of the throat. This more specific thinking process gets results once the tongue has fully relaxed.

Notice that I have begun to suggest that you go higher in pitch as you exercise. Having established some consciousness of relaxation, you can now feed in greater demands and use your consciousness to abolish unnecessary efforts in meeting those demands.

As you go higher, observe whether the tongue wants to behave differently from the way it does on the lower, easier notes. Does it roll forward as loosely and simply?

Is it still soft underneath the lower jaw? Put a finger in the soft place behind the chin bone on the underside of the mouth—there you can feel the condition of the tongue muscles, which should always be soft, even when moving. Is the tongue falling flat on to the floor of the mouth on the second part of the movement, or is it starting to pull back?

Do not rely on your subjective awareness of these points; your awareness is not yet to be trusted. Use a mirror to check for any tiny changes in the behavior of the tongue when dealing with higher and lower notes in the range. The work will bring you to a point where there is no difference in the behavior of the tongue whatever the vocal demand, be it higher pitch, larger emotion, or greater volume. These demands must be responded to with breath and resonance. The tongue must be left free to cope with articulation.

As you continue to practice Step 8 with the aim of gradually increasing your upward range, be aware of what is happening in the breathing musculature whenever the tongue begins to harden, contract, retract, or become tense. You will find that when the tongue tenses you are also tense in the breathing area or that nothing appears to be happening there at all.

Your tongue tightens to provide support as compensation for weak, lazy, dead breathing. In order to leave the tongue free as you move higher in your range, all you need think of doing is sigh from deeper down with more and more relief. This will provide the essential breath, and, if you can honestly induce a real feeling of relief at the beginning of each sound, you will release your mind from its habitual reaction to greater demand, which is either "I can't" or "If I try harder, if I push, if I am determined and really work perhaps to the point of suffering a bit, I'll make it." Don't suffer, don't try, don't work, just sigh with relief. This attitude can initiate a blueprint of psychophysical response leading to a mutually beneficial interdependence of a free voice and free emotions.

Floor Work for the Tongue

As you continue to play with your tongue stretching and relaxation, it is helpful to explore the experience from the vantage point of the floor. Focusing on the tongue you may have lost your awareness of the connection to breathing deep in the body.

STEP 1

- Relax down onto the floor and lazily drop into the diagonal stretch.

- Let your mind's eye travel down to the hip socket nearest the floor and feed in a thought-feeling impulse for a deep sigh of relief that enters that space and then releases out along the wide diagonal channel of your torso.

- Now play with a rather strange picture: imagine that the roots of your tongue are planted in that hip socket and that your tongue lives in the long diagonal river channel that connects to your mouth. With the tip of your tongue down behind the bottom teeth, stretch the middle of your tongue out of your body and into the air—then relax it back into your mouth.

- Next—sigh a long river of vibration out from hip socket to mouth and as the vibrations escape, stretch your huge tongue out of your body and relax it back in.

- Repeat several times on varying pitches.

- Stretch and relax your huge tongue three times.

- The basic sound will be

- Haa—aa—aah

The throat must yawn wide enough to give the big stretching tongue space to roll forward and out of the mouth. The whole mouth and throat will move into the animal-roar stretch.

When the tongue stretches, the resultant sound will be

- Haah-yaah-yaah-yaah

- Repeat in the diagonal stretch on the other side.

- Repeat on descending and ascending pitches as often as you need in order to make the experience your own.

STEP 2

- Float your knees up over your belly and drop one foot to the floor. Clasp your hands over the front of the other knee and gently shake it toward your belly. Picture the shake going through the thighbone to the hip socket. Let the shaking become a vibrating movement that shudders the very top of the thighbone in the hip socket.

- Imagine that the roots of your tongue are in the hip socket. Feed a deep sigh-impulse down to the hip socket where it connects with sound, and as you sigh the sound out, vibrate the top of the thigh-bone with your hands, and at the same time loosen the middle of your tongue in the middle of your mouth.

It is as though you were shaking the tongue loose from the hip socket.

- Huh-yuh-yuh-yuh-yuh

- Repeat on ascending and descending pitches—with a new sigh-impulse for each new pitch-thought.

- Drop that foot to the floor and float the other knee up. Repeat the knee/thighbone/tongue-shaking.

- Drop that foot to the floor.

Alternating legs, repeat several times on different pitches.

- Next, swing your knees over to one side with the torso and arm following—you are now in the semifetal or half-moon position; curled up on your side with your spine in a C shape, one arm comfortably under your head.

This is almost a sleeping position—use it to enjoy the peace and quiet, the baby-rounded belly, and play with a new picture of your natural breathing impulse center; this time see the breath entering and leaving a little pocket just behind your navel.

- Allow a tiny impulse for sound to enter the navel breath-pocket and leave on the outgoing breath:

- Huh

- Now feed in a medium-size sigh of relief and release it on an easy "hu-uu-uh" and as you do so, loosen the middle of your tongue inside your mouth as you did in Step 6

- Hu-yuh-yuh-yuh-yuh-uuh

- Slowly and luxuriously unfold into a stretch on your side, arching and stretching backward, arms stretched above your head, legs extended, making a long arc from fingers to toes—this is called the banana stretch.

- Induce a smiling yawn—maintain the animal-roar opening and let the sigh-impulse go all the way into your stretched belly and then sigh out with a big tongue stretching and relaxing

- Haah-aah—yaah-yaah-yaah-aaah

- Suddenly relax back into the semifetal position and immediately roll over to the other side—let your knees swing you over.

- Repeat the tongue loosening in the semifetal position followed by the tongue stretching and relaxing in the banana stretch.

- Relax back into the semifetal position.

- Now swing your knees all the way over to the other side, let your torso follow and continue the momentum until you are on your knees with your buttocks on—or near—your heels and your forehead on the floor.

This is the folded leaf position: it has other names in the Yoga tradition— *the child, the rock,* but I prefer *the folded leaf.*

In this position you must look deep inside to find your natural breathing rhythm. Stay here for a minute or so until you have relaxed all your muscles. Gravity takes your spine into a long curve from tailbone to head; your shoulder blades drop away from each other. Soften your belly onto your thighs.

The minute exchange of breath that keeps you alive from moment to moment is now apparent in a space just in front of the sacrum—a space that may seem to exist between the sacrum and the pubic bone.

In this position find the touch of sound deep inside, near the sacrum.

- Huh-huh

- Repeat the tongue-loosening exercises in this position as you picture the vibrations running from the sacrum along your spine, over the back of the neck and the top of the head, through the middle of the face and onto the floor.

- Hu-uu-yuh-yuh-yu-uu-uh

- A new sigh-impulse goes all the way down to the sacral pocket with each new pitch-thought.

Now roll the vibrations into your top teeth.

- Heeeee-yuh-yuh-yuh

men: one octave lower   Δ = breath   continue up 4 or 5 pitches, then come down again

hee yuh yuh yuh   hee yuh yuh yuh   hee yuh yuh yuh   hee yuh yuh yuh

mid-tongue   blade of
rolls   tongue
forward   shakes loose

- Rock yourself up onto all-fours, as if you were going to crawl, then tuck your toes into the floor and float your tailbone up the sky with your head hanging down. You are now in the familiar spine-dropped-to-gravity position.

Maintain the picture of the sound starting in the sacrum, running through your spine over the top of your head and out through the roof of your mouth.

- Slowly build up your spine, sighing out and rolling the vibrations forward as you loosen your tongue on descending pitches.

- Heeeee-yuh-yuh-yuh

men: one octave lower   Δ = breath

hee yuh yuh yuh   hee yuh yuh yuh   hee yuh yuh yuh   hee yuh yuh yuh   hee yuh yuh yuh

- Keep your sense of self in the lower part of your body as you come up. It should take at least five sigh- and tongue-loosenings to arrive at an upright position.

Maintain the sense of dwelling in an alive place in the pelvic/sacral region—don't allow your sense of self to come up into your head now that you are upright.

- Find the touch of sound

Huh-huh

- Walk around. Speak some text. Notice if anything feels different.

■ COMMENTARY

In the floor work you have just completed, I have been encouraging you to take the picture of the starting place for your thought/feeling breath impulse deeper down in your body and have asked you to play with an image of the breath coming from the sacrum, or from behind the navel, or from a place between the sacrum and the pubic bone. Let me emphasize that with all these pictures the diaphragm is still the prime instigator of breathing. The deeper pictures are introduced in order to stimulate the inner abdominal breathing muscles and the crura that I described when I first introduced the floor work. The diaphragm is connected to the lumbar vertebrae and the sacrum through the tendonous musculature of the crura.

There is a continuum from the thin, mushroom- or dome-shaped diaphragm down through muscles connected to the inside of the spine all the way to the pelvic floor that, of course includes the hip sockets. Some voice practitioners refer to "the pelvic diaphragm," but the importance of developing an awareness of these deep, inner abdominal breathing muscles has mostly to do with the large nerve center that radiates out from the sacrum.

>

I spoke earlier about the solar plexus as our inner sun and the sacrum as the source of creativity. The sacral plexus is home. It is where we experience ourselves most profoundly and most powerfully. Complex feelings are often aroused when we allow ourselves to linger in the sacral region. Back in the mists of time and presumably in ancient Rome, someone named this part of the body "sacrum;" the Latin word shares its etymological root with the English "sacred." In preclassical times the triangular sacral bone was sacrificed to the gods. In the Tantric tradition the sacrum is the home of "kundalini," the most powerful (sometimes dangerously so) of spiritual energies. Kundalini is seen as a serpent whose power can bring transcendence or destruction. In the Tantric tradition the sexual and spiritual powers of kundalini must be carefully separated and controlled in action—but sex and spirit cohabit in the sacrum.

In the Middle Ages in Europe, before the Church put a safety cordon between the two, there was no experiential division between sex and soul. The word spirit meant both, which is why, a couple of centuries later, Shakespeare made use of the, by then, double meaning of the word to such good effect: "Th'expense of spirit in a waste of shame. Is lust in action . . ." (Sonnet 129) means, on one level, that lust leads the soul into disrepute, and on another, quite literally means that lust is the ejaculation of sperm into a shameful body (waist).

If we can condition our mind/body-breathing message system to encompass both the sacral and the solar plexus, there is an increased likelihood that we will be open to instinctive, spontaneous, reflexive action in the creative and the emotional realms.

This floor work is particularly aimed at that conditioning. Once you have established it and kept it active through regular exercise, there is nothing special about it—it will become your "natural" way of functioning.

As you continue working on freeing the channel, remember your deep breathing connection. One of the by-products of the floor work should be that by now you have experienced the vibrations of sound in the bones of your body from pelvis to skull: you are the embodiment of your voice. These rich, embodied vibrations need a wide, unencumbered channel through which to travel. Work on the jaw and the tongue helps to keep the throat channel open, but there is another vital part of the throat that must be attended to for maximum freedom in the channel—the soft palate. The soft-palate area sometimes causes traffic jams, even fatal crashes. If the part of the channel that leads from the throat to the mouth is closed, it will kill the vibrations; if it is half-closed, it will hold them up and distort them.

PRACTICE

It can take a long time for the tongue and the jaw to relax. Daily life will tense them on a regular basis. Just as regularly, you should massage and shake your jaw, and stretch and loosen your tongue. This is a lifetime's resource. Be patient and explore the preceding exercises over at least a week before adding the next channel exercise.

7
Workday Seven

Freeing the Channel: The soft palate
Opening and limbering . . . space

■ Prepare to work for:
ONE HOUR OR MORE

I took you on the *via negativa* to work on the jaw and the tongue: do nothing in the jaw and tongue muscles so that the breathing muscles can do their job freely. Remove tension in order to allow something new to happen. For the next part of the channel for sound we will work more positively and directly to limber up certain muscles. In fact, the *via negativa* still holds true because the aim will be to remove a condition of desuetude in the soft-palate musculature, restoring a natural ability to respond on the involuntary level that will give full functioning back to some unused resonating channels.

The palate that forms the upper part of the mouth is hard and bony in front (the upper gum ridge just behind the top teeth), hard and domed in the middle (the roof of the mouth) and soft and fleshy at the very back (the soft palate). From the middle of the soft palate, the uvula hangs down above the back of the tongue, a small, fleshy, vestigial appendage. In some people the uvula is rather long, and in some it has virtually disappeared. A long uvula can contribute to a somewhat hoarse or guttural tone; sometimes it prevents a clear use of the upper register. In such cases, regular and conscientious exercise of the soft palate will result in a shorter uvula and a clear passageway.

On either side of the uvula, the soft palate is all flesh and muscle. For working purposes you can regard it as either the doorway from the throat into the mouth or as the trapdoor leading up into the middle and upper resonators.

Without regular, extended vocal exercise, the soft palate tends to become lazy or stiff. If it is lazy, it hangs down like a heavy curtain at the back of the mouth absorbing and muffling vibrations. In this condition it is hard for the sound to travel clearly through the mouth cavity. Some of it will stop at the doorway, and some will be rerouted up through the nose. Nasality nearly always results from a lazy, dead soft palate. If the soft palate is stiff the voice will be monotonous. One of the functions of the soft palate is to respond to changing pitches with tiny changes in muscle tone that almost invisibly lift and lower it as the pitch goes up or down. In a free-speaking voice, pitch is constantly changing in response to thought inflection, so the freedom of the soft palate to respond on an involuntary level is essential to accurately nuanced communication. Stiffness or laziness in the soft palate muscle blocks this response mechanism. Movement in the soft palate is very subtle in speaking, but it can easily be seen to lift in response to the thought of a sung high note. Open your mouth wide and look in a mirror at the soft palate. Think of a high note—without voicing it—and you should immediately see the soft palate lift in involuntary response to the thought. It may not do this so readily if you actually sing the note. The relationship of thought to involuntary soft-palate response may be intact even though habitual effort may inhibit that response in producing sound.

I cannot overemphasize the fact that these movements occur naturally on the involuntary level of the nervous system. The work you will be doing is aimed at restoring and revitalizing this involuntary connection. If, having observed that the soft palate lifts in response to the thought of a high note, you proceed to lift the soft palate whenever you want to sing a high note, you defeat the aim of a free, natural voice. The conscious mind cannot operate these muscles with enough subtlety to preserve the expressive integrity of the natural voice. It can, however, tone up and tune up the muscles so that they respond with more agility to the involuntary demands. We shall begin to work on the soft palate in its capacity as the doorway from the throat into the mouth. As the muscles tone up, vibrations will be released more easily into the face and skull resonators; hence its second name, trapdoor.

STEP 1 Establish where the soft palate is by looking at it in a mirror with light shining directly into your wide-open mouth.

Put the mirror down and relax your mouth without closing it.

- Very gently whisper (just breath, no voice at all) the syllable "kaah." The vowel is the same in the first syllable of the word *father*.

- Focus into the place where the "k" is formed and observe minutely and in slow motion what happens physically for that little noise to occur, using your physical awareness and your mind's eye.

  (1.) The thought "kaah" is formed in the brain.
  (2.) Breath goes in.
  (3.) The back of the tongue rises to touch the hard palate just in front of the soft palate.
  (4.) Breath is momentarily trapped behind the soft palate.
  (5.) The breath is released with a sharp pop as the two surfaces spring apart.

For the following exercises, think of the "k" being formed between the back of the tongue and the actual soft palate—a little farther back than the "k" used in speaking.

Think a definite "aaah" after the "k" not "uh" or "aw," so that the tongue and the soft palate will be quite far apart and the breath will neither gargle over the uvula nor scrape down into the throat.

- Again whisper a clear, clean "kaah" focusing on the touch of soft palate to back of tongue.

- Then whisper "kaah" on an incoming breath.

  (1.) Before the breath goes in again, the back of the tongue rises to touch the hard palate just in front of the soft palate.
  (2.) Breath is momentarily trapped in front of the soft palate.
  (3.) As the two surfaces spring apart, the breath flies in on a whispered "kaah."

- Breathe out again normally on "kaah," then whisper "kaah" as the breath goes in.

- In the rhythm of ordinary breathing, whisper "kaah" as you breathe in and as you breathe out.

On the incoming breath the "k" will happen as the back of the tongue and the soft palate are blown apart by the breath trying to get in. On the outgoing breath it will happen as they are blown apart from behind by the breath trying to get out.

As you continue letting the breath in and out on whispered "kaah"s, be aware of the different temperatures of your breath incoming and outgoing: cool, coming in; warm, going out.

Register which surfaces of the mouth are hit by the cool air.

Check that the front of the tongue stays relaxed, tip touching the back of the bottom teeth.

Put your hand on your breathing area to feel a springy central response to the springy channel.

Now put your focus specifically into the sensation of cool air hitting your soft palate as it rises off the whispered ingoing "kaah."

- Begin to give the cool air more space in the soft-palate area.

- When you whisper "kaah" on the outgoing breath, the aim is to give the warm breath as much space in the soft palate as the cool air had.

You are now working on the flexibility of the soft palate by asking it to respond to sensory stimuli. At the same time you are training your mind to be able to connect with an esoteric set of muscles normally not under conscious control. This you can do only through sharpened awareness.

- Now yawn wide and examine the behavior of the soft palate in the mirror as you yawn. It will spontaneously lift and stretch much farther than you can consciously lift and stretch it, but if you focus your attention into the yawn muscles you can use that awareness to extend your conscious work on the soft palate.

Yawning is so pleasurable that it is easy to get lost in the overall sensation, but you can make good use of a yawn, so it is worth harnessing your attention to the specifics that make up the whole, and even reprogramming the yawn a little to spread its benefits farther.

■ COMMENTARY ON THE YAWN

Do you yawn vertically or horizontally?

Most people favor the vertical yawn, and most of the stretching occurs in a downward direction. The face pulls down and the jaw pushes down. If you begin to think more horizontally as you yawn you can reprogram the act so that you arrive at a completely circular opening, stretching both vertically and horizontally. You can develop a big, deliberate stretch in the soft palate, the throat, and the middle of the face. As you yawn you should be able to see your top and bottom teeth exposed, the soft palate stretched high and wide, and you should have a clear view through to the very back wall of the throat.

If you have managed in the course of this exploration to induce several genuine yawns, you will be in a good, healthy state to continue. Your eyes and nose will run and so will your saliva, your breathing apparatus has been stimulated and you have been in perfect touch with involuntary processes while being aware of them.

STEP 2

■ Looking in a mirror, repeat the exercise in Step 1. As you start giving the cool ingoing air more space in the soft palate, use your awareness of the yawn muscles to induce exactly the same stretch on the ingoing "kaah" as you had when you yawned. (The horizontal yawn and your focus clearly on lifting the soft palate, rather than moving the tongue downward, will prevent a tendency to gag.)

■ Now use your awareness to lift the soft palate consciously into the yawn stretch on the outgoing "kaah."

■ Breathe in and out on a whispered "kaah," lifting and stretching the soft palate to its fullest extent each time.

■ Repeat two or three times, then rest, swallow, and moisten the throat, which may have become rather dry.

Make sure the exercise is isolated to the soft palate and the back of the tongue. Your ever-eager jaw may well try to get in on the act. If necessary, restrain it manually.

Make sure the ingoing breath goes down to the diaphragm and even lower —don't let the upper chest take over.

As your throat becomes more accustomed to the cold air traveling through it, you will be less bothered by dryness or the coughing that sometimes happens in the beginning. Don't be put off by the unfamiliar feeling of so much cold air going into your throat. It will not harm you, and if you avoid the process you may be perpetuating a habitual unwillingness to open the throat, which, though a vulnerable area, can suffer badly from an exaggerated instinct to protect it.

You will probably have realized that this opening is the same as that of the animal roar. The difference is that now you are directing your attention to the interior musculature at the back of the mouth.

Practice the exercise again with the following observations:

The movements should be springy, and the yawn stretch should be elastic.

Do not hold the yawn-stretch position.

The breath should feel and sound light and transparent.

Be careful not to drag the breath in. It should feel as though it is traveling through the spaces of the throat, not scraping over the walls.

Gradually speed up the process, so that the exercise becomes staccato, fast, light, and elastic while you still experience a good stretch.

Read through the following steps so that when you do the exercise they can go in a fast sequence. Use a mirror.

STEP 3

- Breathe in cool air on a whispered "kaah" with a full smiling yawn-stretch.

Picture the air going down to the breathing centers.

- Release warm vibrations from the pelvic floor on "hi"—as in "high" not "hit"—letting them travel up and over the stretched soft palate, the roof of the mouth, and the top teeth and then out into the air. As the sound releases out, roll the middle of the tongue all the way forward and out of the mouth and relax it back three times, the resultant sound being "hi-yi-yi-yi." Keep the tip of the tongue down behind the bottom teeth.

In this exercise you are giving the sound the experience of escaping through a much larger channel than usual. The larger channel should stimulate a larger release from the source, giving the opportunity for tasting a larger sense of freedom. At the same time you should be incorporating the tongue-stretching device so that you do not start to push in a habitual response to larger impulses.

- Practice Step 3, using a mirror to check that the soft palate remains up and stretched throughout the whole "sentence" of the exercise. You should be able to see through to the back wall of the throat even when the middle of the tongue rolls forward.

Induce a yawn impulse throughout the exercise. You will not actually yawn because a yawn happens on the ingoing breath, but if you can think yawn on the outgoing sound your soft palate will stay up.

- Repeat the process on ascending pitches, breathing in on "kaah" each time and then sighing the vibrations out freely through the space while stretching and relaxing your tongue three times on the outgoing sigh.

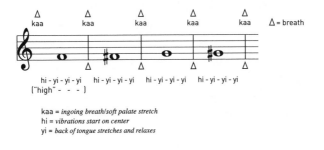

hi = vibrations start on center
yi = back of tongue stretches and relaxes

- Hi-yi-yi-yi.

- Feel the breath and the vibrations on the stretched dome of the soft palate and on the dome of the roof of your mouth.

- With each new breath/thought, picture the outgoing sound starting from the pelvic floor and flowing up and out of the body with a soft, silky release of the diaphragm up through the rib cage.

- Let everything relax.

STEP 4   Having limbered up the channel muscles on a fairly technical level, I'd like you now to observe how they react to an imaginative stimulus.

Read through this first, and then, with your eyes closed, play it, frame by frame like a movie through your mind/body imaging apparatus. *Do not anticipate the result.* If you can get someone to read it to you frame by frame, so much the better.

- The back-story is that you have been out in the country walking all afternoon and now are on your way home for a quiet, solitary evening. You are contented. You come to the shoreline of the small lake near your house.

- Frame 1: You are standing at the edge of the lake looking down at your feet, which are almost touching the water that laps lazily in and out.

- Frame 2: You slowly and pleasurably begin to look up from your feet and out across the surface of the lake—very slowly—looking at the ducks and the wavelets—suddenly you see a fish jump. You then see a little island in the middle of the lake.

- Frame 3: Idly you look past the island across the water to the other side of the lake.

- Frame 4: You see someone standing on the opposite shore.

- Frame 5: To your surprise and delight you see it is a good friend and you are filled with the desire to call—and you call, "Hi—i-i-i."

- Repeat this scenario as if for the first time but this time in slow motion, *and* whisper the call.

You will notice that when you suddenly see your friend, not only does the desire to call fill you with breath but your soft palate lifts as the breath enters. There is a simultaneous response to the desire impulse in both the source and the channel that prepares the vocal apparatus for expression.

- Repeat the whole scenario at normal speed. The exercise is to re-create the circumstances without predetermining the result. Let the result happen—don't make it happen.

■ **COMMENTARY**

This, of course, is the everlasting foundation of good acting: to create and re-create as if for the first time every time, and to set the circumstances step by step so that they lead to the surprise of something unexpected happening—every time. You can help to condition your thinking/feeling/doing process to commit to moment-by-moment causal experience as you continue to work on the "technical" aspects of your voice. The ingoing desire to speak imprints the inner workings of the body and all you need to do is release the desire. Communication is the by-product of desire and freedom.

All too often communication is effort. One works to reach the other person, to make oneself heard. The head, even the body, pushes forward; the shoulders tighten; the abdominal muscles push. But communication can always be experienced as release, if one commits to feeding in the causal desire.

Translate the image of your standing on the edge of a lake calling to your friend into an image of you standing on the stage aware of your audience. You want them to hear and understand not only what you are saying but why you are saying it. Your desire to be truly heard gathers the energies of the central nervous system into a communicative force that flows out to your audience. You are not "projecting;" you do not necessarily need volume; you are fully present on the stage—and at the same time you are in the audience. Communication has happened if you are free.

STEP 5   With an awareness of the spaces now apparent at the back of your mouth but without consciously opening your soft palate, return to the tongue exercise.

- Heeee-yuh-yuh-yuh

- Observe whether you feel any new vibrations or different spaces.

As you go higher, notice whether the soft palate responds without your consciously lifting it to provide new paths for the higher pitches.

- Is it easier to go higher?

STEP 6

- Put the back of the tongue and the soft palate together. Notice that you must now breathe through your nose. Add vibration and you will make an "ng" sound. This is the sound at the end of the word "sing." You are humming through "ng" instead of "mmmm."

- Continuing the vibrations, slowly lift your soft palate and drop the back of your tongue into the yawn stretch. The sound will open to a wide "aaaah."

- Repeat with three closings and openings of the soft palate.

- Ngaah-ngaah-ngaah

- The mouth is in the animal-roar stretch. Once the jaw has opened, it must not move. All the movement is in the back of the mouth.

- You should be able to see all the way to the back wall of the throat on the "aaah."

- Repeat on ascending pitches.

  Speak:

- Ngaa-i

- Then add three tongue stretches:

- Ngaaa-i-yi-yi-yi

STEP 7

- Roll your head on a hum and be aware of the soft palate and the back of your tongue. The space between them should be constantly changing as you roll. When your head is dropped back there is more space, when your head is forward there is less space, but the soft palate and the back of the tongue should never touch each other as you hum.

- Drop your spine down on a hum looking for any differences there may be in the quality or disposition of the vibrations. Build up your spine, humming, and release the sound at the top.

- Speak "huh-hummmmmmuh."

You should sense more natural space in your mouth/throat cavity than before. You may feel vibrations coming from that cavity. You should feel in general that there are more vibrations as a result of the greater space. Take advantage of whatever greater sense of freedom this gives.

When you come back to the tongue and humming exercises, allow the soft palate to adjust as it chooses. Do not attempt to keep it lifted or you will end up sounding false, plum voiced, and pompous.

I suggest that when you next explore the soft-palate exercises you do so lying on the floor, in the diagonal stretch positions, so that you can connect the wide throat channel with the hip-socket spaces. The banana stretch is also ideal for exercising the soft palate. Be creative in your application of the floor work to the channel exercises.

PRACTICE

The progression of exercises from breathing to touch of sound, humming, and floor work with a particular focus on the jaw, tongue, and soft palate continues for at least two weeks.

8

Workday Eight

The Spine and the Channel:
Connection . . . source, journey, destination

■ Prepare to work for:
ONE HOUR OR MORE

Before our final exploration of the channel for sound I'd like to revisit the spine. Now that you have spent a considerable amount of time visualizing different parts of the vocal anatomy and sharpening your ability to access rather esoteric areas such as the hip sockets, the soft palate, and the back of the tongue, your enhanced imaging abilities can be deployed to develop a subtler relationship with your spine. A subtler relationship means one that is more awake, more alive in the two-way street between body and brain. The message systems that run the human organism travel in both directions along the spinal column. The brain depends on the electrical circuitry of the body for its intelligence.

By detailing the connection of breath and sound with the spine, you will further encourage the instinctive reflex actions of your inner abdominal breathing musculature—the ones knit into the lower vertebrae and the pelvic floor—and at the same time train your brain to think specifically. I will be asking you to see and move independently the individual vertebrae of your spine, the three or four at the very bottom and the very top will move together. If your brain can think each vertebra into action then it is more likely that you will have the precision to think each word in a line of text.

STEP 1

- Go down onto all-fours, as if you were going to crawl. Start with your spine parallel to the ground and your hands underneath your shoulders. Keep your elbows straight but not stiff, your hands pointing forward. Let your head hang down.

- Move your mind's eye down to your tailbone, the coccyx. The tailbone is located deep inside the buttocks. Relax your buttocks and relax the backs of your thighs.

- Tell your tailbone to move slowly and subtly up toward the ceiling and then down toward the ground.

This is a very small, very internal movement. Obviously the tailbone is attached to the sacrum and the sacrum is part of the pelvis so the pelvis will also move, but the action should be pictured in the tailbone.

- Now very slowly move the tailbone up toward the ceiling and notice that if it continues to move upward, the sacrum and the next lumbar vertebrae will start moving *down* toward the ground. *Picture each vertebra moving independently, one by one* down toward the ground—all the way through the small of your back and between your shoulder blades.

When your mind's eye visualizes the bull vertebra, it will see that inevitably it *must* now *rise* toward the ceiling. So must the vertebrae of the neck.

Think of your skull as the final vertebra that rises up off the neck vertebrae as if it would like to meet your tailbone.

Your spine is now arched down toward the ground.

- Immediately send your mind's eye down to your tailbone. Specifically, move your tailbone slowly toward the ground. Notice that as it continues *downward,* your sacrum and the next lumbar vertebrae start moving up toward the ceiling. *Picture each vertebra moving independently, one by one* up toward the ceiling.

When your mind's eye reaches the bull vertebra it will see that inevitably it *must* now *descend* toward the ground with the neck vertebrae following so that the final vertebra, your skull, hangs down.

■ Leave your belly muscles completely relaxed.

Your spine is now rounded up toward the ceiling. Your belly hangs from it like the belly of an old tigress.

■ Immediately send your mind's eye down to your tailbone. Specifically and slowly start the movement of the tailbone upward and let your mind move vertebra by vertebra along the spine until your head comes up and the spine has arrived in an arch.

■ Your belly muscles are relaxed.

■ Immediately send your mind's eye down to your tailbone and slowly travel in the other direction.

■ Sit back on your heels.

If you merely arch your spine and round it you will successfully ruin the exercise. It is like saying in one rush: Tobeornottobethatisthequestion. You might try speaking that line all as one crammed thought as you quickly arch your spine. Then try speaking it as though the thought "to be" begins in your tailbone and travels word by word "or not to be" along your vertebrae through the small of your back. Then the words *that is the* are between your shoulder blades until the word *question* comes out as your skull rises.

■ Repeat the physical exercise starting with the tailbone, and let your vertebrae thoughts run a little faster through your spine without jumping a single vertebra. Keep sending your starting impulse down to the tailbone whether your spine is moving into the arch or into the round.

■ Leave your belly muscles completely relaxed.

■ Now play with the notion that your tailbone initiates your breath and see if you can let your tailbone tell you whether the breath likes to go in as it descends or ascends.

- Then letting your mind's energy run faster along your spine from tailbone to skull, so that your breath goes in on one whole movement and out on the other, see if your whole spine can reveal when the breath likes to go in and when it likes to go out.

Find out how your spine likes to breathe — don't let your belly dominate.

You may find that when the spine arches, the breath goes in most easily, and when the spine rounds, the breath releases out most easily.

Or you may find that when the spine rounds, the breath goes in most easily, and when the spine arches, the breath releases out most easily.

- In the spirit of objective research, now lie down on your belly— head to one side, arms down at your sides.

- Without sound, feed in a deep sigh of relief and let it fall out of you. Notice in which direction the small of your back moves as the breath comes in: then notice in which direction your tailbone moves.

I think you will agree that in this position it is clear that for the ingoing breath, the tailbone moves subtly groundward and the small of the back clearly moves up toward the ceiling. The directions reverse as the breath escapes.

In this position you can experience the natural, organic engagement of the lower spine in the breathing process.

Notice also that as the breath enters, your stomach moves down into the floor as the small of your back moves upward, thus creating the largest space for the diaphragm.

- Come back onto all fours and apply the observations you have made. As the tailbone goes *down*, with the belly dropping and the spine rounding *up*, the breath enters: as the tailbone goes *up* and the spine arches *down*, the breath releases out.

There is always a lot of discussion with my students around this exercise. Anyone who has done modern dance will have learned how to contract her abdominal muscles in conjunction with rounding the spine. It will seem almost impossible to let the stomach drop while rounding the spine. But in the interest of the freedom of your breath and emotion you must be able to detach your abdominal muscles from your back muscles. You must be able to move your spine independently of your abdominal muscles. Your diaphragm cannot drop freely as long as spine and abdomen are like conjoined twins. Play with the image of the old tigress; imagine a Buddha belly. You won't suddenly become obese!

Those of you who have conscientiously done sit-ups and push-ups also have a conditioned relationship of your stomach muscles to your spine. Sit-ups and push-ups do not help your breathing.

The best way to recondition this area is to keep going back down onto your belly, observe the organic response to the deep sigh, and immediately come back onto all fours and apply the picture.

Do not try to coordinate or impose—just picture.

STEP 2

- Practice the spine movements—always starting with the tailbone—with this thought: "Tailbone drops; belly drops; breath flies in" then "Tailbone goes up; spine arches down; breath escapes all along the spine on a fffff."

- Run your mind quickly through the vertebrae on each movement.

- Sit back on your heels.

You are now going to add sound to these movements. Read the instructions first and then follow them step by step:

- The tailbone will drop, and breath will fly in as the spine rounds.

- As the tailbone goes up let it create the touch of sound

- Huh-huh

- As soon as the lumbar vertebrae move, close your lips on a hum.

- Mmmmmm

- Let the hum travel along the vertebrae of your spine as it arches.

- When the final vertebra, your skull, comes up off the end of your spine you will find that the vibrations escape

- U-u-u-u-u-u-uh

- Tailbone drops; belly drops; breath flies in as the spine rounds.

- Huh-hu (in the tailbone as it rises)
  Mmmmmm (all along the spine)
  U-u-uh (as the skull lifts up, leaving the jaw behind).

- Repeat on ascending pitches.

- Sit back on your heels.

- When you do this again add a playful picture: your spine is a toy railroad track, the hum is the train. You start the engine in the tailbone, "huh-hu-uuh," as soon as your lips close on the hum, the toy train travels swiftly along the railroad track—not skipping any ties—and at the end of the track your top jaw lifts up and the toy train flies out to the wild blue yonder.

- Don't hold on to it. Let it go. Immediately return to the tailbone station for the next hum-train trip.

- Repeat the exercise with the same picture. Enjoy it. Smile if you can as the hum-train flies off to the wild blue yonder. This will lift your cheeks and open your soft palate.

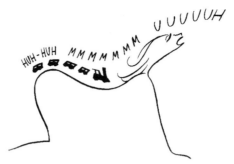

- As the vibrations release with your skull rising off your bottom jaw, stretch and release your tongue three times to prove you are not using it for the sound.

You can picture the hum train flying off into the distance while your tongue waves goodbye.

STEP 3 The Squat.

- Tuck your toes into the floor and rock yourself back into a squatting position—your feet should be far enough apart for the soles to be flat on the floor.

- Put your hands together and push your knees away from each other with your elbows.

- Drop your head onto your clasped hands.

- Feel your tailbone sinking down toward the floor and feed a deep sigh into your hip sockets that releases out along your spine.

- Let the sigh find sound.

- Now gently stretch one leg out to the side. Massage the leg muscles. Point and flex the foot, encouraging the leg to elongate.

- Imagine that your mouth is in your foot and breathe in and out on a whispered "kaah" to stretch the soft palate.

The picture to play with is of the sole of your foot as a mouth and your leg as a throat while you widen the actual outgoing throat channel.

- Keep your outstretched heel on the floor, then shift your pelvis toward it, bending that knee. The opposite leg stretches out to the other side.

- Repeat the in and out soft-palate stretching on whispered "kaah"s.

- Moving from one leg stretch to the other, breathe in on a "kaah" and sigh out on

- Hi-yi-yi-yi

- Sigh as though the sound runs from foot to foot through your legs.

Come into the middle of the squat and once more sigh the sound out over your spine—as if your mouth is in the back of your neck.

- Float your tailbone up toward the ceiling and gently uncurl until you are standing.

- Shake your legs out.

- Shake the sound down through your legs.

- Speak a speech, a poem, or some text on all fours, in the squat, while shaking your legs out. Let the words release through the movements. When you come back to standing, maintain an awareness of the connection to your lower body.

PRACTICE

Daily.

9
Workday Nine

Throat Awareness:
The open throat . . . chasm

■ Prepare to work for:
ONE HOUR OR MORE

We have become aware of the jaw, the tongue, and the soft palate as component parts of the channel through which sound travels. Intrinsically the throat is the major portion of the channel. In dealing with the soft palate, you have also been dealing with the throat. When you yawn the stretch is not restricted to the soft palate but affects a mass of pharyngeal muscle as well. I should refer to it as the pharynx from now on, but since *pharynx* is not a word in common usage, I shall use the word *throat*, meaning the part of the channel that runs behind the soft palate from the height of the nose down to the collar bone. The throat contains the larynx and provides the primary resonating cavities in the spaces around, above, and below it. The back wall of the throat is lined with muscle tissue that reacts to changing pitch with a toning response that tunes the throat cavity to give resonating feedback appropriate to that pitch. The resonating aspect of the throat will be explored more fully in the next chapter. Here, the interest is in the throat as part of a free channel for sound.

The main working point here is the sharp angle at which the throat passage turns into the mouth passage. If the soft palate is lazy and the tongue tense, this angle quickly becomes jammed.

Behind and below this corner, the throat should be pictured—for working purposes—as a wide, unblocked passageway all the way down to the diaphragm and the pelvic floor. The less interest taken in the larynx the better.

The only work to be done with the throat at this point is to clear the angle at which a traffic jam can occur, stimulate the sensation of spaciousness, and explore a more direct and freer connection with the breathing centers as the channel frees.

STEP 1

- Lengthen the front of your neck so that your head is as far back as it will easily go without collapsing into your shoulders. See how the picture of the channel changes in this position.

There is now a straight column through which breath or sound can flow unimpeded from the pelvic floor to the sky. No corners to turn; no traffic jams.

- In this position sigh out a whispered "haaaa."

- Then, using the back of the neck, bring the head up on top of the spine.

- Visualize the shape of the column now that the head is up, and sigh from the breathing centers a whispered "hu-u-u-uh."

When the head is back it is almost impossible to use the throat to support the sound, the breath must take over. You can, in this position, have a very distinct impression of the connection with the deepest breathing areas. When the head comes up again, maintain that impression so that the connection is graphically clear as you release breath into the whispered "huh" and realize that, despite the angle the breath must now follow, there still need be no interference in the throat.

STEP 2

- Lengthen the front of the neck as before. Think of the tongue and jaw as belonging to the front of your body, and the soft palate and skull to the back of your body. Picture a wide chasm between your front and your back. At the very bottom of the chasm is a warm pool of vibrations.

- Release vibrations from the pool up through the chasm like a geyser, "haa-aa-aa-aaah."

The throat remains totally uninvolved. The impulse for sound should be felt springing powerfully from a center of energy down below.

- Lengthen the neck up on top of the spine, the head floating on top. Leave the jaw hanging loose. The chasm changes its shape but it does not close. Release vibrations from the unchanged warm pool of vibrations below, "hu-uh-uh-uh."

As you continue to relax the throat and remove its ability to support sound, you should find your connection with the centers of your breathing becoming clearer.

These breathing centers become energy centers.

- Repeat the first part of this step, but this time focus your attention both on the starting point of sound deep in your body and on a spot on the ceiling (or in the sky) to which you want the vibrations to travel. Release "haa-aa-aaah" from the central pool of energy/vibrations and picture an unbroken stream of sound flowing all the way up through your body, through the chasm, through the air to your chosen arrival point.

- Bring your neck and head up—don't let the channel close—pick a spot straight ahead of you (on a person if possible) and release vibrations from the warm central store to that spot.

- With your neck and head back, imagine the pool of vibrations with color. If a color does not immediately occur to you, try blue. Release a long blue stream "haa-aa-aa-aah" of blue vibrations to paint the ceiling blue or to join the sky.

- Bring your neck and head up. Release your vibrations of color (perhaps in this position they change color) to paint the wall or the person opposite you "hu-uh-uh-uh."

- Repeat any or all of the tongue, soft palate, humming exercises in conjunction with (1) your increased connection with the breathing/energy source, (2) your awareness of a relaxed throat, and (3) colors in the vibrations of sound—if they stimulate you.

The use of colors helps initially to bring some extra life into the sound. The mind and the imagination will be more actively involved and the sounds will have some specific content, they will not be vibrations for their own sake. If you begin to use your imagination in this way you may find that different colors evoke different feelings in you. Experiment to discover which are more peaceful, which more stimulating. But make sure you visualize them centrally, connecting with your feeling in the solar plexus and the sacral plexus. You can get lost in inventive doodling if the colors emanate from your head.

PRACTICE

Incorporate this awareness into your daily practice.

Part Two

The Resonating Ladder

The Next Six to Eight Weeks of Work
Developing and Strengthening

10

Workday Ten

Developing and Strengthening: Chest, mouth,
teeth resonators
Finding resonance . . . purple, blue, yellow

■ Prepare to work for:
ONE HOUR OR MORE

What is the Resonating Ladder?

You have now, in theory at least, freed the breathing process and therewith
the source of sound, and you have freed the channel for sound through the
relaxation of tensions in the jaw, the tongue and the throat. In practice you
may have only become dimly aware of some of the components of your vocal
apparatus, making occasional, haphazard contact with them. In theory, you
cannot go on to develop your voice safely until you have freed it, but in
practice you cannot wait for such a perfect process, so you will now proceed
with the development and discover more liberation at the same time.

The next stage of the work is based on the assumption that you can isolate resonating cavities throughout the body and increase the vibrations in
those cavities. In physical fact, the exercises are perhaps diversionary, and
employ the mind in such a way that the muscles governing the vocal folds
are strengthened and the folds themselves function more and more efficiently. As the mind becomes conscious of the three to four octaves of range
available in the speaking voice and of the endless variety of resonating quality within that range, the breathing musculature and vocal folds respond with
more subtlety and with more strength.

We will be looking at the resonating system as if it were a kind of ladder.
The resonators are a series of cavities going from big and broad at the base
and gradually getting smaller and narrower toward the top—like a certain

type of ladder. They have many different shapes as well as sizes, built in as they are to the skeleton. I shall use as clear a set of working pictures as I can, imagination, emotion, analogy, absurdity, or fact—to make tangible the complex coordination of the involuntary nervous system with a highly sophisticated acoustical mechanism.

Each part of the voice has its own resonating rung on the ladder, and the ladder is the body from the chest to the mouth, teeth, sinuses, nose, and skull. In the following exercises you will be directing your voice to move up and down the resonating ladder until every part of it is available, familiar and safe. Weak rungs can be strengthened, and gaps in the ladder can be filled in ways that are palpable. Your vocal range of three to four octaves can be mapped clearly and your use of it can become physically familiar through regular travel.

We will begin to work with two large resonating cavities, the chest and the mouth, but before working with sound it is necessary to do some physical preparation exercises.

STEP 1

■ Lengthen the front of your neck so your head is back as in the throat-freeing exercise. Picture the resulting wide channel down into your chest. Imagine it broadening out into the rib cage as though into a great, hollow cave.

■ Focus clearly on the back of your neck, and be sure not to use any jaw muscle strength. Do not tighten your stomach muscles as you lengthen the top seven vertebrae that comprise your neck until your head floats on top of the topmost vertebra. Notice that the channel has changed its shape but has not closed.

■ Drop your head forward without letting your mouth close. Notice that the channel has again changed its shape but that it need not close, although the opening in this position is narrow.

■ Bring the top seven vertebrae of the neck back and up into alignment with the rest of the spine, the head floating on top. Leave the jaw muscles loose enough for the jaw to drop slightly as the head comes up. The space between the teeth is a little wider than it was when the head was forward.

- Lengthen the front of your neck, leaving the bottom jaw behind so that the wide channel—the chasm—through the throat to the chest appears again.

The primary action here is to shift all the responsibility for moving the head into the top seven vertebrae of the spine (the back of the neck). The by-product of this action as the neck moves from front to back is that the shape of the channel automatically changes as the relationship between the skull and jaw changes. This spontaneous response depends on complete freedom in the jaw hinges and, as it is possible that there is still some tension there, you may, for the time being, consciously have to drop your jaw when you bring your neck up from the forward position and over to the back.

- Practice Step 1 until you feel you have made strong contact with the back of the neck and that you can move it through the three positions without any tightening in the stomach muscles. Put your hand on your stomach and insist that your breathing continue in a natural easy rhythm as your head and neck go back, up and forward. Remember the great chasm that opens as the neck goes back and never quite closes in the other positions.

STEP 2

- With your neck and head back, as in Step 2 of the throat exercises, find a warm pool of vibrations deep down at the bottom of the chasm, and with a lazy released sigh, warm the chest on "haa-aa-aaah."

Let it be a low, very relaxed, warm sound. Make sure it is all vibration, not breathy at all.

Put your hand on your chest and register the vibrations of that sound throughout your chest.

- Repeat the sounds three times, long and slow:

- Ha-a-a-ah—ha-a-a-ah—ha-a-a-ah

- △

- Repeat the sounds five times long and slow:

- Ha-a-a-ah—ha-a-a-ah—ha-a-a-ah—ha-a-a-ah—ha-a-a-ah

- △

- Repeat the sounds five times a little faster and more conversationally:

- Haah-haah-haah-haah-haah

- △

- Bring the back of the neck up, head floating on top: know that the shape of the channel has changed but not closed, and allow the sound to flow into your mouth cavity on "hu-uh-uh."

- Let the speaking pitch rise a little and you will find the sound that awakens a strong sensation of vibrations all through the roof of the mouth. Repeat the sounds until you find resonating feedback from the bony mouth cavity:

- Hu-u-uh hu-u-uh hu-u-uh

- △

- Huh-huh-huh-huh-huh

- △

- Huh-huh-huh

- △

- Lengthen the neck back again, this time as though you are removing the bony mouth-box resonator from the picture, leaving yourself only with the lower throat and chest resonators.

- Find a low sound on "haa-aa-aah" that rumbles around the chest cavities. Indulge and wallow in the sound. Go as low as you can without pushing down in the throat in any way.

- Beat your chest with your fists to shake up and awaken more vibrations.

- Bring the neck up again, picturing the mouth-box resonator restored as the head floats up.

- Find a sound and a pitch that will awaken the optimum resonating feedback from the bony walls of the mouth-box.

- Go from mouth resonator (neck straight) to chest resonator (neck back) and back again several times:

- Huh-huh-huh-huh-huh   △

- Neck back

- Haah-haah-haah-haah-haah   △

- Neck up

- huh-huh-huh-huh-huh   △

- Neck back

- Haah-haah-haah-haah-haah   △

Observe the change of speaking pitch and the completely different quality of resonance in each cavity.

- Go from chest resonator to mouth resonator, and then drop the neck forward.

- The channel is now very narrow and sound falling forward through it will arrive on the front teeth, shaped by the channel into "heeeeee."

- Feel the vibrations on the front teeth and find the speaking pitch (slightly higher than the mouth pitch) that awakens the clearest resonating feedback from the front teeth.

- Now move the head from the front, to the top, to the back, using only the back of the neck to move it. Allow the shape of the resonating channel to change as spontaneously as possible in response to the changing relationship of the skull and jaw and release a flow of vibrations from deep in the body that focuses on the front teeth, the mouth, and the chest according to the altering shape of the channel:

- Hee-hee-hee (front teeth vibrations: neck forward)

- Huh-huh-huh (mouth vibrations: neck straight)

- Haah-haah-haah (chest vibrations: neck back)

- Haah-haah-haah (low pitch: chest resonance)

- Huh-huh-huh (middle pitch: mouth resonance)

- Hee-hee-hee (slightly higher: front teeth resonance)

- Hee-hee-hee (front teeth vibrations: neck forward)

- Huh-huh-huh (mouth vibrations: neck straight)

- Haah-haah-haah (chest vibrations: neck back)

There is a fine distinction in this exercise between placing the sound in the different resonators and letting it happen in them as a result of causal conditions. To begin with, you will certainly have to think "haa" "huh" "hee" and think about changing the pitch from lower to higher. Try, however, to explore this exercise in terms of the let-it-happen concept. While it may not yet hold true, because of residual tensions, letting—not making—should be continually borne in mind.

STEP 3   In pursuit of "letting it happen," go through the whole sequence of resonator awareness without sound, whispering. "Sound" implies vibration or sound-waves; "whispering" is soundless, just breath.

- With your neck and head back, picture the breath sighing from the pelvic floor into the chest, warming it gently.

- Lengthening the neck and head up to bring the mouth resonator into focus, feel the warm breath brushing the roof of your mouth in a whispered "hu-u-u-uh."

- With your head dropped forward, sigh the breath from the pelvic floor through the front teeth in a whispered "hee-ee-eeh."

- Repeat, moving from teeth, to mouth, to chest.

When you whisper, listen for the natural changes that occur in vowel and pitch according to the position of the head and neck.

First observe that when your head is back and your throat wide open, the only sound that can happen without your changing the shape and without moving an extra muscle, is "haah." The shape dictates the vowel and the vowel is the by-product of the shape. When your neck straightens, the head comes up and the jaws swing into their median position; if the tongue is completely relaxed, the only sound that can happen without changing the shape of the channel and without moving an extra muscle is "huh." This is sometimes difficult to experience because of lurking tensions in the back of the tongue that secretly distort the shape. When you drop your head forward and the channel narrows, if the tongue is relaxed so that it falls forward but does not block the opening, the only sound that can happen without changing the shape or moving a muscle is "hee."

- With a heightened awareness of the condition of the channel in the three positions, go through them once more with one long sigh of breath only (no sound) from deep inside. You should hear the whispered "haah, huh, hee" as the breath is automatically molded on its way out through the changing channel.

Do not linger over this point if you do not get a completely satisfactory result. What I have described depends on totally free breathing and a totally free jaw, tongue, and throat.

The second observation of the let-it-happen concept is that pitch, within the exercise, will also change spontaneously as the structure changes its shape. Larger spaces create a lower frequency of vibrations than smaller ones. Eventually all you need do is provide a steady supply of vibrations from the impulse source, and as the head and neck move through the three main positions, those vibrations will automatically rise from lower to higher because the cavity gets smaller.

This concept, however, is a refinement, and for the time being it is enough to awaken the voice to three major resonating areas using whatever is necessary to experience some of the different qualities of vibration re-sounding from different surfaces.

STEP 4   In order to provide a stimulus for the breathing centers, which may be suffering from neglect as the attention moves elsewhere, try the whole sequence again with a new image behind it.

- Neck and head back, throat wide.

- This time imagine the throat as an old-fashioned chimney widening down into the chest. The chest-chimney widens on down to a fireplace that glows on the pelvic floor. In the big, old-fashioned fireplace there is a large fire. Picture yourself sitting in a comfortable armchair beside the fire, feeling relaxed and warm. Let the warmth of the fire and your feeling of contentment release on a deep, warm "haa-a-ah" up and into the chest chimney.

- Keep in touch with your fire. Bring the neck and head up. The chimney changes its shape but does not close. Let the warmth of the fire rise to warm the roof of the mouth on "hu-u-uh."

- Drop your head and neck forward. Keep in touch with the fire feeling. Let the warmth and vibration stream on to your front teeth "heee." The "heat" is more focused and sharper in this position.

- Head up, "huh-huh-huh," (a warm spot focused on the roof of the mouth).

- Head back; relax back down by the fire; let the warmth spread all through your torso "ha-aa-ah ha-aa-ah."

STEP 5

- Repeat the exercise with a different image. This time imagine you have a store of paint in your breathing area, perhaps spray cans of paint with buttons in the diaphragm.

- With your head back, chest resonance, paint a great swatch of purple on the ceiling, "haah-aaaah."

- With your head up, mouth resonance, paint a large blob of royal blue on the opposite wall, "huh"; then three blobs, "huh-huh-huh."

- With your head forward, teeth resonance, paint a thin line of bright yellow on the floor from your middle, "heeeee."

- Reverse the process, going from yellow to blue to purple.

Keep the paint coming from your middle. See the colors arrive where you aim them. Notice the resonators as a by-product of your game.

Other images you can play with:

- Sound coming up from under the earth to reverberate through your chest resonator; then turning to honey coating the roof of your mouth for the mouth resonator; then turning into clean and refreshing toothpaste for your front teeth resonance.

- The inside of the torso is like a mineshaft, it is a goldmine and there is rich, glistening gold at the bottom of the mine that is all yours. Your pleasure reverberates in your chest on "haah-aa-aaah." When your neck comes up and your mouth resonator is restored, you use some gold to buy a Fabergé egg, which you hold in your egg-shaped mouth, glittering with emeralds and diamonds that sparkle with "huh-huh-huhuu-uu-uh." Head and neck forward, you become a pirate with a sharp cutlass between his teeth coming to steal the Fabergé egg. He expresses his gleeful intent, "hee-hee-hee-heeeee." You return to the safely guarded treasure sparkling in the roof of your mouth with "huh-huh-huhuu-uu-uh" and then go back down to the bottom of your goldmine to revel in your plenteous riches with "haah-aa-aaah."

■ It is worth spending a great deal of time with these basic resonance exercises. First get familiar with the concept and the general picture, then develop variations of your own within the concept. You may experience different energy or emotional content in each area, particularly when you are playing with colors, and there are intrinsically different energies that come with changes of pitch. It is a sign of increased organic awareness when you begin to apprehend the connection among energy, imagination, and resonating response; embark upon an exploration of emotion, mood, color, and resonance and you will enrich your vocal palette, broadening and revitalizing your expressive scope.

STEP 6   When you have become thoroughly familiar with the resonating jumps from chest to mouth to teeth you can begin to fill in the resonating ladder rung by rung, with ascending and descending pitches.

■ Introduce the picture of the resonating ladder and think of the sounds walking up through your chest and throat, rung by rung, over the soft palate, into the roof of the mouth, over the upper gum ridge, and onto the front teeth. The neck and head are coming up and dropping forward.

■ Reverse the procedure.

■ Let the voice travel up and down in pitch in even intervals, each interval finding its appropriate resonating rung. This should be explored in speaking inflections, not singing ones.

Practicing this isolation of resonating cavities develops parts of the vocal range that might otherwise lie dormant. In natural speaking such isolated response is rare and will occur only in the case of a locked emotional state or extreme tension. Normally we blend vibrations from several resonating areas, constantly changing the proportion of higher and lower overtones according to the changing intensity of what we think and feel.

STEP 7   In this step the aim is to blend the resonators as you free your voice on a call. Be aware, as you call, of the blend of vibrations from chest, mouth, and front teeth. It is a blend of colors, too, a rainbow.

Let the impulse to call originate in the breathing centers.

Let the objective be to free yourself.

The sound is a long, easy, unforced "hey."

- Relax the jaw, the tongue, and the throat completely and let the call spring from the energy center of the solar plexus/diaphragm as you free yourself on a long "he-e-e-e-ey."

Let it gather vibrations from all available resonating surfaces in the chest, throat, soft palate, roof of mouth, and teeth, on its way out of your body to the far distance.

- With the next long call, paint a rainbow across the space.

PRACTICE

One week.

11

Workday Eleven

Releasing the Voice from the Body:
Calling, triads . . . the rainbow

- Prepare to work for:
  ONE HOUR OR MORE

Most of the emphasis in the preceding exercises has been on a physical awareness that permits specific routing of impulses from the mind to stimulate new areas of physical response and to deactivate old habitual responses. As you focus on such specific consciousness you may have difficulty feeling free at the same time, yet that is the overall aim of this work—to liberate the natural voice and yourself with it. This next section of work offers some very easy general ways of releasing the voice from the body with more emphasis on *what* you are releasing than *how* you are doing it. The only image to create and recreate is that of sound emanating from the depths of the body.

STEP 1

- Set up a simple scenario in your mind's eye. For example, you are standing on the sidewalk of a busy street and you see someone you know on the other side whose attention you wish to catch. Or, you look out through a window and across a garden and are surprised to see someone you know there.

- Put your mind's eye down into the solar plexus region.

- In response to either scene you call out on "hey" to your friend. Notice the blend of resonances from chest, mouth, and teeth.

Think, feel, and imagine the scene in clearly defined steps. For example:

- You look out of the window to see what the weather is like.
  You see your friend. (A specific person and one you like).
  What you see fills you with the need to call to him or her.
  The need draws breath down into your solar plexus/pelvic regions.
  You release the need in a call.
  You relax, breathe, and wait for the response.

Throughout the scene your body is acted on: first by the outside stimulus, then by the desire to communicate. There should therefore be no need to push or strain in order to call.

- Practice feeding the desire to call down into the feeling/imaging centers and releasing that desire through a free channel that picks up vibration from your chest, mouth, and teeth.

STEP 2 Remove the image of calling to someone.

- Easily sigh a long "he-e-e-ey" out from the breathing centers. The impetus originates deep in the pelvic floor and engages the diaphragm in its easy swoop upward through the rib cage. Let the vibrations be suffused with the colors of the rainbow. Perhaps the image of Iris, the messenger of the gods, can inspire you.

Here, now, are seven ways of freeing your body from tension as you call or speak:

(1.) As you release your voice on "he-e-ey," gently bounce your shoulders blades up and down, bouncing the rainbow-colored sound freely through your upper body as it flows out.

(2.) Then bounce your knees so that your whole body bounces loosely on "he-e-e-ey." Let your knees bend loosely and restore your balance in an easy, bouncy movement. Let your arms be loose, shoulders loose, stomach muscles loose, head loose, jaw loose as you bounce a loose, long sound out of your body. See how the colors move and change.

(3.) Imagine that there are springs under the soles of your feet and that the rest of your body is like a loose-jointed rag doll. Release the "he-e-e-ey" from deep inside and bounce on the springs all over the room, your body flapping everywhere and sound and color flying out of you quite uncontrolled. Don't preserve the sound at all, let it be utterly influenced by the shaking out of your body. Don't let the vibrations or the colors get stuck anywhere in your body.

(4.) Stand still. Call "hey"s from the pelvic/diaphragm centers and slowly drop down through your spine until you are hanging head down, with the "hey"s dropping out through the top of your loosely hanging head in response to gravity. Let your breath replace easily, and then slowly come up the spine calling "hey." Let there be a new breath whenever you need it. When you reach the top, decide to abandon yourself in a long, releasing, pleasurable "he-e-e-ey." Swing your upper torso from side to side as you call. Reintroduce the images of color if ever the sound seems forced or mechanical.

(5.) Lie on your back on the floor. Go through your body to relax all tensions and then call "he-e-ey" freely from the middle of your body to the ceiling. Check that your throat and jaw are relaxed.

(6.) Roll over on your stomach. Put your forehead on your hands so that your face is toward the floor. Sigh with relief several times deep into your body. Notice that in this position your spine lengthens toward the feet as your breath goes in, and shortens as the breath goes out. The small of your back lifts on an incoming breath and drops on an outgoing breath. With this awareness, call "he-e-e-ey" from the prone position.

(7.) Roll loosely from lying on your stomach to lying on your back; to your stomach, to your back, while letting loose, easy open sounds release from your body.

- He-e-ey

  and

- Hu-u-u-uh

- Let your whole body be sloppy. Be sure you are not holding tension in your jaw, neck, or throat. Don't protect or preserve sound in any way. Each time your body falls heavily onto your stomach or heavily onto your back, the sound should be bumped out by the impact. Find a way to do this out-of-doors, rolling down a grassy hill.

■ **COMMENTARY**

You may try many of the voice exercises lying facedown on the floor. It is a position that immediately reveals any unnecessary head movements that imply tension in the back of the neck or jaw. The sounds can be pictured falling forward and out of your mouth in response to gravity. Remember this graphic-forward energy when you are standing upright. Also, once you get the feeling of breath affecting your lower spine you are less likely to slip back into shallow breathing without noticing.

- You can use any or all of these physical loosenings to advantage while speaking a speech or a poem. Choose something you know well. Let your attention focus one hundred percent on the thoughts and feelings of what you are saying but rid yourself of any physical tension by shaking out your body in one of the seven ways suggested. You will have to sacrifice many of the external results you might have previously established for a particular piece. All your inflections will be shaken out, all your external controls removed. Take advantage of this. Be concerned only with the inner content and let that come from you in new ways that you had not planned. You may be surprised to find new meanings and feelings that come to you as your body is freed from habitual thought patterns and emotional ruts.

Extending the flexibility of your range
from chest to mouth to teeth.

I hope that by now you are taking great interest in the experience of voice as a product of impulse, breath, and resonance. I hope that you are exploring your investment in causal impulses of thought, images, and feelings with your voice coming into action as a result of your desire to speak. I hope that you are experiencing some freedom from unnecessary effort in the stomach muscles and the throat. At the very least, I hope that your awareness of these possibilities has increased.

I'd like you now to draw more satisfaction from the chest, mouth, and teeth resonators with some sounds that can help develop variety and flexibility in your speaking voice. These sounds will look as if they are to be sung. They are not! They are to be sighed. You will be sighing triads going up in your range and then down. The vowel is "hey."

> The "hey" vowel comes naturally more into the front of your mouth than "huh." It is an extrovert sound.

Start standing up while being aware of your chest, mouth, and teeth resonators, feeding a sigh of relief deep into the feeling centers and sighing out relief on vibrations that flow through the pitches illustrated.

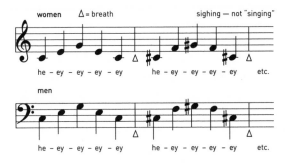

Commit yourself to the sigh.
Picture the bony resonating cavities.
Leave your jaw, tongue, and throat completely relaxed.

As the notes go higher, keep your mind down in the lower part of your body. Picture the sounds sighing out on a horizontal path from your mouth. (Don't let the picture of the sounds go up and down vertically with the notes.)

As you continue, go through the releasing movements and positions described in Step 2 and in the floorwork you have done:

- Bounce your shoulders.

- Bounce your knees.

- Put springs under your feet, jumping like a loose-jointed rag doll.

- Drop your spine down on the triads letting them drop out through your head to gravity.

- Lie on the floor.

- Sigh the triads through the diagonal stretches.

- Bounce them from the pelvis.

- Shake them out from the hip sockets with your hands on one knee and then the other.

- Flop over onto your belly and sigh them down to gravity.

- Sigh them out through the banana stretch and the semifetal positions.

- Sigh them through your spine in the folded-leaf position.

- Sigh them through your arching spine on all fours.

- Come to hanging head downward and sigh them again.

- Take four or five triads to come up your spine.

- Shake out.

PRACTICE

Combine with previous exercises daily.

INTERMISSION WORKOUT

At this stage of working on yourself through work on your voice, you
should be able to plan a twenty- to thirty-minute run-through of exercises to
be done regularly before learning new ones, before any rehearsal of a play or
a scene, before acting class, or before an actual performance. You have
accumulated the contents of a vocal warm-up—partial as yet, but effective.

I would remind you that these movements and sounds are designed to
help recondition your whole way of communicating. Such reconditioning
takes time and constant reprogramming before it sticks and the communicating process forms reliable new habits. Old habits and daily tensions fight
hard to be retained, so these exercises are for daily use in the life of a working actor.

Here is the outline of a suggested warm-up; all the exercises have been
described in detail in the previous pages.

Workout (30 minutes)

Warm-up
Stretch and drop down the spine.

> Build up.

> Roll the neck and head.

> With your hands loosen your jaw.

> Stretch and relax the tongue.

> Limber the soft palate. Yawn and stretch all over.
> Roll the head again.

> Drop down the spine again build up.

> (This should take approximately four minutes.)

Breathing
Stand with an awareness of alignment and balance.

Close your eyes and be aware of your skeleton.

Turn your attention inward and be aware of your everyday rhythm of breathing.

Allow your breath to release on small "fff"s.

Stay with this awareness until the involuntary rhythm takes over.

(This should take approximately one minute.)

Touch of Sound
Central awareness of vibrations on

> Huh-huh

> Pitches going down and then up

> (This should take approximately one minute.)

Vibrations
Lip Vibrations

> Huh-hummmmmmmmuh

> Move your lips around on vibrations.

> Blow out through your lips.

> Stretch your lips sideways with your fingers in the corners. Let them go.

> Blow out through your lips on sound. ∿ ∿ ∿ Repeat.

> Huh-hummmmmmmuh

> Repeat several times going down one tone at a time on pitch.

Then go up.

(This should take approximately three minutes.)

Head Vibrations

Roll your neck and head on a hum.

Alternate directions, changing pitches, six or seven times.

Body Vibrations

Drop your spine down on a hum.

Come up and release sound at the top.

Repeat several times on descending and ascending pitches.

Bounce your knees as you release at the top.

Bounce your shoulder blades as you release at the top.

Huh-hummmmmmh (Speak it).

Go down onto all fours and send the hum into your spine on the hum-train several times.

Come up again through your spine

Huh-hummmmmmh (Speak it).

(This should take approximately six minutes.)

Tongue
With the tip of the tongue behind your bottom teeth, stretch and relax your tongue several times.

Sigh vibrations from deep down and loosen tongue:

Hu-yuh-yuh-yuh-yu-uuh

Sigh out from deep down and roll the sound into your teeth as the tongue goes forward and back

Hee-yuh-yuh-yuh-yuh-yuh

Repeat on ascending and descending pitches

Hee-yuh-yuh-yuh

Hee-yuh-yuh-yuh

Repeat it hanging head down and relaxing onto the floor.

Stretch and relax your tongue in the diagonal stretch.

Lie on your back with one knee up, hands clasped over it, and shake your tongue from the top of the thighbone as you shake the knee toward your chest:

Huh-yuh-yuh-yuh-yuh

Alternate knees.

Roll into a semifetal position: loosen your tongue:

Hu-yuh-yuh-yuh-yu-uuh

Roll over to the folded-leaf position and sigh the sound into your top teeth with your tongue rolling forward.

Hee-yuh-hee-yuh-hee-yuh

Tuck your toes into the floor, send your tailbone up to the ceiling, and come up your spine.

(This should take approximately five minutes.)

Soft Palate
Breathe in and out on whispered "kaah," stretching the soft palate into a yawn. Stretch while the ingoing breath goes down to the pelvic floor.

Breathe in on whispered

> Kaah's

> Sigh out over the stretched soft palate on ascending and descending pitches:

> Hi-yi-yi-yi

> Stretch your tongue forward and back three times on one sigh.

> Call on "hi."

> (This should take approximately ninety seconds.)

Throat
Lengthen the front of your neck back to free your throat and find a connection with your deep impulse centers:

> Haaaah

> (This should take approximately thirty seconds.)

Resonators
Experience chest, mouth, and front teeth vibrations with, respectively,

> Head back:

> Ha-a-ah ha-a-ah ha-a-ah

> Neck straight, head up:

Huh-huh-huh

Head forward:

Heee-heee-heee

Reverse the process, then alternate it, from front to back and vice-versa.

Repeat with colors and/or imagined scenes.

(This should take approximately two minutes.)

Freeing
Call to free yourself.

He-e-e-e-ey

Shake the "hey" out, bouncing the shoulders, the knees, the whole body; jumping.

Roll your head around, calling.

Drop down your spine, calling

(This should take approximately one minute.)

Relax onto the floor.

Sigh triads out from all the floor positions we have explored.

(This should take approximately five minutes.)

Stay on the floor and speak a text in any or all of the floor positions.

Come up to standing; walk about; speak your text.

■ COMMENTARY

Here, under an "umbrella" heading, is a simple summary of the work you have done thus far.

Physical Awareness (centered on the spine)
Awareness of Natural Breathing (small fff's and the sigh)
The Touch of Sound (huh-huh)
Freeing the Vibrations (lips, head, body)
Freeing the Channel (jaw, tongue, soft palate)
Developing and Strengthening the Voice (chest, mouth, teeth resonators, calling, triads)

There are a variety of exercises under these broad headings; the floor work involved helps to lead the mind deep down in the body in search of the source of free, uninhibited impulses for breath, emotion, and voice. Each stage of the progression of exercises is designed to release the energy of the voice organically—to arrive at an experience of letting sound happen rather than making it happen. In the last series of exercises, before the intermission, calling and sighing triads began to make greater demands upon the breathing musculature. The impulses for calling are organically stronger than the impulses engendered in the earlier freeing experiences; the triads constitute longer "sentences" needing more breath.

In a logical progression of work to develop resonance, strength, and range, we should now proceed to the next rungs on the resonating ladder—the sinus, nasal, and skull resonators. However, these higher, more extrovert resonators make an increasing demand on the breathing muscles. You are going to need more breathing power to carry out the next part of the journey. You are going to need both increased breathing capacity and stronger, more flexible breathing muscles.

We step off the resonating ladder to renew our interest in the breathing process.

12/13

Workdays Twelve and Thirteen

Beathing Power: Diaphragm, intercostals,
pelvic floor . . . breathing gym

Sensitivity and Power: Enlivening and strengthening
impulses . . . free weights

■ Prepare to work for:
TWO HOURS OR MORE

Earlier I referred to the respective responsibilities of the three large consti-
tuents of the breathing musculature. Here again is a useful, much-simplified
breakdown of their functions and interdependence:

■ The diaphragm muscle is the primary breathing muscle; the home of
 the solar plexus; and the main receiving and transmitting center for
 emotional impulses.

■ The inner abdominal muscles and crura connect the diaphragm to
 the sacrum and the pelvic floor. They are responsive to primal energies and instinctive impulse.

■ The intercostal muscles are responsible for capacity and are responsive to greater demand from the solar plexus and the sacral energies.

 Up to this point the emphasis has been placed on the diaphragm as the
key muscle in breathing. There is no convenient space underneath the diaphragm so that when you breathe in and the diaphragm descends, the stomach is pushed down and the intestines are moved around to make room.

Consequently the stomach area must stay relaxed so as not to inhibit the ingoing breath. It is useful to imagine the breath going down into the belly so that two mental processes can become one. Although the direct effect of this imaginary device is to relax the inhibitory contractions in the lower abdomen, it indirectly stimulates the inner abdominal breathing musculature, which, attached from the fourth lumbar vertebra both to the pelvic floor and the diaphragm, pulls the latter down, flattening it as part of the process that draws air into the lungs.

I have laid heavy emphasis on relaxation in the realm of breathing. It takes so long for such deep relaxation to become familiar and for organic awareness to develop as a result, that it is wise to postpone work that increases breathing capacity and strengthens the breathing musculature until it can be done with awareness and sensitivity that ensure the connection of breath with inner energy impulse whatever the demand. Larger breath capacity and more powerful breathing muscles should imply larger emotional capacity and a more powerful desire to communicate. Otherwise there will be sound and fury signifying nothing. Large lung capacity *per se* is almost irrelevant to the problem of whether a breath lasts through a sentence. For instance, the capacity developed in underwater swimming does not serve the needs of a dramatic event that demands a big, and perhaps emotionally long-winded speech.

Any attempt to sustain breath by holding it back or preserving it sets up tensions that defeat the objective. This is why the old-fashioned exercises in "rib reserve" are so counterproductive. This idea of breathing asks the speaker to take in breath and then hold it with expanded rib muscles while the diaphragm expels air until the ribs have to release their reserve of breath. The effort involved in holding the ribs open in order to maintain a reserve tank of air creates tension that contracts the natural capacity. The intercostal breathing muscles expand and contract in the involuntary rhythm of natural breathing. If they are interfered with and asked to perform an unnatural task such as holding the rib cage open, there is severe dislocation in the deep, instinctual connection between emotion and breath. If you are tensed and holding muscularly, you are tensed and holding mentally. Elasticity in the breathing muscles is essential to mental agility, and strength must not be acquired at the expense of subtlety. Strength, however, must be acquired in order to deal with larger expression.

By expanding your awareness of mind-body unity, you can explore the expansion of your breathing capabilities in the interest of greater expression, not just greater noise.

There are three sets of breathing muscles that make up the whole apparatus: diaphragmatic, inner abdominal, and intercostal. The "costae" are the ribs; the "intercostals" are the muscles between the rib bones, and it is to these that we will now apply the stretching and relaxing process, first to make them elastic and flexible, then to make them longer so that they create a larger cavity inside so that the lungs can expand farther. Increased breath capacity will be the aim. It is important that you are now capable of sending specific messages to stimulate activity in the rib muscles isolated from the stomach muscles. Work on one part of the breathing apparatus can have an unnoticed negative effect on another, so that gain in one area is offset by loss in the other.

You may, in the previous exercises that paid total attention to the diaphragm and inner abdominal breathing, have allowed the ribs to give in to the nether regions. You may have even become quite sunken in the chest as you focused more and more on the satisfactory depths of the lower belly and pelvis. Without losing that deep access, it is now time to add upper expansion.

One of the duties of the intercostal muscles is to lift the sheer weight of the rib bones off the lungs without losing mobility. Imagine for the moment the weight of bone in the twenty-four ribs that make up the rib cage, and imagine that weight lying on two sponges. The lungs are roughly in the state of the two sponges when the intercostals are not doing their job. The upper part of the spine is, of course, the most vital element in suporting the rib cage. The intercostal support is secondary. If the section of the spine that runs up between the shoulder blades is weak, the posture of the rib cage will demonstrate one of two results: either the upper chest will hollow and the lower ribs will disappear as the spine droops, or the rib muscles will take over the job of supporting the chest. The latter response deploys the strength of the intercostals to such a degree that there is nothing left with which to move the lungs.

In order to develop the most effective division of labor between diaphragm, inner abdominals, and intercostals, we must first redress the balance of attention hitherto placed solely on the first two areas of the breathing musculature by now focusing exclusively on the ribs.

You will pretend for a little while that your intercostal muscles are your only means of respiration.

The easiest way to begin this exclusive relationship with your ribs is on the floor.

STEP 1

- Lie on your right side, curled up in the semifetal position.

- Put your left hand on the left-hand side of your rib cage—thumb to the back, fingers to the front of your lower ribs, elbow pointing up to the ceiling.

- Introduce this very precise imaginary picture: your only lung space is in the left-hand side of your ribs, under your left hand. You *cannot* breathe into your stomach area, your lower belly, your upper chest, or the right side of your rib cage.

- Feed a sigh *without sound* into the left side of your ribs. Feel the left ribs rising up toward the ceiling. Then release the sigh out of you and feel the ribs drop suddenly toward the floor.

Imagine there is nothing underneath your ribs so that your bones fall clattering to the floor.

- As you feed in the next sigh—still on breath only, no sound—ask the ribs to go half an inch higher toward the ceiling before they again drop suddenly toward the floor.

Don't hurry on to the next sigh. Wait until you can organically induce a new thought and feel an impulse of relief.

- With each new sigh impulse, ask the ribs to move another half-inch toward the ceiling before dropping. After four or five sighs, when you think they have gone up as far as possibly can—ask your ribs to go at least another quarter-inch up with one more sigh.

- Roll onto your back and rest with your knees up and your feet flat on the floor. Check out the sensation in the left-hand side of your ribs as contrasted with the right-hand side. Undoubtedly you will feel a considerable difference—shape, mass, density, openness. Register the differences.

- Now roll onto your left side in the semifetal position. Put your right hand on the right-hand side of your rib cage and repeat the exercise slowly, with careful attention to the detailed messages and the detailed picture.

- Roll onto your back. Notice the enhanced spaces inside your side ribs.

- Roll again onto your right side with your left hand on the left side of your rib cage. This time as you sigh exclusively into the left-side rib space, let the outgoing sigh fall onto sound.

- Hu—u—u—uh

Imagine that the vibrations of sound are living under your left ribs and that, as they drop suddenly toward the floor, the ribs fall onto the vibrations, bumping them out of you.

- Repeat the sighs, the ribs going a little higher each time. Now let the ribs drop onto a triad.

- Hey-ey-ey-ey-ey

Sigh, don't sing. Let your ribs drop, as if clattering to the floor, without any sense of sustaining your breath. Imagine that the triad "lives" under your side ribs.

You should find that although you apparently let all your breath drop out at once, there is enough left for the triad. The rib-drop helps you release mentally and therefore there is ample breath for this relatively short "sentence."

- Repeat on your left side in the semifetal position with your attention exclusively on the right side of your rib cage, sigh, let your ribs drop, and drop into a triad.

- Now roll over onto your belly—forehead on your hands or arms so that your face is toward the floor—and, *without sound*, feed a deep thought/ feeling impulse for a sigh of relief down into your lower back *and then out into your side ribs*. Let the sigh fall out from the impulse center without restraint.

This becomes a really huge sigh of relief because you have added the extra dimension of your ribs. You will feel your belly going down toward the floor as the breath enters and you should be able to get a very clear picture of the response movements in your diaphragm, your lower back, and pelvis, then a split second later open your side ribs to add even more space for the feeling of relief and the accompanying breath. The outgoing breath obeys the impulse to escape, registered fleetingly in the solar plexus center and perhaps the sacral region, and flies out.

- Now roll onto your back (knees up, feet flat on the floor) and feed a deep thought/feeling impulse for a sigh of relief—*without sound*—into your pelvic floor, your back, and your side ribs, picturing clearly all the spaces available and then triggering the release impulse in the diaphragm.

Because you now have so much space for breath and so much more breath available, you can now double the length of the "sentence" that you create.

- Feed in the thought/feeling sigh impulse for two triads that release on one outgoing breath, still on "hey."

- Hey-ey-ey-ey-ey-ey-ey-ey-ey

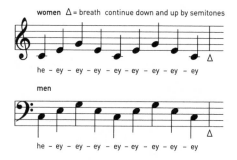

women △ = breath continue down and up by semitones

he – ey – ey – ey – ey – ey – ey – ey – ey

men

he – ey – ey – ey – ey – ey – ey – ey – ey

Do not try to make the breath last. Feed in the sigh-thought to the belly, the back, and the side ribs and freely release it from the diaphragm center.

You should want to expend all of your relief on the two triads. Be generous. Be spendthrift. Don't hold back. Keep the picture of the diaphragm clear as it billows through the rib cage.

- Continuing with the double triad, loosely roll over into the folded leaf. Keep picturing your belly, back, side ribs.

- Rock yourself up onto all fours. Feed in the sigh to your "belly-back-side-ribs" as you round the spine toward the sky and then sigh the double triad out along the spine as you arch it down toward the ground. Be sure to initiate the movement and the sound from your tailbone.

- Hey-ey-ey-ey-ey-ey-ey-ey-ey

- Repeat several times.

- Move into a squat and then float your tailbone up till you're hanging head downward. Keep picturing "belly-back-side-ribs" for the ingoing breath impulse and slowly build up your spine. Take at least three double triads to come up.

- Keep feeding in the picture and walk around the room sighing out the double triads.

- Stand still. Call out on a long "hey-ey-ey."

Rib Awareness Standing

As you proceed slowly through the following exercises, bear in mind that the layer of intercostal muscles that directly activates the spongy lungs—called the sub-costal muscles—is on the inside walls of the rib cage. This layer demands powerful mental pictures in order to stimulate powerfully subtle movements; it is only through the imagination that you can exercise the involuntary musculature deliberately.

Remember also your response to the ingoing breath in your lower back when you were lying on your belly on the ground. Accurately picture the lungs and the shape of the rib cage: the lungs go down slightly lower in your back than they do in the front of your body. The dome of the diaphragm is asymmetrical, sloping down farther at the back than the front. The front of the diaphragm is connected to the front ribs and the inside of the abdominal wall while the back of the diaphragm connects to the lower back ribs and the spine.

There is more capacity for breath inside the back ribs, though there is greater potential for expansion in the lower front ribs. You need it all.

You need to monitor the tendency that the side ribs have for taking over too much responsibility in the breathing process. They pump very efficiently but often at the expense of the sensitivity of the delicate diaphragm/solar plexus connection.

In the interest of capacity, here is the next exploration of how to encourage the ribs to open in response to greater demand.

STEP 2   Rib Stretching

- Standing, feel the edges of your rib cage from the collarbone to the descending breastbone to the bottom of the front ribs and around to the spine. Dig your fingers firmly enough into the bottom of the back ribs to leave a clear impression as to their location.

- Imagine that there are two short, strong pieces of elastic that attach your lower back ribs to each elbow point.

- Lift the elbows a little, straight up and out from the sides, and feel the back ribs respond as the imagined elastic pulls. Make sure that the shoulders do not lift at all and that the upper spine is straight. Do not bend forward. Establish a powerful mental connection between the elbows and the lower back ribs.

- Let the elbows drop.

- Lift the elbows up from your sides again, this time moving them until they are level with your shoulders. This should have the effect of pulling your back and side ribs well up and out to the sides away from the spine so that the entire back of the rib cage gets stretched and opened.

- Now move your elbows forward about three inches. The elastic will pull your back ribs out away from your spine even more.

- Bring your elbows back, allowing the back intercostals to relax a little.

- Move your elbows forward to stretch the back intercostals.

- Bring them back to relax the intercostals.

- Lower your elbows to your sides and let the back intercostals relax completely.

- Now apply the same process to the front of the rib cage to stretch and relax the front intercostal muscles.

- Imagine short, strong elastics attached from your elbows to the bottom of the front of your rib cage.

- Float your elbows up to shoulder height, pulling the bottom of the rib cage out to the sides away from the breastbone, with the emphasis now on the front ribs.

- Move your elbows back a little, to stretch the front of the rib cage more.

- Bring the elbows forward again to relax the intercostals.

- Stretch; relax.

- Lower your arms down to your sides, letting the front intercostals relax totally.

Your mental picture should be of the actual rib bones moving apart from each other in the stretch, the muscles between the bones being stimulated into stretching by the imaginary elastic connection. Be careful not to lean forward or arch back or pull the elbows too far; it is quite easy to do a superficial stretch that merely engages the big external back and chest muscles (the *latissimus dorsi* and the pectorals).

- Float your elbows up to shoulder height.

- Move them forward pulling the back of the rib cage wide open.

- Keeping the back of the rib cage as it is, move the elbows back a little pulling the front of the rib cage open.

- You should now have a rather uncomfortably expanded barrel chest.

- Wriggle the whole of the rib cage up and even wider until you can picture it as a big opened golf umbrella.

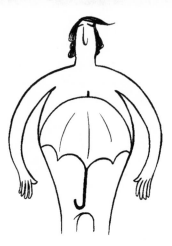

- Keeping the rib cage where it is, lower your arms and relax your shoulders. (You should still be in a grotesque position with your ribs overexpanded, high and stretched, making it hard to breathe.)

- Now release the lower front ribs enough to allow you to breathe easily, but keep the spine long and don't let your back ribs collapse.

- Then let the whole rib cage collapse as though you were dropping your rib bones into your stomach.

- Repeat the whole sequence without the final collapse.

There may be a tendency to pull forward and up in the shoulders that must be vigorously counteracted by increasing the focus of the mind on the lower part of the rib cage. The shoulders should stay relaxed throughout; the stretch runs from the bottom of the rib cage up the sides and along the underside of the upper arms to the elbows—a lateral stretch.

Make sure you do not arch the small of your back as you stretch the front intercostals. A good check on this is to keep your knees a little bent and your tailbone dropped. Locked knees and an over-arched lower spine nearly always go together.

If you can stretch and relax the intercostal muscles without breathing in as you stretch and out as you relax, so much the better. Try counting out loud on one long outgoing breath while you stretch and relax the back and front intercostals. This will counteract a tendency to breathe in as you open the rib cage, back or front, and breathe out as you release it. If you can make direct contact with the actual intercostal muscles through your image of the structure, you can separate them from their habitual breathing patterns. Once reconnected with the intercostals the breathing impulses will find that new spaces are available to respond to greater need.

■ **COMMENTARY**

As with most of the voice and breathing exercises described in this book it is the introduction of consciously accurate visualization of the breathing apparatus that will enhance its function. Your body otherwise operates on its own unconscious visualization that leads to a state of benign neglect in muscles that yearn for loving and lively attention. Your whole organism benefits when you play with the gamut and nuance of your breathing. When you pay attention to your breathing, more oxygen enters the bloodstream and stimulates circulation, waking up glandular and cellular processes. The body/brain union that constitutes the central nervous system profits from your enhanced breathing process to the extent that you may find yourself more alert, more responsive to stimuli, even, seemingly, more intelligent.

"The central nervous system is connected to every point of the body by nerves, which are bundles of axons originating in the cell body of neurons. The collection of all nerves connecting the central nervous system (brain, for short) with the periphery and vice versa constitutes the peripheral nervous system. Nerves transmit impulses from brain to body and from body to brain. The brain and the body are also interconnected chemically, by substances such as hormones which course in the bloodstream." (From *The Feeling of What Happens*, p. 325)

By now it should be apparent that when you explore the full extent of your breathing you are exploring your Self. The sensitivity with which you observe the tiny exchange of air that keeps you alive from one

>

moment to the next requires that you are sensitive to your Self—to some central, personal aspect of You that asks that you drop away external distraction and dwell—perhaps for a few moments only—in intimate proximity with a simple, true You. Then when you feed in a deep impulse for a sigh, searching for a genuine feeling of relief and releasing it with something akin to gratitude, your mind begins to penetrate down to the lower depths—not only of your pelvic floor but of your psyche. I remind you that the word "psyche" used to mean "breath and blood" and "soul" in ancient Greece. Sighing deeply, you may trigger emotional release that is not immediately discernible as relief. Or not "pleasurable" relief.

A breath that goes deep down into body, blood, and soul and awakens those parts of the central nervous system that house memory may bring up inchoate feelings of sadness, fear, anger, or (more rarely, alas) hilarity. It can be a great relief to allow these emotions to release on a sighing, soughing, wailing, moaning, roaring, growling, shouting breath or sound. If you enter into this kind of experience, make sure that you consistently allow the breath to replace, leaving yourself and your body open so that the emotion can change. The nature of emotion is to change once it has been freely and truthfully expressed.

As we continue the exploration of breathing capacity the challenge is again to ask your Self: "What is my capacity for imagination, for emotion, for desire? What could I say through these large spaces I find within myself?" Let your developing breathing capacity suggest the development of your creative capacity.

We are going to move into an organic process for strengthening all the breathing muscles. In the old days of singing and voice production work, teachers would ask their students to lie on the floor with two or three *Encyclopedia Britannica* on their bellies while performing breathing exercises or *vocalizations*. The assumption was that the abdominal wall muscles had to be strengthened in order to strengthen the voice. We now know that the big external muscles are poor substitutes for the delicate complexities of the involuntary breathing musculature. But still there is the need for strength. We must look for strong organic stimuli to provoke strong respiratory reaction as exercise for the moment when powerful emotional content demands a powerful voice for its expression.

STEP 3   Breathing-impulse barbells — or free weights

The next exercise is designed to stimulate the whole breathing apparatus as vigorously as possible using strong involuntary reflexes. It is called "vacuuming the lungs," partly because there is a sense of cleaning the lungs out, but mainly because it uses the natural power of a vacuum to stimulate the breathing muscles into powerful action.

The exercise takes a very short time to do but a long time to explain, so read all the instructions first, then follow the quick step-by-step action. You are entering the gymnasium of imagination and respiration. Your brain and body will be exercised by the free weights of impulse.

Explanation:

You are going to empty all the air out of your lungs as though you were squeezing water out of a sponge. You will do this by blowing out on ""fffff" quickly and then squeezing the last remnants of air out until you feel there is no more inside you. (Don't take too long over this). Quickly close your mouth and pinch your nose shut with your fingers so that no air can get in. Now open up your rib cage with the image of the open golf umbrella from the previous exercise. See an image of a large vacuum inside. The best way of doing this is to try to breathe in through your nose while it is still pinched shut. Put your other hand on your lower back ribs and allow the intercostal muscles to respond to the demand despite the fact that no breath can get in. Register the pull of the vacuum for a moment. Then, keeping your mouth closed, let go of your nose. Air will rush in through your nose to fill the vacuum. Don't help by "breathing in." Let the breath be sucked in by the law of nature that abhors a vacuum.

Action:

Stand,

- Empty your lungs on "fffffff."

- Hold your nose; close your mouth.

- Try to breathe in so that your ribs expand as far as they can (the open umbrella position.)

- Picture the vacuum you have created.

- Let go of your nose, keeping your mouth shut, and let the air rush in to the vacuum.

- Return to natural breathing.

Some people have a moment's panic when they feel the vacuum. It is, after all, a very unnatural condition. But remember that it would only be dangerous to be without air if the condition were controlled by anyone but you. All you have to do is open your mouth and things will return to normal.

The reason for only letting the air enter through your nose while keeping your mouth shut is that the nasal passages are narrow. The breathing muscles must thus work harder to take the air in. This activity strengthens them.

Think of your lungs as filling the whole torso from hip sockets and pelvic floor to the collarbone as you repeat the vacuuming.

- Blow all the air out of your body.

Your whole torso will collapse inward.

- Hold your nose; close your mouth.

- Put your other hand onto your lower back ribs.

- Drop the pelvic floor, open your belly, your back, and your side ribs to create a "vacuum" through your whole torso.

- Let go of your nose and feel the air rush down to the pelvic floor, into your back and your front, your sides, and finally your upper chest.

- Relax and return to natural breathing.

The vacuum impulse is like an imaginative barbell or free weight that you pick up on entering the breathing gymnasium and employ judiciously to build a muscle that must be responsive to thought and feeling, not just command.

You may be dizzy with all that extra oxygen rushing in. If you are not, it could be a sign that you are not doing the exercise fully. It could also mean that your breathing apparatus is in good shape already. Don't be afraid of the dizziness, but don't reinforce the condition by repeating the vacuuming too quickly. Rest, do other exercises, and then come back to this one. As you exercise your breathing apparatus, the dizziness will disappear.

Be careful not to suck for air with your throat muscles. The "suction" must come from your lungs and you should focus your attention on the lower back ribs so that you feel a direct connective pull from nostrils to back ribs.

■ COMMENTARY

Rib stretches and vacuuming the lungs limber up the energies. They fit into a vocal warm-up just after the chest and mouth resonator work and provide extra support for moving onto the middle and upper part of the range. Vacuum three or four times, sometimes slowly, sometimes quickly. It invigorates the whole system and is a generally healthy exercise, but its main purpose at the moment is to strengthen the breathing muscles by the use of natural reflexive movements. If you practice "deep breathing" exercises to achieve strength, you build muscular control that will not serve spontaneous communication. The relationship between impulse and muscular activity must be diligently maintained as we move into the more vigorous exercises that are necessary for the vocal apparatus and the emotional apparatus of an actor to develop simultaneously. If the voice develops independent strength, it can substitute sound for feeling, and there is nothing more insidiously corrosive to an actor's artistry than the consciousness of growing vocal energies that are more accessible than emotional energies. Conversely, the actor may be developing the emotional instrument faster than the vocal one, and the resulting short circuit can blow all the fuses in the house. It is idealistic to suggest

>

that an actor can maintain a strict balance while working on body, voice, and creativity, but if the aim is idealistic, at least there is the possibility of quality along the way.

Actors who have "good voices" and have been complimented on them are sometimes surprised, if not offended, when I commiserate with them on their gift. It is nearly always those actors who have the greatest trouble finding their emotional resources. Those who start with weak vocal instruments tend to be better off in the long run, as dependence on the inner life pays off and the voice gradually learns to serve it freely.

In the next exercise you will be entering the breathing gymnasium to play with impulse free weights designed to restore reflexiveness, develop swiftness of response, and encourage flexibility. Perhaps the notion of free weights or barbells can be replaced now by juggling balls. The larger capacity found in the total picture must incorporate growing flexibility if sensitivity is not to be sacrificed to power. The next point of attention will focus on the diaphragm as the instigating breath activator with the pictures you have been establishing of your belly, your back, and your side ribs as coresponders.

STEP 4

- Prepare for this by stretching, relaxing down and up the spine, rolling the head and neck, and vacuuming the lungs twice.

- You are going to feed four huge (really *huge, gargantuan*) impulses for sighs of relief—genuine, deeply felt, pleasurable relief—into the full length, depth, and breadth of the torso. Replace one impulse immediately after the other. Don't hurry them, but don't wait in between them.

Let the impulse move the breath and let the breath move the body. Treat the pleasurable relief as though it were an acting exercise if necessary. Think of something bad that was about to happen but didn't, leaving you with a huge sense of relief. If you program this once or twice you should then be able to go directly to a real sigh without its being merely a big breath with no content.

Let your breath fill you from the bottom up every time. When you fill a jug with water it does not fill from the top down. So, too, with your lungs.

- Create four huge sighs in a row and then rest. If you do more than this, you court fainting.

If you picture the process, the diaphragm appears to be blown down and up by a gale of wind raised by the impulses. Its movements can be imagined as a silky billowing parachute. Your insides will be quite discombobulated by the disturbance if the sighs are gusty enough. The external abdominal wall must be like jelly being moved quite violently by the inner turbulence but not actively controlling it. The whole inner torso swells and deflates with the entry and exit of the impulses.

- Repeat the four big sighs of relief.

- Rest.

- You are now going to feed in six repeated impulses for sighs of relief. This time, however, they will be slightly smaller and faster and affect you more toward the center of the dome of the parachute diaphragm. These are medium sighs of relief. Your job is to create and re-create the six relief impulses. Only on the very last one will the whole breathing torso collapse with a final deep yielding to the relief pouring out.

This will now seem rather like panting; it is, but do not take the short cut of calling it panting yet. Program the impulse connection conscientiously until you can be confident that the muscle movement can trigger the impulse as surely as the impulse triggers the muscle movement. Then you can work from the inside out or the outside in safely.

- Exercise your ability to re-create repeated impulses of relief without their becoming shallow, thoughtless, or mechanical.

- Repeat the four huge, turbulent sighs.

- Repeat the six medium, faster sighs more toward the center of the parachute/diaphragm area.

- Rest.

- Focus your attention on the very center of the dome of the diaphragm and now feed in many quick, lively impulses of pleasurable anticipation that flutter tiny breaths in and out of that center. Let the anticipation stimulate the breath and let the breath flutter the center of the parachute dome of the diaphragm, so that little breaths fly in and out fast and loose and then move through a transition that results in a final sigh of relief.

Leave the outside muscles of the torso really loose; they will be moved but should not get tight at any point. The breath goes in and out evenly; that is, you should not get fuller as you go on, nor should your lungs empty in the course of the exercise. In theory you should be able to continue for a long time with these tiny breaths going in and out this quickly because as much goes in as out each time. In practice, the muscles may get tighter as you go faster, so do the exercise in short sequences.

The exercise therefore is this:
ten or so quick, light anticipatory impulses, then a transition
release on relief
anticipation-relief-anticipation-relief.
The quicker, the lighter, the more central, the better.

In the first part of this exercise the repetition of four big sighs of relief is intended to accustom the whole breathing capacity to supplying a large demand quickly, and to release quickly without controlling. In the second part, more energy is generated and the agility of the breathing muscles is tested. In the third part, the agility increases, flexibility is essential, and an important reconditioning process is introduced: to remain free of tension while the intensity of emotional energy increases. This, of course, is using the word "tension" with the common meaning of "holding." Emotional energy stimulates a great deal of activity in the muscles. The muscles must be conditioned to allow the energy to ripple and fly without clutching, holding, or stopping the flow.

The quick light impulses designed to stimulate quick, reflexive responses to changing emotions can be enlivened by the picture of a puppy who knows that his/her owner is going to take it out for a walk. The knowledge excites a rapid in-and-out of breath. If you look at a happy, excited puppy you will see that the breath flies in and out of its body with no tension apparent in the outside belly—movement, yes, tension, no. I will now start using the word "panting," trusting that the movements will not become mechanical thanks to the puppy. The happy puppy is panting with pleasurable anticipation. A happy puppy picture can help stimulate the fast inner action of the diaphragm.

It is often necessary to remind an actor not to hold onto an emotional condition. It feels so good when the feeling suddenly comes that the actor often wants to nurse it, holding on with the surrounding muscles; yet in doing so the feeling dies. If the actor has the courage to *spend* feeling freely at such a moment, more feeling will be naturally generated. Muscles that hold onto feeling kill it, but muscles that are conductors of that feeling help propagate more feeling through the mutuality of neuro-muscular function. Panting helps restore organic reflex action to the diaphragm allowing it to release and replenish breath in a natural response to impulse.

The panting exercises, if done with true mind/body unity, not only make the breathing musculature fit enough to serve the emotional instrument but also can be used to stimulate pure energy when you are physically lethargic and unreceptive to inner stimuli.

■ **COMMENTARY**

You may by now be questioning the repetition of the sigh. Sighs of relief, pleasurable relief, are now joined by pleasurable anticipation. This choice as a means of stimulating the breath is made because it is easier to learn to respond to increased energy and intensity through positive, optimistic content rather than that which is unpleasant.

The deconditioning of protective muscle reaction and the reconditioning of uninhibited giving and receiving energy happen faster under pleasurable circumstances. Eventually, however, this reconditioning must pay off in the interest of an exchange of human experience that includes fear, pain, misery, anger, panic, depression, doubt, hate, etc. Having established a format of freedom with easier feelings it is usually best to deal with the more difficult emotions in the context of a speech or scene. It would

>

be irresponsible to offer in a book the means by which the reader could tap into and release powerful emotions of a dark nature. In the laboratory atmosphere of a classroom or studio, fears can be allayed by common experience, and emotional energy can be channeled into the context of the actor's needs.

All emotions can be labeled as positive after familiarity creates natural controls. But working on self in these areas is difficult because there has to be a moment at which you let go of habitual controls and someone trustworthy must be there to make use of that moment, channeling the new energy into the work at hand. Otherwise the letting go can lead to emotional self-indulgence and/or a blind freakout. Emotional incontinence and indulgent self-expression are the antithesis of communication, leaving no room for listening and responding to others.

The answer to this problem is not that it all belongs in acting class or therapy, but in accepting that voice work must be acting work, and good acting work is therapeutic.

Here is a relatively lighthearted story, which can be used with the panting exercise to illustrate ways in which you can safely inject some variety of content into any exercise. If you can get someone to tell it to you step by step, so much the better. Otherwise practice being able to visualize a sequence of events specifically and without anticipation, even though you know the story.

Preamble:
This morning in the mail you received an anonymous note telling you that this evening at five o'clock, you should take the nearest train (or bus or subway) to a particular station just outside the city (or town). Once there, you were to go out of the station, turn left, and go down to the end of the road where there would be a large house set back from the road in its own garden. You were instructed that the house would be empty, the door unlocked, and you were to go in, up the stairs, down the long corridor on the left, and into the room at the end where you were to wait.

- All this you have done.

- You are now waiting in an empty room, in an empty house, and dusk is gathering.

The Exercise:

- Let us assume that you are in a state of anticipation. Let the anticipation stimulate your breathing quite arbitrarily into a loose panting rhythm such as you have just explored. Feed everything that happens from now on directly into the panting center.

- You are standing in the middle of the room, listening. Suddenly, downstairs, you hear the front door open and close. Hear this with your breathing.

- You hear footsteps going slowly across the hall below. (Let it affect your breathing in the center—don't let the muscles tighten—just let the breathing quicken.)

- The steps come slowly up the stairs and start down the corridor. (The panting should quicken—still centered. Leave your outside muscles loose.)

- The steps come slowly closer and closer to your room and stop outside the door. (Very fast, free panting.)

- The door opens, and it's your favorite friend. (Release the breath on a great pleasurable sigh of relief.)

Try not to be critical of this simple story and make use of the atmospheric elements to introduce sensory provocation to a place in your body where it can arouse feelings that intensify and finally go through a transition in response to new sensory provocation. The panting forbids the muscular contractions, which inhibit productive reaction at various stages along the road, and ensures that breath is constantly leaving the body carrying feelings on it. This is spontaneous communication.

Be sure you really feel the emotional transition from anticipation to relief when you see your friend. (There are various reactions you may have, of course, to such a scene. React as you will, but let it be on panting and a sigh, with a transition between the two.)

The big point here is to decondition a neuro-muscular process that produces tension in response to intensity, and to recondition the neuro-muscular response to one of release. In other words, develop mental intensity without physical tension.

STEP 5

- Practice the quick, central, anticipation breathing on sound.

- Imagine that the diaphragm is a trampoline slung from the bottom edges of the rib cage.

- Picture the sound as a little person—you—bouncing up and down in the middle of the trampoline. (The breath goes in between each "huh" sound, however fast you bounce.)

- Bounce six or seven times, then let the miniature You on the trampoline take a flying leap out of your mouth and across the room.

- Huh △ huh △ huh △ huh △ huh △ huh △ hu-u-u-u-uh

STEP 6

- Working with the picture of the elastic connection between your elbows and your side ribs, float your arms up above your head and drop your clasped hands on top of your head. Lengthen your spine and neck so that you don't give in to the weight of your hands.

- In this position notice that the diaphragm is stretched because it is attached to the bottom ribs which are now more open. The "trampoline" is more taut and more bouncy.

In this position also it is possible to distinguish clearly between letting the ribs drop on the sigh release that comes after the panting *or keeping them open and directing the release of the diaphragm up through the rib cage.*

- *Deliberately choose the latter picture* and pant with anticipation, first with breath only, then with sound, on pitches going up and then going down. Each transition to a sigh release includes the picture of the diaphragm's upward release.

- Drop your arms, keep the ribs open without holding and repeat the panting exercise, alternating a cluster of breath-panting with a cluster of sound-panting.

- Drop your spine down and repeat the panting exercises hanging head downward—notice that now your diaphragm is completely relaxed and that gravity is helping the sigh release through your rib cage.

- Lower your tailbone into a squat: pant and release.

- Put your hands behind you on the floor and sit down; then lay your spine down vertebra by vertebra until you are flat on your back. Your knees up and feet flat on the floor, pant—with breath only, then with sound. Picture the diaphragm moving horizontally through the rib cage on the sigh release.

- Roll over onto your belly: repeat the panting exercises on pitches ascending and descending

- Huh-huh-huh-huh-huh-huh-hu-u-uh

This should be the easiest position for a free and lively panting experience: your belly muscles are out of commission on the floor and the diaphragmatic response should be really evident.

Repeat in the semifetal position, the folded leaf, and on all fours.

Finally uncurl back up through your spine to standing.

Once you have found enough freedom in the solar plexus/diaphragm area to induce fast, even panting on breath alone and with sound—a new, quick breath going in between every sound—you can practice the panting on double triads: the first triad, panting; the second a long sigh of relief.

STEP 7 Repeat the lonely house story with sound.

The link between breath and inner energy is forged in sensitivity and depends on sensitivity for its continuation through the largest expression. The essential attributes for an actor's voice are range, variety, beauty, clarity, power, and volume, but sensitivity is the quality that will validate all the others, for they are dull attributes unless they are reflecting inner energy. Then they come to life, becoming the range of feelings, the variety of the mind, the beauty of the content, the clarity of the imagination, the power of the emotion, the volume of the need to communicate. Energies that fuel the voice muscles need to be attuned with great sensitivity to the still finer energies of psychological creation if the communication from inside to outside is going to be transparently true. When the energy of the content is powerful, the economy of its transmission will preserve the truth of the content.

The concept of working from the inside has been applied from the beginning in this method, and, therefore, economy of effort has been practiced all along. As your physical awareness becomes refined, however, you can apply more and more subtlety. Your next step will be to find how the working concept of impulse centers can be cultivated to achieve greater economy.

I have played with the idea of a central point in the dome of the diaphragm that both touches sound and receives the touch of sound. The word *center* can be used as in feeling-center, breathing-center, energy-center, and center of the torso. I want to suggest a paradox in approaching the idea of a "center." One approach is to pin down more precisely where it is, and the other is to say that it can be anywhere. We will use both.

When the word *center* becomes jargon we fall into a trap supposing we have experienced something because we remember the word that described that thing. *Center* meant one thing to the dancer Martha Graham, another to the acting teacher Michael Chekhov, and yet another to, for example, me. It is a practical word, but only if one does not deify it to the point of searching for it like the Holy Grail containing Absolute Truth. The value of the word in general is that wherever the "center" may be placed in the body, the very fact of looking for it, and working from it, clears the mind and focuses energy. The state of being improves, and consequently so does the performance of the task at hand. The strict, physiological benefit of centering the voice is that the more economically the breath plays on the vocal folds, the better the tone. Too much air blows the folds apart, producing a "breathy" voice. On the other hand, economy must not mean holding back. The use of a sigh of relief in almost all the breathing exercises up to now has been designed to release the mind from any tendency to hold back. Now, assuming that mental condition has been established, we can look for economy in the use of the breath without danger of holding back.

In the previous steps you stimulated fast anticipatory panting in the center of the diaphragm. When you let sound happen with an awareness at the center of the panting movement, you will find that less breath is used, and that it replaces itself more easily than before. The reflex action of the involuntary breathing musculature kicks in. All the movements producing the sound can diminish while the sound remains as strong as the mind thinks it is.

The next exercise refines further the image of the center, thereby transferring still more of the responsibility for sound making from muscle to mind.

STEP 8

- Let the fast panting in the center of the diaphragm happen in such a way that you can hear the outgoing and incoming breaths clearly. Take particular note of the incoming breaths as they tend to disappear with speed, indicating that the diaphragm is gathering tension.

- Now, close your mouth and very lightly induce such a fast version of the panting that it is just a quiver in the diaphragm center that hardly disturbs the breath at all. What breath there is goes in and out through the nose. Then let the breath release out through the nose.

- Quiver—let go; quiver—let go.

- Imagine your rib cage is a birdcage with a hummingbird in it. The speed of the quiver-pant has the quality of the quick flutter of a hummingbird's wings. When you release after the quiver, the bird escapes.

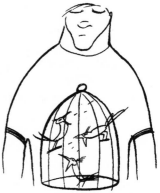

- Open your mouth and do the same quiver and release.

- Without the quiver find the touch of sound on the quiver center; make it a very specific contact.

- Huh-huh

Now I would like you to picture a place I will name the "inner center." The next exercise will lead you to a place that seems to be farther inside your body than the breath. If you follow the instructions addressed to the imagination you will arrive at the most economical and physically subtle use of your voice.

- Read these steps before doing them.

First allow the tiny quiver to happen like an electric current in the center of the diaphragm—then let go, give in, so that almost all the breath leaves your body. Do not, however, push or squeeze it out as in the vacuum. At this point it might seem that there is nothing left with which to make a sound. Without taking a new breath, think of relaxing even deeper into the interior and drop to a sound "huh" that is farther inside than the breath.

- Do the sequence: quiver / release / drop to sound farther inside than the breath; relax, allow breath to drop back in to refill the center.

- Repeat the sequence.

Pinpoint your attention on the place deep inside your body where the sound is found. It may seem to be right up against your spine at the back of the solar plexus. Register it as a definite physical place and label it the inner center.

- Repeat the sequence thus:

- Quiver / let go / yield deeper inside onto a sound in the inner center "huh." Drop the diaphragm, letting your breath replace.

- Now find that "inner center" touch of sound again apparently without using any breath.

It should seem as though, when your thought-impulse touches sound on the inner center, no breath is needed to form that sound. It will only be when you relax after the sound is over that some breath will replace, showing that some breath was used.

- Try it again.

- Quiver / give / give in farther to sound

- Huh-huh

- Release for the breath to replace.

- Don't use that breath.

- Talk again from the inner center.

- "Huh-huh" / release / and realize breath was used though apparently you did not use it.

- Talk again from the inner center "huh-huh." Relax and the breath goes in.

The conditioning being done here is to go yet further in translating physical effort into mental energy. In order to communicate larger content freely, all you need to do is stay connected to the inner center and deliver more voltage from the mind.

STEP 9

- Find the inner-center connection on "huh," then change the sound to "hey."

- Repeat "hey-hey-hey."

- Let the breath drop back in and decide not to use that breath but to let the "hey"s happen again on the inner center. After each set of "hey"s, relax inside and your breath will replace. Familiarize your-self with the mental process that says, "I am not going to use any breath for the sound, but I will let breath replace after the sound."

Here you begin to deal directly with mind-voice unity, leaving out the mid-dleman—breath.

- Go through the preparatory inner-center sequence. Then, starting sound on "hey," continue, building up power and volume in the sound depending solely on mental, not muscular, intensification. Let the "hey"s get louder and louder without going higher in pitch.

- Drop the diaphragm for the breath to replace.

The increase in the intensity of the sound should come from inner strength, leaving the outer muscles almost completely relaxed.

- Try this contrast exercise to clarify the difference between external and internal strength: shout "hey" pulling your stomach muscles in as tight as possible. Make the big, outside, abdominal muscles do a strong movement inward punching out a loud "hey."

- Now leave the outside abdominal wall loose and send the same strong shout impulse to the inner center on "hey."

Go from outer-muscle strength to inner-mental strength several times to experience the changing process and the different results.

Economy of breath means a commitment to image, feeling, and impulse. We are familiarizing the body and the mind with the experience of dropping an image into the breathing areas, inducing a feeling in the diphragm or the pelvic/sacral region, and accepting an impulse and following its reflexive action.

Perhaps the word *center* can mean the center of the image.

The imagination has been flexing its muscles as we journeyed through the inner landscape of the body. Now I'd like you to experiment with images that you create as though you were a visual artist, images that originate internally and culminate externally, images that stimulate and command breathing impulses.

STEP 10

- Stand about twelve feet away from a wall and imagine that the wall is a huge canvas—at least twenty feet wide—on which you are about to paint a picture: a seascape.

- Read the instructions first.

- Paint a horizon line of bright blue waves right across the canvas.

- Paint a large, simple ship—red.

- Paint a mast and two big white sails on the ship. Paint a round, yellow sun.

- Paint the rays of the sun.

- Paint different sizes of white, fluffy clouds. Paint little seagulls flying around the ship. Sign your name right across the bottom. The paint is your breath—"ffff." Each new image creates a new breath impulse. There are large images that need large breaths—the horizon, the ship. There are medium-size images that need medium-size breaths— the sails, the sun, perhaps some of the clouds. There are small images that need short breaths—the seagulls, each ray of sun, the dots on the i's and the crosses on the t's of your name. All impulses connect with the breath on the inner image-centers and travel out through the torso on "ffffff."

- Final instructions before starting: be seized with sudden inspiration and the need to get the picture on the canvas quickly. Go.

- Repeat with sound. All the sounds should be open "hey," "hah," "huh," and "hee."

STEP 11

- Close your eyes and see the images you have just painted inside your body on a level with your diaphragm, merging with your breath.

- Open your eyes. Look at your picture on the wall while maintaining your inner picture.

Let your voice and the following words be paint and paintbrush as you connect the inner and the outer pictures:

- A wide horizon

- △

- A dark blue sea

- △

- The sun burns in the sky

- △

- A great ship floats on the waves

- △

- It has two sails

- △

- Seagulls swoop and call

- △

- Where are the sailors?

- △

Let your voice be the bridge between the inner and the outer pictures.

Transition Back to the Resonating Ladder

The extension of your breathing awareness through exercises that increase capacity, power, and sensitive reflexiveness in your breathing muscles provides you with the potential for more powerful expression, livelier expression, and more range of expression. Let me remind you of the fundamental elements of the voice.

- The need or desire to speak

- Clear thought/feeling impulse

- Breath

- Resonance

- When speech is added to voice, then the lips and the tongue articulate thoughts and feelings into words.

With additional breathing power we return now to enhancing the awareness and effective performance of the resonating ladder.

We have explored the large cavern of the chest resonator that strengthens the lower part of the voice and the resonating mouth cave—smaller, egg-shaped, with a perfect acoustical dome in the cave roof. From there we isolated the resonance found in the front teeth. With each resonating area you found the pitch of voice that would arouse the optimum resonating feedback in that area.

The sinuses, nose, and skull are the next rungs on the resonating ladder. You will need more breath awareness before you move on up because these are the parts of your vocal range most likely to be relying on support from your tongue, jaw, and throat. The middle and upper parts of your voice must learn to depend solely on breath and resonators if they are to be emotionally and psychologically expressive rather than descriptive. Remember Hermes, the trickster tongue god? The tongue muscle must be completely relaxed in the next stretch of the voice journey, and so must the jaw if Iris's rainbow-colored truth is to be revealed through a transparently open middle and upper range.

14

Workday Fourteen

*Sinus Resonators: Middle of the face, middle range . . .
the road out*

■ Prepare to work for:
ONE HOUR

We are now moving into the most subtle, complex, and interesting part of
the voice, halfway up the resonating ladder, in the middle register. It is the
voice's most revealing area, and perhaps for that reason it is often the least
freely used. The resonating corridors here are labyrinthine compared with
the simple chest and mouth chambers. You have to examine an actual skull
to appreciate how many and how varied in shape are the passages and
chambers within the mask of the face. Some are scooped out of solid bone,
some are a millimeter wide and have walls of transparent cartilage. With
such multiplicity of shape and texture there is enormous potential variety
in resonating quality. And yet when most people are in the middle register
of their voices, they tend to employ only one or two notes, sometimes strident, sometimes nasal, sometimes breathy, sometimes sing-y, but seldom
with more than one overriding quality. Even when the sound is very pleasant
to listen to because it is "well placed" and "well modulated," it will not express
more than just that — a well-trained voice. I find a well-trained voice hard
to trust for it implies a well-trained person who knows how s/he wants to
be perceived and can achieve the desired result at the expense of truth. A
person who has enough control to present a consistently "pleasant" tone of
voice is hiding many things.

With the variety of resonating qualities available, it is possible for the
subtlest nuances of thought to be revealed accurately. How dangerous that
accuracy can be in daily human commerce is evidenced by how rarely nuance

is heard. Easily triggered defense mechanisms develop early in life to make the most revealing part of the voice the best guarded. Some of the defensive reactions are instinctual and spontaneous, some of the instinctual harden to habitual; some are semiconscious character choices, some imitative. All result in muscle responses in the tongue, jaw, soft palate, and throat that block access to certain resonating chambers and divert vibrations into others. The primary resonating response is checked, and secondary ones convey a veiled message.

An example of this can be found in a comment such as, "Darling, I think you're driving too fast." There might be a primary feeling impulse of fear, modified by the characteristic "staying calm in a crisis." The energy stimulated by fear would, if expressed directly, activate the breath and the vocal folds to produce a relatively high frequency of vibration that in turn would find amplification in resonators in the middle to upper part of the face. Myriad tiny muscles in the tissue lining the upper pharynx, the soft palate, and the upper sinuses would pick up the energy of the initial impulse, creating muscle tone capable of feeding back more vibrations of the same frequency, thereby relaying accurately the primary fear stimulus.

Tuned-up emotional vibrations generate tuned-up sound vibrations, unless countermanded by a stream of secondary messages from character elements or external influences. In the case of the dangerous driver, the actual sequence of psychophysical reactions in the passenger might be:

(1.) A stab of panic in the solar plexus stimulating a swift intake of breath, and a simultaneous, almost imperceptible tightening in the temples, eyeballs, scalp muscles, and upper pharynx.

(2.) A conditioned, therefore speedy, decision not to express the panic. Habitual depression of the back of the tongue and larynx in order to create a passageway down into the deep, calm resonating area of the chest.

(3.) A manipulation of the laryngeal musculature and lower register to convey in a warm, deep tone the gentle suggestion that it is better to be safe than sorry, to be late than dead—anything that might help reduce the speed.

Another kind of character conditioning might just as easily take the fear impulse and turn it into laughter, possibly a rather high, giggly laughter, as those particular character influences add impulses that increase the tension of the muscle response and spiral everything, including the sound, higher.

Innumerable variations can be played on this one simple example by adding different ingredients: the driver's state of mind; the relationship between the two; the frequency of the incident; the reality of the danger, and so on. They are all more commonly expressed than the basic, simple— as opposed to complex—fear impulse. Until the actor's voice can express pure unadulterated feelings, it cannot be relied on to express complexities with any accuracy: the complexities that the actor chooses or that the role demands will be filtered through unchosen mixtures of habitual defenses and individual characteristics, and will emerge sounding quite different from the mental conception.

In summary, the pure connection of thought and feeling energy with breath, vibration, and resonating response underlies this exploration of range. You can do it by treating the voice as a musical instrument, sound only, divorced from feeling, but you can also open your mind to the marriage of feeling with sound, and allow feeling and sound to be mutually stimulating.

The following exercises will provide some clues as to how to make all the mid-face resonators available.

- Physical preparation for work on the middle of the voice

- Do not think of your face in terms of a mask, with just the dimensions you can see when you look in a mirror. Meditate a little on its inner dimensions, its depth behind the nose, and the bony catacombs hidden by the skin.

- First, you must activate and limber up all the muscles of your face that run vertically, horizontally, and diagonally. These can either mobilize to aid communication or remain immobilized and block it.

Face Isolations

- Lift and lower the right eyebrow several times.

- Lift and lower the left eyebrow several times.

- Bunch up the muscles of the right cheek and then relax them several times.

- Bunch up the muscles of the left cheek and relax them several times.

- Lift and lower the upper lip several times.

- Pull the lower lip down and release it several times.

- Stretch the right corner of the mouth sideways and release it.

- Stretch the left corner of the mouth sideways and release it.

- Alternate stretching the right and left corners of the mouth.

- Wrinkle the bridge of the nose up and release it.

- Move the bridge of the nose up and down.

- Squeeze the right eye shut.

- Stretch the right eye open.

- Squeeze the left eye shut.

- Stretch the left eye open.

- Alternate vigorously opening and shutting the right and left eyes.

- Lift the left eyebrow up and stretch the right corner of the mouth sideways simultaneously. Don't let your jaw move.

- Release.

- Lift the right eyebrow up and stretch the left corner of the mouth sideways simultaneously.

- Release.

Devise any combination of movements to stretch the face vertically, horizontally, and diagonally. Make intentional movements and check them in a mirror to see whether you are connecting as you think you are.

Finally:

- Squeeze the whole face into a tight ball.

- Then stretch the whole face as wide as it can go — eyes and mouth wide — as in a silent scream.

- Relax your face and shake the skin of your face off the bones.

- Massage your face with your hands.

The Middle Sinus Resonators

Sinus means a recess, cavity, or hollow space. A hollow space scooped out of bone makes a perfect resonating cavity, and the following work will focus on the two most familiar pairs of sinus cavities, those on either side of the nose that I shall call the middle sinuses, and those above the nose and eyebrows, the upper sinuses.

STEP 1

- With your fingers get to know the topography of your face. Feel the shape of your face from the nose out across the top of the cheekbones. Bring your imagination into the survey and picture your nose as a small mountain peak while your cheekbones are rounded hills. You will find a slight hollow between the mountain peak of the nose and the cheek-hills that we might name "the soggy sinus valleys." From beside the nose spreading out under the cheek-hills, there are cavities, sinuses, which are soft and spongy to the touch, sometimes sensitive. Gently massage these areas with your fingertips in small circles moving up and outward from the nostrils and on out below the foothills of the cheeks.

  Having made this initial survey, the next task is to isolate the muscles that run across the soggy sinus valleys from the nose mountain to the cheek-hills. Imagine these muscles as two small rope-bridges that lead from mountain to hills over the valleys.

- Now move these rope-bridge muscles up and down.

This is the movement you use to push a slipping pair of sunglasses back up on the bridge of your nose when your hands are occupied.

Look in a mirror and check:

  (1.) That the movements are isolated to the mid-sinus muscles on either side of the nose

  (2.) That any movements in the forehead and upper lip are reactive not active

  (3.) That the jaw is not moving

Now massage the sinus area with your middle fingers.

Alternate massaging the sinus area with your fingers and moving the sinus muscles up and down independently.

STEP 2

- Let the tip of your tongue fall loosely forward onto your lower lip.

  The tongue should slide, thick and relaxed, forward and out of the mouth. If it is really relaxed, it will be wide, touching the corners of the mouth, thick and unmoving. If it tenses anywhere along its length, it will try to pull back into the mouth again, become pointed or thin and flat or scooped down in the middle.

- With your tongue lying relaxed on your lip, move your sinus muscles up and down.

- Here you are gradually conditioning your mind/body awareness to perceive a pathway to the mid-sinus area and to deactivate any support the tongue may habitually offer.

- Now, with the tip of your tongue still out on your lower lip, sigh a whispered "heeee" through the narrow space between the front of the tongue and the top teeth.

- Next—as you sigh a whispered "heeee" through the narrow space between the front of the tongue and the top teeth with the tip of your tongue still out on your lower lip, move your mid-sinus muscles up and down several times.

At this point you are actively detaching any habitual tongue response from the picture of the mid-sinus and the release of breath.

If you find that activating the sinus muscles with your tongue out while releasing a good free sigh feels like patting your head with one hand while rubbing circles on your stomach with the other, then you have pinpointed a major habitual pattern of effort.

- So—keep at it until the breath and the movement in the sinus area detach easily from the tongue, which can remain calmly resting on the lower lip throughout.

  Use a mirror.

The next step is to add vibration to the sighed "heeee."

- With the tip of your tongue relaxed on your lower lip, sigh a long "heeee," aiming it clearly through your mouth on a mid-register pitch—approximately an F above middle-C for women and an octave lower for men—and at the same time move your mid-sinus muscles up and down several times.

- Let the breath replace and release another sigh on "heeee," one semi-tone higher, moving your mid-sinus muscles, leaving your tongue on your lower lip as you repeat this for several ascending notes.

- As you continue sighing out "heeee"—going higher until you feel effort creeping in, then coming back down—alternate moving the mid-sinus muscles up and down with massaging the sinuses with your fingers.

Aim the "heeee" very deliberately through your mouth: out through the top teeth and past the tip of the tongue.

Do not let the sound be placed in the sinuses, although you are awakening vibrations in that area and you may notice the sound being affected by the movements. If you aim the sound into the sinus movement, it will in fact arrive in the nose. This will do no harm but will deny the exploration of the many other qualities of vibration to be found surrounding the nose, in and around the cheek-hills, and throughout the facial catacombs.

It is an intensity of thought that brings the sound out past the top teeth and tongue. Not pushing, but an intensely focused sigh.

A vital point of awareness in this exercise is the tongue. The back of the tongue, as explained earlier, commonly starts to tense as the voice goes higher, substituting its muscular strength for the support of breath. As the sinus resonators open up, they will begin to provide true resonating strength for the voice. The voice can begin to transfer its dependence from the back of the tongue to the real strengths of breath and resonance. The more you relax the tongue, the more the voice will demand support from the breath and find its true resonators in the whole breadth of mouth and face. The corollary of this is that the more the voice finds its true resonating power, the more the tongue can relax.

STEP 3

- Again let the tongue slide, thick and relaxed, forward and out of the mouth. Check that it is really relaxed, wide, touching the corners of the mouth, thick and unmoving. Don't let it pull back into the mouth, become pointed, thin, flat, or scooped down in the middle.

- On a triad, sigh out the "heeee" through your mouth and over your tongue, through the narrow space between the surface of the tongue and the top teeth. Move the sinuses up and down on the triad "heeee"s, checking that the tongue stays totally relaxed throughout the triads.

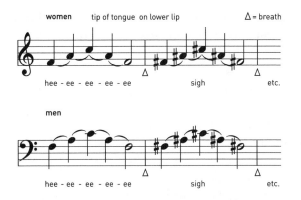

- Relax for a new breath.

- Picture the triad sound traveling horizontally out through the mouth into the air—not moving up and down vertically with the pitches.

Use this series of ascending triad "heeee"s to check out the interrelationship of tongue and breath. If the tongue goes hard on the underside of the jaw area, massage it loose again with your fingers while continuing the sound. You can push upward into this area quite vigorously as it is insensitive. There should be the same soft condition as when you are silent, whatever the pitch. Whenever the tongue tightens, become aware of your breathing and sigh out with more release, more freedom, from deeper inside.

For the basic freeing of the voice, make a general rule—as you go higher in pitch, sigh more fully from deeper inside.

- Let the tongue release back into the mouth and, forgetting the specific focus of the preceding work, call freely on a long easy "he-e-e-ey." Shake the sound out—loosen your whole body on sound.

Do not be anxious if the quality of the sound is not aesthetically satisfying at this stage. Be content to focus solely on causal things—the freedom of the breath in response to the thought of higher pitch, the loosening and awakening of the face muscles, the continued freedom in the throat, tongue, and jaw. The results may be very strange initially, and it is sometimes better that they are, because your old aesthetic standards may have to give place to new standards. In the freeing stage of training, aesthetic judgment is usually an inhibiting factor and should be postponed to a much later, refining phase. As long as you are clinging to an aural criterion and inwardly commenting, "That's a hideous sound;" "I sound much better when I'm singing properly;" or "That's not my voice," you may be sure you are not directing all your attention to the physical and sensory aspects of the work, and the results will never be satisfactory.

The reconditioning involved in meeting the demand of a higher and higher pitch is not only designed to help open up your range or to develop your singing voice, though it will do both. It is also a basic reprogramming designed to change the response to all large demands on the voice from greater effort to greater release—the demand of a powerful character you must embody, the demand of a huge theatre in which you must be heard, or the demand of a strong emotion that has to be communicated. Such powerful communication should be the byproduct of abundant inner energies of an appropriate nature—the open, free communicative channels of voice and body; the strong, generous desire to communicate; and the promise of the great pleasure inherent in such communication. The most powerful emotional expression offers the most powerful and satisfying release.

■ **COMMENTARY**

The reason for sighing more as you go higher is to break a common conditioned reflex of pushing for high notes. Reaching, bracing, working harder, and simply refusing to go higher are all common psychophysical reactions to going up in pitch. If you consciously decide to sigh with more and more relief as you go higher, you do three things: (1.) you undo automatic preparatory tensions in the breathing muscles because tension and sighing are a contradiction in terms; (2.) you deliver a greatly increased gust of breath to help release and support the pitch; (3.) you undermine the pushing, working, suffering, and/or "I can't" syndrome by substituting a palpable sensation of relief that has to be allied with pleasure. If you can decide that it is a sigh of pleasurable relief and that each ascending pitch can connect with more and deeper pleasurable relief, then you will generate enormous energy, enormous quantities of breath, and a new attitude to high notes that will make them a great deal easier to produce. Economy will come later.

STEP 4　In order to counteract the tendency for the impulse and breath sources to move—almost imperceptibly—higher up in the body as the pitch goes higher, all the sinus exercises should now be combined with floorwork.

- Lying on your back—knees up, feet flat on the floor—begin on a comfortably low pitch to sigh out triads on "hey"s. Notice which resonators are engaged in the lower sounds and then, as you go higher, notice the mouth resonance coming into play.

- As you feel you are entering the middle of your range, roll over onto your belly: change the vowel to a long, loose "heeee" as you continue with the triads. Make sure you are feeding the sigh impulse deep down into your lower back, feeling the small of your back moving up to the ceiling on the ingoing breath and falling toward the floor as you sigh out. Picture the vibrations falling through your teeth toward gravity.

- Then move into the folded leaf, let your tongue fall out onto your lower lip, and continue on "hee" triads while moving your sinuses up and down. Be conscious of your lower back opening for the ingoing breath and picture the sound flowing out from your tailbone, along your spine, over the *back of your neck and the top of your skull* and falling out to gravity through the middle of your face.

- Tuck your toes into the floor and move into a comfortable squat. With your elbows inside your knees, put your thumb pads onto your sinus area and massage/vibrate the sinuses with your thumbs as you sigh the triad "heeee" out along your spine, over the *back of your neck and the top of your skull* and falling out to gravity through the middle of your face.

- Float your tailbone up in the air so that you are hanging head downward. Put your elbows on your knees and again massage/vibrate the sinuses with your thumbs as you feel/see the diaphragm falling to gravity on the outgoing sigh triad.

- Slowly come back up until you are standing, keeping your own center of gravity low in your body while maintaining the buzzing clarity of the sinuses.

By now you should be very aware of the spaces behind your face, particularly those behind the cheekbones. The cheekbones themselves are beautifully shaped for resonance

- Bounce your knees if you feel dizzy.

STEP 5 This next exercise demands focus and clear, mental energy.

- To prepare, push your lips forward into a pouting position, as if you're about to blow a kiss. Then vigorously draw them sideways into the widest grin you can manage.

- Repeat this several times: forward, sideways, forward, sideways; pout, grin, pout, grin.

- Be sure not to involve your jaw. Check: put the tip of your little finger between your front teeth as you do the lip exercise.

Be sure that the tip of your tongue remains behind your bottom teeth. You are exercising the horizontal and diagonal muscles of the face that inevitably include the sinus areas and your cheek muscles. Be aware that your cheeks bunch up under your eyes as you grin and that the skin over your bones stretches as you pout.

- Push your lips forward into a pouting position. Picture a tiny ball of vibration that you can hold in your pouting lips. Find a middle range sound, and play with the feeling of vibration within your pouting lips, squeezing it and releasing it a little and squeezing it again. ("Oo-uh" on a very small scale.)

- Now imagine the ball of vibrations as a small pebble and your lips as a slingshot that will catapult the sound forward and off your face as you pull your lips sideways into a grin. The catapulted vibrations fly forward in a strong sharp "wey."

The sound of *w* is composed of two vowels "oo" and "uh." In the syllable "wey" the two vowels are "oo" and "ey."

- When you repeat this, look in a mirror and observe the diagonal stretch from your cheekbones to the corners of your mouth when you push your lips forward. Think of the sideways movement of the lips as a release from that stretch, having the quality of a strong slingshot being stretched and let go. As you let go notice that your cheeks are pushed up under your eyes. With a strong movement, a strong sound should result. Do not feel you are shouting, but rather that a strong, sharp sound is the natural outcome of the movement.

This sound picks up and intensifies the sinus/cheekbone resonance and helps develop strength in the middle and upper range of the voice. It is very extroverted, and the result is a short, sharp shout. It happens because of your energy being focused, not because you are shouting. By *extroverted* I mean a quality that occurs outside rather than inside. It is open and unveiled.

- Now renew your interest in the breathing energy centers: feed in four huge sighs, six medium sighs, and many, many quick lively anticipation impulses.

- Right at the end of a cluster of anticipation panting, send the impulse directly from the pant-center to your lips and cheekbones on "wey"!

- Repeat "wey" several times on one breath

- Forward "oo;" sideways "ey"

- Forward sideways; forward sideways; forward sideways

- Oo ey oo ey oo ey

All this is done while keeping the vibrations in tangible contact with the lips.

- Repeat with the tip of your little finger between your front teeth on several ascending pitches—from about F sharp to E flat.

men: one octave lower   continue to D or E ♭

oo – ey – oo – ey – oo – ey   oo – ey – oo – ey – oo – ey

There must be no strain at all in the throat. The soft palate is open. The tongue is relaxed with the tip behind the bottom teeth. The jaw does not move. There is a clear space from the breathing source to the front of the face.

■ Use a mirror to make sure you still go fully forward and fully sideways with your lips.

■ Blow out through your lips to relax them.

■ **COMMENTARY**

The old idea in voice training was that you had to "place your voice in the mask" and "project" your voice in order to be heard.

This one-dimensional image of a "mask" not only denies the complexity of the facial bone structure and its rich resonating capabilities but also suggests that the face is a "mask" behind which to hide. The word *project* means "throw forward." If you are "throwing" your voice forward at the same time that you are trying to be truthfully engaged in playing the scene, you are splitting your energies.

To replace these counterproductive terms you must commit yourself to truthfulness, freedom, and openness. You must want the listeners in the back row of the theatre to share the thoughts and feelings of the character you are playing, and you must have open and relaxed channels of voice and body that can serve that desire. You must be able to expand your circle of awareness to encompass the inner world of your performance and the outer world of your audience without one diminishing the other.

If you are committed to the truth of the thought/feeling that is to be communicated, if you have a real desire to share that thought/feeling, and if there are no blocks or tensions in the breathing and vocal musculature, the voice will carry the thought/feeling content from deep inside to the front of your mouth and out to the audience.

To strengthen this middle part of your range you must devise and practice sounds that stimulate the resonance in the very front of your face. This is the open, extroverted, carrying part of the voice that allows your innermost thoughts to be intimately revealed and your most lively, ebullient, stormy feelings to be freely expressed without effort.

In order to help create the conditions for this kind of communication, here are some playful extensions of the "wey" exercise. Their many repetitions will eventually lead you to natural usage.

■ Instead of "wey," but with exactly the same face and lip actions, substitute

Will you will you will you

This changes the emphasis on the two-way diagonal cheek muscles to an active pull sideways on "will" and a release forward on "you." The tongue also gets a little workout on this exercise as it ripples the sound from its front on *l* to its middle on *y*. The *i* vowel rings into the cheekbones as the "wey" did.

■ With a full grin and a full pout explore the mid to upper range of your voice on the triads.

Willyou-willyou-willyou-willyou-willyou

Then extend this to:

■ Will you wait will you wait will you wait will you wait

■ Each time feel the "i" in "will" and the "ey" in "wait" pinging off your cheekbones. The "oo" in "you" goes into the lip pout.

■ Triads: willyouwait-willyouwait-willyouwait-willyouwait- willyouwait

Then extend to:

■ Will you wait for Willie (Same full lip movements sideways and forward)

- Triads:

  WillyouwaitforWillie-
  WillyouwaitforWillie-
  WillyouwaitforWillie-
  WillyouwaitforWillie-
  WillyouwaitforWillie

- You should check all of these for unnecessary jaw activity with the tip-of-the-little-finger test.

- Then speak this as a very quick question.

  Add:

  Will you wait for Willie and Winnie (etc.)

- Gradually increase the pace and develop agility. As you go faster, relax the stretches a little; let the corners of your mouth flicker in and out. Keep your voice releasing through the cheekbone/sinus resonators.

- Use the ascending range to ask a long question and the descending range to answer it—"No I won't wait" or "Why won't you wait." Repeat this pattern of question and answer covering the middle and upper range with:

  Will you wait
  Will you wait for Willie
  Will you wait for Willie and Winnie
  Will you wait for Willie and Winnie Williams
  Will you wait for Willie and Winnie Williams the well-known welterweights

And so on.

WILL YOU WAIT WILL YOU WAIT FOR WILLIE WHY WON'T YOU WAIT NO I WON'T WAIT

You can improvise with "Whether they are Welsh" and "World-famous," or you can answer the question with "Why won't you wait for Willie and Winnie Williams" and other variations.

Play with the forward resonance and increasing speed.

This, incidentally, is not an articulation exercise as such. You would not use such exaggerated movements for speaking. It is an exercise to wake up extrovert, forward resonance and involve the lips and tongue in the outgoing impetus. Unquestionably this makes a good foundation for the more precise articulation exercises that come later.

PRACTICE

Daily, in conjunction with the workout plan.

15
Workday Fifteen

Nasal Resonator: Carrying power . . . mountain peak

■ Prepare to work for:
ONE HOUR

A clear distinction must be made between the terms *nasal resonance* and *nasality*. Nasality is the quality heard when, finding the opening into the mouth obscured, the voice escapes through the nose instead. The physical causes for nasality are a lazy, soft palate that may sit flaccidly on the back of the tongue, and the tongue itself when it bunches up at the back driving the sound sharply into the nose. Nasality inevitably implies torpid breathing. Nasality can be heard in deep voices, high voices, or middle-register voices and means that the pall of a single resonating quality hangs over all utterance. When a deep voice is nasal it tends to be richly adenoidal and monotonous; when a medium-pitched voice is nasal it tends to be aggressively strident and monotonous, and when a high-pitched voice is nasal it is piercingly monotonous.

Nasal resonance, on the other hand, is a vital part of the whole resonating system. It provides brilliance and carrying power for the voice and is a major component of the front-of-face resonating structure. Its power must be tempered by balance, since it can easily dominate and distort the whole. Many actors have found that if they place their voices up in the nose/cheekbone area they can be very easily heard in the back row of the balcony. So easily, in fact, that they need hardly exert themselves in any other respect. Being heard is perhaps only a third of the battle, and clear, empty voices often sail up to ears that hear the words and wonder what cargo they carry. Those whose aim is to share what they feel with an audience will allow emotional energy to activate the breath and generate vibrations. These vibrations, reinforced by all appropriate resonating feedback, will flow out through the body, gathering a mix of sinus, cheekbone, and nasal vibrations as they travel through the face, creating sound waves with a carrying power faithful to the initial aim. Communication is a by-product of desire, intention, and freedom.

As with the other resonators, the nasal cavity must be discovered, isolated, developed, and then left to react automatically in the general interplay of speech. It is the penultimate rung on the resonating ladder.

Here I remind you that the resonating ladder is an energy ladder and we are approaching the high-intensity rungs. Excitation in the breathing area is a prerequisite for excitation of the higher resonators.

The nose resonator is the farthest forward resonator in the body—literally the most extrovert. Be aware first of the shape of the nose bone and realize that vibrations arriving in that sharply concave structure will resound with great intensity. If, for instance, you stand close to the corner of a room and make sounds into the angle, you get a much stronger resonating feedback than if you speak to a flat wall.

STEP 1

- With your finger, press the right side of your nose to close off your right nostril. Wrinkle up the left side of your nose and breathe in through the left nostril in short, sharp, quick sniffs. Five or six sniffs should fill you up, then release the breath out through your mouth on "ffff."

- Close off the left nostril with your finger and bring five or six short, sharp, strong sniffs up into the bridge of the wrinkled-up right nostril—then let the breath out through your mouth.

- Repeat this several times for each nostril registering the feeling of cold air in the nasal passages.

STEP 2 Having sniffed up each nostril several times, rest and become conscious of the cool places that the breath rushed through.

- Now close off the right nostril and wrinkle up the left side of the nose and hum on a medium pitch—A or A flat; an octave lower for men—picturing the humming vibrations focused exclusively in the left nostril and warming the cool spots.

- Close off your left nostril, wrinkle up the right side of the nose and hum, feeling the vibrations traveling through your right nostril.

- Wrinkle up the bridge of the nose, and while it is wrinkled, pant in and out through both nostrils. (You may need to blow your nose before doing this.) Your mouth will, of course, be closed.

- Aim a hum where the wrinkle is and while humming, massage with your fingertips from the nostrils out in small circles. Repeat on ascending pitches, a new breath between each new pitch. The hum will become stronger and more focused in the nose as you massage.

- Now, aiming the sound one hundred percent into the nose, let the hum turn from a focused "mmmmmmmm" into a narrow "meeeee" with the "eeee" coming exclusively through the nose.

Here is a ridiculous image that may facilitate this exercise: picture your lungs in your head, your vocal folds between your eyebrows, and your nose as your only resonator.

- Speak

Mee-mee-mee

Aim the "mee" into the wrinkled bridge of your nose, picturing the sound coming into the nose from above. Don't let any of the vibrations go into your mouth.

- Relax. Drop your spine down and uncurl back up to standing. Roll your neck and head.

Speak the "mee-mee-mee" into the nose on the top part of your speaking voice—*not in falsetto*. Feel the vibrations ping into your nose.

By *falsetto* I mean the head singing voice for women and the counter-tenor part of men's voices above their daily speaking range.

Falsetto is a term that is still commonly used. It originally came from the misconception that the false vocal folds that are muscles existing above the true vocal folds came together to produce the high sound above the speaking voice. Once voice science had developed the instrumentation to see the vocal folds in action the misconception was cleared up. Those high sounds are created in true vocal fold action. The term *falsetto* remains.

■ Relax. Drop your spine down. Build up. Stretch and relax the tongue. Breathe in and out on a whispered "kaah" to release the soft palate. Then, forgetting the focus of the preceding exercises, call "he-e-ey," long and free from your center. Shake out your body on sound.

Remembering that there is a correlation between increasing inner energy and ascending pitch, do not pull back from the strength of the intense, ringing vibrations the nose bone produces. To begin with, you may feel you have to push slightly in your throat to get the sound focused sharply enough, but gradually you should find that you can transfer such effort from the body to the mind. The mental image of the path to the nasal cavity strengthens; the power of the thought of the sound increases; and the ability to bypass the throat develops further. If you use your lips they will help propel the sound directly into the nose without the aid of your throat muscles.

You can also explore the nasal resonance from the back of your mouth.

■ Send the nasal "eee" into the wrinkled bridge of the nose from an "ng"—formed between the back of the tongue and the soft palate. "Ng" is a single consonant sound despite its spelling—the "g" is silent.

An important aspect of the psychophysical nature of the voice is its resilience. If you treat it tentatively, always afraid of strain, you will never stretch it or tap its unknown potential, for you will always stay within what is safe and familiar. If you are tentative, you may think you are just being physically careful, but you will also be holding back on essential energies that are the very fuel the voice needs. Carefulness, of the wrong sort, can create a vicious cycle. It is worth taking the risk of occasionally scraping your throat or getting a little hoarse in order to find new possibilities. You know enough to restore your voice to a good state if you should happen to strain it (and I must stress that it certainly need not ever happen): go through all the basic relaxation exercises with particular emphasis on the tongue and throat loosening. Then, gently humming, roll your head, drop down your spine, massage your face, and so on. Humming provides a natural massage for the vocal folds, and this treatment, administered as soon after the strain as possible, is much better for your voice than resting it by being silent. It is also healthier psychologically to remove the fear of "losing your voice," the very kind of energy-sapper that contributes most to the condition.

If you have conscientiously practiced the sequence of exercises in this book, you will have acquired experiential knowledge of your voice. You are on your way to becoming your own authority on your own body and how to guide yourself. Your voice is the prime instrument of your artistry, and your creativity is its master. Awareness will be the monitor of what works and what does not work. Playing safe will only mean you never move beyond your known boundaries, and a limited, comfortable artist eventually ceases to be an artist of any kind.

STEP 3

- Wrinkle the bridge of your nose and again prepare the path by sniffing in and out.

- Send the "mee-mee-mee" pinging into your nose.

- Put your fingertips on the bridge of your nose and imagine that you can, with your fingers, draw the vibrations from the bridge of the nose across your cheekbones. Let the sound expand slightly from "mee-mee-mee" to a very narrow "mey-mey-mey." This sound must still come through the nose but is now influenced by an extended resonating surface. It fans out in opposite directions from a point on top of the bridge of your nose across the upper ridge of your cheekbones.

- Repeat two or three times.

Repeat using the "ng"

- Ngee-ngee-ngee

- Ngey-ngey-ngey

- Relax your throat, soft palate, and tongue and shake sound out from your whole body.

Keep your eyes open—don't bunch up your whole face when you do this exercise.

STEP 4 You are now going to redirect the vibrations from your nose into your mouth.

The idea to work with is that, having developed an intensely packed crowd of vibrations in your nose, you are now going to free them out through your mouth. They will still be nasal vibrations, but they will go through the mouth instead of the nose. In order for this to happen, the soft-palate trapdoor, which has automatically closed in response to your direction that sound be diverted into the nose, must fly open at the appropriate moment, restoring the mouth channel.

- Send the "mee"s into the bridge of the nose as before. Put your fingers on the bridge of your nose and, with your fingers guiding your thoughts, spread the vibrations across the cheekbones on the "mey"s as before.

- Then—and this is where the soft palate flies open—using your hands to guide your thought, redirect the vibrations consciously out through your mouth on "mah-mah-mah" while the palms of your hands open out into the air in front of you.

Do not let the jaw substitute for the soft-palate opening.

The whole face, including the jaw, will stretch to the "animal-roar" opening for the "mah."

It is the mid-face and cheek muscles that articulate the "mah-mah-mah"— not the jaw. Activate the top lip and the cheeks.

- Relax—breathe.

Repeat the whole sequence on one breath on ascending pitches

- Mee-mee-mee-mey-meY-mEY-MAH-MAH-MAAAAH

(Nose) (Cheekbones) (Mouth)

- Use your palms to direct the "mah" out away from your face and through your mouth. Feel the stretch in the center of your palms imitating the stretch in the soft palate.

- Speak the whole sequence in the upper portion of your speaking voice.

Do not drop the pitch.

This is the upper part of your speaking voice.

Do not make the mistake of dropping into a speaking pitch that could belong to the mouth resonance or lower.

- Repeat the whole sequence starting with an "ng" sound—remember that this a single consonant in which the *g* is silent.

- Ngee-ngee-ngee

- Ngey-ngey-ngey

- Ngah-ngah-ngah

- Relax; breathe; shake out.

■ **COMMENTARY**

This is a difficult part of the voice to discover, and once it has become available, may be hard to understand. It is between the middle much-used part of the range and the very high, excited part in the skull that is used in expressing high-energy and hysterical states. The rungs on the resonating ladder leading from the bridge of the nose to the forehead are often skipped completely in vocal development, and it is usually here that the famous "break" in the singing voice, which everyone asks about sooner or later, occurs. This break is not necessary. The voice knows how to move smoothly from a speaking to a singing register. Any break that occurs is because of tension.

In my observation, the part of the voice that goes from the nasal reso-nance up through the upper sinuses—those above the eyebrows—and to the skull is the most vulnerable part of the voice. By *vulnerable* I do not mean the weakest. Rather it is the part of the voice that expresses the most ingenuous, open, and vulnerable feelings and thoughts. It is there to respond to quivering, naked fears, to innocent surprise, to sud-den, amazed joy, to naive, open questions that go up at the end. (It is surprising how few questions are asked with a simple, rising inflection. Start listening, and you may hear how many have a preconceived answer implicit in them that turns the inflection away from vulnerability.) As is the case with vulnerable areas, this part of the vocal register has become guarded. High-octane impulses are rerouted away from it, and although such impulses may send the pitch into the upper register, the resonating response will be more safely found in the nose, or it will be reduced to half by an excessive rush of breath. When such energy impulses end up in the nose they are extremely piercing and not endearing; the excess volume is an interesting defense against direct response. The opposite method is a breathy reaction where words are heard through a misty filter that suggests the defense of appeasement: "Look how weak and

>

unprotected I am—I dare not even commit my thoughts to a whole voice. In a way I hope you won't quite hear what I have to say in case I'm wrong."

To give an example of what I mean, here are three versions of the same scene:

Two people who were in love with each other ten years ago and haven't met since meet by chance, at a party or some public event. For the sake of the example, use this one sentence to communicate three possible reactions:

"How wonderful to see you; did you know I'd be here?"

Applying the defensive postures suggested above, here are two possible sequences of psychophysical events.

First sequence
1. At the sight of the former lover, the person's adrenalin floods the blood, the knees go weak, and breathing increases as the heart pumps faster.
2. Thinks: "I can't let him/her see how much I'm affected."
3. Method: Add social energy to make a slightly exaggerated and inappropriately extroverted joy that activates the muscles in the throat and face more vigorously than the breath.
4. Result: Channel muscles drive the sound into the nose, creating a high pitch of delight that smothers the initial vulnerability in social noise:
   "How WON-derful to SEE you: did you KNOW I was HERE."
   (Exaggerated surprise and delight: The question safely assumes the answer is yes.)

Second sequence
1. At the sight of former lover, the person's adrenalin floods the blood, the knees go weak, and breathing increases as the heart pumps faster.
2. Thinks: "I wonder if he/she feels the same as I do. Until I know I don't dare express what I feel or I might get hurt."

>

3. Method: Let out all the breath in a rush while holding the feeling in. Empty breath floods the vocal folds left flaccid by the withheld emotional impulse, creating half-voice, half-whisper that lacks the vibrating energy to stimulate resonating feedback or lively inflection.
4. Result: The person half-whispers, "How wonderful to see you. Did you know I'd be here." (The monotone throws the responsibility on to the hearer to project what has been heard into the unrevealing sentence, thus showing the hand first.)

Third sequence

In the event of an open revelation of feeling the psychophysical sequence could be:
1. At the sight of former lover, the person's adrenalin floods the blood, knees go weak, and the heart pumps faster.
2. The excitement energizes the laryngeal musculature that governs the vocal folds: the excited breath and excited folds create high frequency vibrations that are picked up and amplified by simultaneously toned-up muscle tissue in the upper pharynx and upper facial areas.
3. Pitch jumps: Light, high resonating quality responds and the ex-lover hears the surprised, half-fearful delight and the genuine need to know whether the ex-partner has chosen to seek him/her out or if it has occurred by chance.

STEP 5

- Start with the "mee-mee-mees" in the nose, then, drawing your fingers from your nose up through your eyebrows, bring the "mey-mey-mey" up into the upper sinuses.

Still direct the vibrations through your nose.

The upper-sinus hollows are behind the forehead, above the eyebrows.

- Repeat—and this time move your hands up to the top of your skull. Imagine a trapdoor opening up and out from the top of the skull and let the sound escape—soft palate open.

- My-my-my-my.

- Repeat and end on one long "my-y-y-y" on an upward inflection as though for an ingenuous question

- Mee-meeee-mee-mey-meY-mEY-My-my-mY-Y-Y-Y?

Try not to go into falsetto.

Check that your eyebrows don't go up at the idea of a question. If they do, your voice won't go as far as it might. (The eyebrows tend to substitute for the soft palate.)

- Repeat; and at the end of the questioning "my-y-y?" say "why?" on the same breath, in the same resonance, on the same rising pitch.

- Mee-mee-mee-mey-meY-mEY-myY Y-WHYYY?

- Send the "why-y-y?" out through the top of your head.

- Repeat "meemeemeemeymeymeymy? why?"

- Then add "why fly?" Δ "why fly so high?"

Do this with the accumulated energy of the pitch, the resonator, the question, and the urgency of your need to know the answer coming from your diaphragm.

STEP 6

- Imagine you are standing on top of a mountain. There is a narrow deep valley between it and another peak. On the other peak stands a friend of yours. The sky is blue; the air is clear and crisp.

- Let the scene affect your inner state. From an exhilarated center of the solar plexus/diaphragm call a long, high, curving "hi-i-i" across to the opposite mountain peak.

- Imagine the same scene exactly—the same feelings—the same desire to call. This time whisper the call, just allow the impulse from the breath center with breath flying out through the wide channel of your throat to produce a whispered "hi-i-i."

■ Voice it again.

Here you are providing yourself with the kind of scene that can stimulate the energy that needs the upper to high part of the vocal range and resonating ladder in order to express itself satisfactorily. All the technical work must be trusted to pay off automatically. The calling impulse should travel naturally to the diaphragm without being subverted by the throat muscles; the diaphragm should spontaneously draw in enough breath to supply that impulse and willingly release the breath and impulse with energy sufficient for the demand. By now the throat, the soft palate, and the jaw should be naturally limber and agile enough to open a passageway for the call, which will be impelled into high, carrying resonators capable of amplifying the vibrations enough to accomplish the goal of communicating with your friend on the opposite mountain peak. The diaphragm, intercostal, and inner-abdominal breathing musculatures are lively and responsive to the largesse of the need.

It is important now that you begin to create your own simple scenes so that you can alternate between the technical, conscious work, which tones your vocal instrument, and the imaginative work that knows the voice must function involuntarily if it is to be true. In the technical work you carve out paths from the mind to chosen muscles; in the imaginative work you know those paths are there and you run along them. You are reconditioning your use of yourself, not just something called "your voice," so when you follow a scene, you feed the initial impulse of image to the place where the path begins before you start. Start from the central energy source, feed in the images, nurture the feeling response—then release the images and the energy from the deep wells of thought/feeling/breath and sound and see what happens. If you stumble or fall, go back to do a bit more carving in the technical department. Then deliver yourself up again to your creative self. From technical to creative and back again, but at this stage, do not try consciously to do the two at once or your energies will split and lose their strength.

PRACTICE

Daily in conjunction with the workout plan.

16

Workday Sixteen

Range: Three to four octaves . . . from basement to attic

- ■ Prepare to work for:
  ONE HOUR

Within the framework of the resonating ladder, only the domed top of the head remains to be explored. The top of the resonating ladder has a perfect acoustical shape and texture. It resounds simply and strongly to the high frequency sounds that find amplification there, but unless you are a practicing soprano, tenor, counter-tenor, or daily screamer, you may not be familiar with the feeling of skull resonance. There is intense energy in the sound that must be created centrally if it is to serve some human purpose. It is easier to lead into the exercises for developing skull resonance from doing simple work on the whole range, which will allow energy to generate naturally, rather than making a direct assault on it. In theory, the work on skull resonance goes before that on range, but in practice it is more helpful to work on the range exercises first. In the following exercises you will be using your developing awareness of a resonating ladder to free your voice into its widest possible range.

STEP 1

- ■ Standing easily while maintaining an awareness of the skeletal support of your body, close your eyes and turn your attention inward. Imagine your body is a house. Put a sub-basement (foundation) below the rib cage, the basement in the chest, the lobby floor in the mouth, first floor from the mouth to the eyes, second floor from the eyebrows to the hairline, and the attic in the top of the skull.

■ Picture your voice as an elevator with an electrical mechanism in the sub-basement. Using a long "he-e-ey" as the sound in which your voice/elevator is manifested, travel from sub-basement to attic, visiting all the resonating floors on the way, going from the lowest part of your voice to the highest.

Take into account the fact that a house does not move when the elevator runs. Let your mouth drop open, but otherwise do not allow your shoulders, jaw, tongue, lips, or eyebrows to move in any way as the voice/elevator moves.

■ Let the breath replace after you have arrived in the attic; and, renewing the electrical power from the sub-basement, travel down through the house again, making sure you do not skip any of the floors and that the elevator runs at the same smooth pace all the way down.

There is a tendency to skid out of control on the way down, jumping from attic to lobby and spending a great deal of time in the basement.

■ Repeat the exercise several times until you are familiar with the idea.

■ Points to look out for:

The power that moves the elevator comes from the sub-basement, whether starting from the bottom or the top.

If you feel you are running out of power halfway up or down, don't squeeze the last volt out, get a fresh boost from below. This is not an exercise to test how long you can sustain one breath.

Let your attention be on the accuracy of the image and the sensory perception of resonance; let pitch be a by-product of these.

STEP 2   Having visited the resonating chambers of your body, now deal with your range carelessly and freely.

- Drop down your spine very quickly and build up as quickly.

The drop down goes in two unequal stages: a sudden, heavy drop of the head and a quick undoing of the spine. (Make sure your knees bend as you do this or you will be thrown off balance.)

The build-up starts as a rebound from the sudden drop, goes fast up the spine, the head floating up last.

- Standing—start the "hey" at the bottom of your range in your belly, drop your head and begin to go *up* through your range as you drop *down* through the spine. Let the ascending pitch and the descending spine accelerate so that the sudden, bumpy drop at the bottom expels the top part of the range out through the top of your head very freely towards gravity.

- New breath. Start the "hey" at the top of your range. Build *up* your spine as the sound travels *down* through the range arriving back in your belly by the time your head floats up on top of your spine.

Go *up* the range as you go *down* the spine, and *down* the range as you go *up* the spine, being aware of the following:

Mentally take advantage of gravity to allow the top of your range to go higher in pitch each time you drop down. Think of the sound as falling upward out of your skull.

Be loose, free, careless: the bump as you suddenly drop down should shock the sound upward.

Don't hold on to the top note—let it swoop out giddily.

Don't adopt too serious an attitude to the exercise or you will destroy its purpose.

A useful picture to play with is that, when you are standing, the "hey" starts in your tailbone and travels up your spine to your head where it escapes through a hole at the top. When you are upside-down, it starts under the ground, then flows from your head down to the tailbone again by the time you are upright.

STEP 3   Lie on your back on the floor and travel slowly through the range, examining and relishing all the rungs of the resonating ladder.

Again, the spinal picture can be useful: this time, while supine, think of the spine as a railroad track and the sound as a train traveling from the tailbone depot to the topmost vertebra terminal and vice versa.

In this position you can really check that you are moving through the whole range of your voice using only your mind and your breath. You do not need to open your mouth wider as you go higher or lower; you do not need to push with your throat muscles to reach the high notes; you do not need to press your head back or lift your eyebrows. Thought and breath are all you need. The resonating spaces are built in.

STEP 4

- Stand up and repeat Steps 1 and 2 with the awareness of Step 3. "he-ey-ey-ey."

STEP 5

- Go through your range from bottom to top and top to bottom on "he-ey-ey-ey."

- Bounce your knees.

- Bounce your shoulder blades.

- Blow through your lips.

- Shake your jaw.

- Loosen your tongue.

PRACTICE

Daily, in conjunction with the workout plan.

17

Workday Seventeen

Skull Resonator: High intensity . . . playing the dome

■ Prepare to work for:
ONE HOUR

In Step 1 of this lesson we will link the range-freeing process with skull exploration exercises. I am going to reintroduce a concept here that can be very useful if grasped clearly. In Step 2 of the previous lesson the physical process of suddenly dropping your body upside down propelled the sound up in pitch without obvious muscular effort. All your abdominal muscles should have felt totally relaxed at that point with the diaphragm dropping through your rib cage. It should be clear that you do not need extra muscle power to support a high sound. Yet extra energy has to be generated.

■ Repeat Step 2 of the previous lesson. Then, remaining upright, consciously transfer the physical energy of dropping down into mental energy that imagines gravity existing in the sky: release the "hey" from bottom to top of your range.

The physical energy generated by a body dropping through space in response to gravity is great. The mind can use the experience of such release to generate mental energy that is as great as, if not greater than, the physical energy.

This means that high sounds can be produced with very little extra work in observable muscles. High notes are produced through increased aerodynamic pressure between the breath and the vocal folds; this increase in pressure is created by increased effort in the breathing musculature and the laryngeal musculature. The danger is that anatomical knowledge encourages effort in the form of conscious abdominal support, thus spoiling the delicate balance of energies on the involuntary level of neurophysical response. Economy of effort is essential to truthful results. To put it another way, as soon as the abdominal muscles pull in, push out, or do something to boost sound, they substitute physical effort for mental energy. Mental energy, in the high part of the voice, usually implies emotional energy, so muscular substitution would be a critically false intrusion.

STEP 1

■ Drop your spine down quickly, moving up through your range on a long "hey."

Register the topmost sound that flies out through the attic when you are upside down: It should by now be a high falsetto sound for both men and women.

■ Allow a new breath and, still upside down, release a high, falsetto "keeee" on the same pitch as your voice was in the attic. Move it out through the trapdoor in the top of your head to gravity. The "keeee" can be something like a yodel and should not be sustained on one note for too long.

■ Relax and slowly build up the spine without sound. When you are upright, release the high falsetto "keeee" again. You should feel it ring into the dome of the skull.

■ Keee-eee △ keee-eee △ Keee-eee

Men should start a little lower in pitch, but most can soon go as high as the preceding suggested pitches.

As a variation and for greater flexibility think the following pattern as a quick, light oscillation in the falsetto release

■ Keee -ee-ee -ee-eee-eee △ keee-ee-ee -ee -ee -eee

In response to the lively mental energy needed to create these sounds, you will feel a lively breath reaction in the center of your diaphragm.

Let that happen but don't add to it. Don't add any extra pull from the external abdominal wall muscles. The abdominal wall will move, but with a passive strength, pulled from inside as the diaphragm releases up. It is necessary to know the difference between a strong physical movement that is active on the muscular level and a strong physical movement that is reactive on the involuntary level. The muscles should respond from inside, but because everything is connected, the outside abdominal wall will move, too. The internal breathing musculature is stimulated by powerful impulses into powerful activity, and the energy thus generated is of a different quality from that produced by effort in the large external muscles of *rectus abdominus.*

STEP 2

- Inject the impulse of the thought of a high, falsetto "keeee-ee" such as you created in Step 1, but this time whisper it. The strong thought impulse will arouse a strong response from the center of your diaphragm releasing a strong breath hissing through your front teeth.

- Whisper "keeee-eee" several times, concentrating on reproducing the thought of the falsetto pitch and allowing the body to react to that thought with appropriate energy. Use a new thought impulse and a new breath impulse each time.

- Then voice the impulse, dealing with thought, breath, and inner energy and allowing the sound to be a by-product of them.

- Repeat on ascending pitches, alternating the whispered and the voiced "keeee-eee"s.

Feel the sounds ringing around the dome of your skull.

When you fully commit to the strong thought-impulse you are dedicating communicative energy to cause.

STEP 3

- Drop your voice down to the bottom of your range and, with your mind relaxed, let your breath rumble deep into your chest resonance on "hey."

You may find that the resultant sound is deeper than before as your vocal folds relax more fully after their unaccustomed stretching.

STEP 4

- Experiment with calling on "hey" as high as you can without slipping into falsetto.

Men, particularly, can find a strong, ringing sound that has an intense existence in the top of the dome of the skull and is easy to maintain there once it is free of the throat and connected to appropriately strong energy from the energy-breath center.

- Women can experiment with a high, falsetto "keee-eee" extending their range into mouselike squeaks. Do this lightly and playfully—swooping the sounds, never holding onto the last or first note, letting the energy spring as though from a jack-in-the-box from the center of the body.

Your first objective in working to free the very top of your range is to remove fears and dissolve the boundaries that skirt unfamiliar territory. The quality of the sound is irrelevant, although as the vocal folds strengthen and the throat frees you will develop excellent raw material for a soprano or tenor voice and rich counter-tenor quality. But beauty must wait.

Falsetto work increases the elasticity and strength of the vocal folds and the breathing muscles. (This part of the range is scientifically referred to as the "loft" register. Above this is the "whistle" register.) It is useful for both men's and women's voices because the whole range will benefit from such strengthening if it is done as the final part of a well-balanced workout on the voice. Men are no longer as culturally averse to experimenting with the falsetto part of their voices as they used to be, although some still make a subconscious protest at its unmanliness by being unable to find it. Similarly, many women still seem to feel subconsciously that chest resonance is not for them, preferring the "feminine" appeal of their upper register. A man can compete easily with a woman's soprano range and develop at least two octaves in a falsetto that is mellow and unforced. For both men and women, work in the high, falsetto, skull-resonating area develops flexibility and strength in the rest of the voice. It also removes inhibitions, releases powerful energies, and provides a familiarity with intense vibrations of feeling and sound. This allows the expression of emotional extremes with ease, without trauma, and without straining the voice.

As with all the exercises suggested so far, these top-of-the-skull sounds should be done in context, and their context is the top of the resonating ladder. You should not plunge into any of the high sounds until you have thoroughly limbered up the voice. I strongly recommend that you develop a sequence of exercises that takes you from conscientious physical relaxation through all the steps laid out thus far, and that you are faithful to this progression. Do not alter the sequence or make arbitrary jumps within it until you are quite sure of what you are doing. In the beginning it may seem nonorganic. Your body and your voice may tell you that you don't need such-and-such an exercise. Unfortunately your "instinct" may be some ingrained, crafty habit fighting to maintain your vocal status quo; if you doggedly persist in doing the most unpopular exercises along with the others you will regularly cover every aspect of the whole. It is easy to become enamored with your chest resonance, your middle resonance, even your falsetto, and if you give any one area more time than other areas, you will end up with as unbalanced and inflexible a voice as you previously had.

PRACTICE

Daily, in conjunction with the workout plan.

18

Workday Eighteen

Exercising Your Range: Strength, flexibility, freedom . . .
swinging

■ Prepare to work for:
ONE HOUR

Now that you have experienced the freedom and expansion of your breathing, the embodiment of sound, the release and amplification of vibrations, the relaxation of jaw, tongue, and soft palate that liberates the channel, and the full gamut of your resonating apparatus, you are ready to enter the gymnasium of your voice, flex its muscles and tap into the inherent joy of the three to four octaves of speaking and singing notes that are your birthright.

I will introduce you to the "arpeggio" and then suggest ways in which you and the arpeggio can play together in dozens of different liberating games. The arpeggio is the triad's big sister (or big brother). It goes farther, it swings more, it swoops and has no fear. It goes out on a limb, but always comes back home.

The triad covers five full notes, or pitches. The arpeggio covers eight. They both enjoy more freedom than a scale, which carefully moves step by step, so you can let yourself go on them. The main reason to play with arpeggios is to be free.

■ Here is an arpeggio:

You can familiarize yourself with the pattern of sounds on a long, easy "hey-ey-ey-ey-ey-ey" and then let go of any sense of staying in tune or of singing. It is a longer sentence, a longer, bolder thought, and it sighs out of you on a long horizontal path. You can throw an arpeggio out of you as though it were a yo-yo that moves horizontally out to the end of the string and then reels back into your hand. The key sounds are the home notes at the beginning and the end, and the farthest out (or top) note. You can picture your voice on a swing, swooping and flying.

Once you are familiar with the arpeggio, you can check your voice for relaxation and freedom:

Take your time. These ideas for developing freedom, strength, and range can be read very quickly. But in practice they should be slowly and repetitively savored.

■ Hey-ey-ey-ey-ey-ey-ey-ey

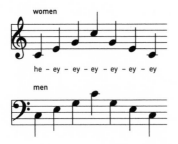

STEP 1 First, explore the deep, relaxing pitches.

■ Sighing out on an arpeggio,

Bounce your knees

- Going down in pitch, sigh out on an arpeggio,

Bounce your shoulder blades

- Sighing out on an arpeggio,

Roll your neck around

- Then, begin to go up in pitch on

Hu-u-u-u-u-uh

- Sighing out on repeated arpeggios,

Hold your jaw with your fingers and thumbs and shake it loose

- Sighing out on arpeggios,

Shake your tongue loose.

This will result in:

- Huyuh-yuyuh-yuyuh-yuyuh-yuyuh-yuyuh-yuyuh

- Sighing out on arpeggios,

Stretch your soft palate on

Ngah-ngah-ngah-ngah-ngah-ngah-ngah

Return to

- Hey-ey-ey-ey-ey-ey-ey-ey

- Releasing higher and higher in the pitches, sigh out on arpeggios while dropping your spine down so that you are hanging head down and the sound is dropping to gravity through the top of your head, then slowly come back up your spine on descending arpeggios—bounce your knees when you reach the top so that you do not become dizzy.

- Blow through your lips ∿ ∿ ∿ ∿ ∿ through the arpeggio

- On descending arpeggios, drop your spine down and then sink into a squat. Picture the sound sighing from your tailbone over your spine and through the top of your head.

- Put your hands behind you on the floor; lower your buttocks to the floor; roll down on your spine until you are lying flat on the floor, knees up.

- Drop your knees over into the diagonal stretch and sigh the arpeggios out from your lower hip-socket out along the wide, diagonal river channel from hip socket to shoulder socket.

- Repeat on the other diagonal.

- Roll again onto your back. With a picture of the two hip sockets and the wide pelvic basin full of breath and sound, sigh out the arpeggios.

- Add a clear picture now of your resonating chambers. See the deeper sounds rumbling through your chest, then as the arpeggios go higher, visualize your bony mouth-cave resonator; the sinus/cheekbone/front-of-face and nose resonators, and the free swoop-up-into-the-skull resonator.

Reminder: This not singing—it is freeing, releasing, and sighing.

Maintain a clear picture of the diaphragm's steady, silky parachute-like release through the rib cage on the outgoing sound and its sudden drop to allow breath to fly in.

- If you start to push, then you know what to do—loosen your tongue, loosen your jaw, open your soft palate, and sigh from deeper down.

- Roll onto your belly and sigh out arpeggios on "hee-ee-ee-ee-ee-ee-ee." Be aware of your access to the lower back and side ribs.

- On arpeggios do "hey"s again and roll over to the folded leaf.

- Rock up to all fours. Sigh the arpeggio out along your arching spine.

- Hanging head downward, build up your spine on *descending* arpeggios.

When the single arpeggios begin to seem easy, double them—two arpeggios on one breath, then three. Exercise your capacity by increasing the demand and expanding the thought. Three arpeggios are a longer thought. As this longer thought enters, it stimulates a greater response in the intercostal and lower-back spaces and draws in more breath. You don't have to "sustain" the breath; you have to think the long thought, and your breath will last.

Some other suggested physical activities to help free the extended voice from the body.

Swings:

A swing of any sort uses gravity and momentum and generates natural energy.

Arm swings and leg swings are wonderfully helpful as a reliable means of releasing genuine energy, but you must be aware when you enter into them in order to ensure maximum effect. Once the general principle is grasped, variations on swings are easy to follow.

Lateral arm swings:

With the last exercise I said: *"These ideas for developing freedom, strength, and range can be read very quickly. But in practice they should be slowly and repetitively savored."*

With the next exercise I urge you to: *Read the instructions slowly, and carefully absorb them. Then give in to the rush and natural fast pace of the movements.*

STEP 1

- Start with your arms extended from your shoulders at right angles to your torso. Your feet should be underneath your hip sockets, and your spine should remain in a straight vertical line. There may be a temptation to let your spine undulate slightly in the course of the swings, or to lean forward; keep it absolutely plumb, vertical to gravity.

- Now let your arms drop suddenly to your sides so that you tune into the force of gravity.

- Float your arms back up to their original position, and this time, as they drop let them fall across the front of your torso where they will swing a couple of times before coming to rest.

Don't let your upper spine drop as your arms drop. Keep your spine long and make sure that you are letting go completely in your shoulder sockets so that the experience is isolated in your arms.

- Float your arms up and away from your sides, and this time, as they drop, let your knees bounce so that your arms are offered extra energy to swing back up to their original position, and then drop again to your sides.

The picture now is that your arms drop, and your knees give in to gravity. Then, as your knees rebound on the momentum from gravity, that momentum surges vertically up from the legs through the spine and then out horizontally through your arms to your fingertips.

As you swing, make sure that you do not lean forward. Your spine is vertical.

As your arms drop across your body and out again, feel the movement in your shoulder blades.

- Now, let your arms drop and your knees give in to gravity and, as your knees rebound on the momentum from gravity, let energy surge up from your legs through your spine and then out horizontally through your arms to your fingertips. Continue by letting your arms drop across your body and immediately let momentum swing them back out to your sides and drop again across your body. The effect of gravity and momentum continues into an ongoing swing.

You now have the opportunity to enter an experience close to that of perpetual motion. You can never drain gravity of its magnetic force; momentum is the flip side of gravity. If you can really drop your arms and release your knees to gravity, if you can catch a ride on the resulting momentum, if you can drop again and ride again, it will seem as if you can go on forever. You are making no effort, you are capitalizing on a natural force.

- Let your mind yield to the fun of the swings and go along for the ride, otherwise it will try to control the whole affair. Give the control over to gravity and momentum.

STEP 2   You are now going to start an arpeggio when your arms are out to the sides and allow your arm swings to help release the sound.

- Continue the picture of energy coming from under the ground in reaction to your arm drop, rushing vertically on momentum up the spine and laterally out through your arms and fingertips, but now that energy *is* voice. The rhythm should emerge organically: the first "hey" and the top "hey" happen when your arms are out; the last note happens as the arms swing for the second time across the body. Then the breath goes in as the arms swing out for the third time. The arm swings have an inevitable steady rhythm, and the arpeggio follows.

Do not hold on to the last note of the arpeggio or you will miss the opportunity for your breath to fly in automatically as your arms swing out.

The arpeggio releases on one long unbroken sound.

- Be sure that your voice is unified with the physical experience. Your voice falls to gravity with your arms and flies out horizontally through the arms and fingertips as they swing sideways. Your voice, your body, your mind, gravity, and momentum are a single thing.

Leg Swings:

You can balance yourself for leg swings by holding the back of a chair with your left hand when swinging the right leg and vice versa.

STEP 1

- Bring your right knee up until your thigh is parallel with the ground. Let your lower leg dangle loosely from your knee. Keep your spine long with a feeling of lifting the weight of your torso up off the left leg. Picture your hip socket. Drop your leg from the knee letting it swing in an arc behind your body and immediately swing back to the front and then drop the foot easily to the floor.

As the leg swings forward and back, the foot should brush gently over the floor. There should be no tension in the calf, ankle, or foot muscles. The activity is in the thigh with the top of the thighbone rocking in the hip socket. Keep talking to your knee. Don't let your foot take over. The knee-joint should remain more or less at a right angle with the thighbone throughout.

- Repeat with the left leg.

The message to the leg is "go away." You are releasing the leg from its obligation to the torso, opening up the hip socket, and undoing any holding tension that may lurk there.

STEP 2 Leg-swings with arpeggios:

- The arpeggio starts in the lower belly and is thrown down into the leg with the leg swing. The first "hey" note releases on the down-and-back swing, the top "hey" note comes as the knee swings back up to the front, and the last "hey" happens on the down-and-back swing. This allows your breath to replace automatically as your knee swings forward again. As your knee swings forward and up, the lower back is lengthened, and the breath flies in.

  Really see the voice going down the leg and out through the foot. Repeat several times with each leg, on ascending and descending pitches.

Although I have broken up the "hey" as I described these exercises, all the arpeggios are always on one long unbroken sound.

Secret tensions often lurk in shoulder and hip joints. Well-executed swings will help release these tensions and allow impulses to run unimpeded throughout the central nervous system, from your fingertips to toes. The two-way street between body and mind means that as the arms and legs let go, so will concomitant inhibitions in the mind.

PRACTICE

Daily, in conjunction with the workout plan.

19

Workdays Nineteen, Twenty, Twenty-one, and Thereafter

Articulating the Voice into Words: Consonants and vowels—voice joints

The word *articulation* means "jointedness"—*articulated* is "jointed" or "having joints." Such a definition is the least ambiguous way to describe the process by which vibrations flowing out through the mouth are cut up into words and become speech. It is an oversimplified account of the complex activity that transforms thoughts into speech, but the simple definition is the safest here as we move into the realm of words because we want to preserve the widest possible range of individuality for speakers. It is from the uniqueness of each individual that rich and creative communication comes. Freedom should be the foundation of that communication. If speech is "the natural exercise of the vocal organs; oral expression of thought or feeling" as the *Oxford English Dictionary* defines it, then rules of "correct" speech do not have any place in the free development of such a natural ability. As long as there is a sensitive connection between the mind and the organs of speech, the natural ability develops as the mind develops.

The exercises in this chapter will deal with speech only through its connectedness with mind. The muscles that articulate words must be freed from limiting conditioning and made responsive and agile enough to reflect the agility of the mind. No standards of "correct" speech will be suggested. Such standards last longer between the covers of a book than on the tongues of living people. They are a lost cause because live communication will not sit still and behave. Much of what has been optimistically labeled Standard American, Transatlantic Speech, Standard English, or even Received

Pronunciation is largely a reflection of class consciousness. As aesthetic rules of thumb, these attempts are doomed to failure. We must be flexible and multi-faceted, becoming fluent in different ways of speaking, in order to hold the mirror up to a multi-dialectal community. Further, we should rejoice in and preserve the rich diversity of sounds that are rooted in different regions and cultures.

Lest the alternative to standards seems to be anarchy, I would emphasize that communication through speech involves not only a speaker but also a hearer. If, therefore, what is said is incomprehensible, however satisfying the speaker finds the saying of it, it fails as communication. Anything that distorts the message must yield to comprehension, be it a personal rhythm that quarrels with the rhythm of the text; a vocal mannerism that leads attention away from the content of what is being said; an accent of such an extreme nature that the listener is always translating; or a lushly beautiful voice whose music is all that can be heard.

The one attribute necessary for dealing with such distortions is sensitivity. Any piece of good writing has its own palpable rhythm, texture, and style. A sensitive interpreter will allow that rhythm to alter personal rhythms, will absorb the different texture to color the voice differently, will let the style shape and transform delivery. A sensitive performer, whether interpreting a text or not, will want a voice that serves the desire to communicate. The exercises in this book are dedicated to that end. Those speakers who are relaxed enough to be able to hear what is going on around them and who respect an audience of one or many, will adapt even the most extreme regional accent to a point where communication is effected without sacrificing individuality.

Many accents owe their definitive regionalisms to a configuration of mouth muscles that traps the voice in one particular place. The nasality of the Midwest or New York accent derives from a habitual posture in the back of the tongue and soft palate. A southern drawl gives all responsibility for speech to the jaw and leaves the tongue lying dormant. The South Kensington drawing-room accent exploits a tiny portion of the tongue and the lips and an overdeveloped upper register to communicate as little as possible from below the neck.

These habits of mind and muscle have developed under the limited conditioning of one environment. Rigid extremes are inevitably modified as new interior and exterior environments are explored; once the whole potential of a voice, its three- to four-octave range, endless harmonics, and unlimited textural quality, is freed, changing styles become available to changing content. The only limitations are of talent, imagination, or life experience.

Our exploration of articulation will offer suggestions for the most economical use of the articulating musculature. In this economy lies the potential for a sensitive connection between mind and matter. With agile lips and tongue, free from the constrictions of habit, the one criterion for clear speaking becomes clear thinking.

The Articulating Surfaces

The most frequently used articulating agents are the front—or blade—of the tongue, the middle of the tongue, the back of the tongue, and the surfaces above that a tongue most naturally touches. All other articulation comes from the two lips in various forms of contact, occasional contact between the top teeth and the bottom lip, and the protrusion of the very tip of the tongue between the teeth for a "th." For all words to be formed in such a small space, the articulating muscles must perform with the energy, precision, and delicate teamwork of a miniature acrobatic troupe. As with the breathing and laryngeal musculature, the coordination of muscle movements that mold vowel shapes while chopping them with consonants is too subtle and complex for conscious manipulation to do a better job than involuntary control. Once more, in the interest of an individual reflection of the mind, we must do no more than free the muscles from tension, limber them up, and leave them to be played on by clear thought-impulse.

The initial work to be done is to exercise the separate articulating agents with the consonants that stimulate them.

Consonants

Lips

STEP 1

- Using a mirror to make sure that the message you are sending arrives in the intended muscles, focus your attention on the whole of your top lip. Move your lip up and down as in a sneer that lifts the top lip, exposing the top teeth and then stops, dropping the lip.

Leave the bottom lip relaxed and isolate the top lip activity.

- Repeat several times. (The muscles that move the lip in a sneer run from the nostrils through the moustache area.)

- Let your top lip relax and turn your attention to your bottom lip. Keep your teeth together so that your jaw is out of commission and pull your bottom lip down to expose your bottom teeth. Then relax the muscles to allow the lip to spring up. The activating muscles run down into the chin.

Differentiate between movement in the jaw and movement in the chin musculature. The jawbone must remain immobile during this exercise and all the lip and tongue exercises that follow.

- Blow out through your lips to relax them.

Repeat the movements several times:

- Top lip: lift, drop; lift, drop; lift, drop.
  Bottom lip: pull down, release; pull down, release.

- Blow out through both lips.

STEP 2

- Stretch your lips sideways as wide as you can into a grin.

- Then push them forward into as pursed a pout as you can.

- Stretch sideways, push forward, keeping your teeth together and your lips apart.

- Repeat several times and then blow out through your lips to relax them.

Put your fingers into the corners of your mouth and pull them to the sides.

- Let them go exactly as a stretched elastic band lets go.

- Blow out through your lips.

Repeat Steps 1 and 2 several times.

These are limbering exercises for the general musculature of the top and bottom lips: more specific sets of muscles are employed in forming consonants. Developing the independence of these muscles from those of the jaw is of prime importance. When the teeth are together, the jaw is immobilized and the articulators must take over.

- Repeat Steps 1 and 2, alternating teeth together and teeth apart, to develop the independent response of the lip muscles. When the teeth are apart the jaw remains quite relaxed and immobile as the lips move.

It is important that as you concentrate on articulation you don't lose your freedom and cut yourself off from your connection with breath impulse. There is a tendency, when working on the lips and tongue, to lose the free flow of breath and vibration so that the sound starts in your mouth. Articulation should involve an increased sphere of awareness, one that encompasses the source of sound along with the agents that handle the sound. Otherwise there is nothing to "articulate," just a series of isolated "joints." Such disjointedness is quite common. It accounts for those actors whose diction is flawless but who remain unintelligible despite the fact that every word is crystal clear. Overdeveloped muscles of the lips and the tongue can destroy the balance between voice and articulation that is essential to full communication.

STEP 3

- Sigh out a hum and move your lips around on the hum, tasting the vibrations. Now play with the vibrations. Catch them and release them to explore a sense of the lips handling the vibrations and passing them on to the outside. Your lips are like jugglers tossing many balls in the air.

- Mmmmmmm-uh mm-uh m-uh mmmmmm-uhmm-uh-mmmm-uh-m-uh Muhmuhmuhmuhmuh

- Getting faster—bounce the vibrations off your lips. Try the following rhythm: ˘ is short, / is long.

$$\breve{\ }\quad \breve{\ }\quad / \quad \breve{\ }\quad \breve{\ }\quad /$$

- Muh-muh-muh-muh-muh-muh

Now change the shape of the stream of vibrations as they leave your lips:

- Mmm-ee mmm-eee

Make sure the "ee" comes out through your mouth. "M" is a nasal consonant and there will be a tendency for accompanying vowels to go into your nose. This tendency can be counteracted by your having a sure picture of the forward flow of vibrations through your mouth and by checking to see that your tongue is relaxed.

Change the shape again:

- Mm-ey mm-ey mm-ey

- Mm-ee mm-ee mm-ee

- Mm-ey mm-ey mm-ey

Change the shape of the escaping vibrations again:

- Mm-aah mm-aah mm-aah

- Mm-ee mm-ee mm-ee

- Mm-ey mm-ey mm-ey

- Mm-aah mm-aah mm-aah

Observe that your lips do not have to change their behavior as the vowel changes. They can still go up and down, gathering vibrations and passing them on. The "ee," "ey," and "aah" shapes are made automatically as you think them. The back of the tongue moves subtly from a relatively high position toward the soft palate for the "ee," down to a flat relaxed position for the "aa." For the time being, let the vowels look after themselves and focus your attention on the sensory experience of consonants.

Practice the slow sensual connection between relaxed lips and the vibrations:

- Mmmmeeee mmmmeeee mmmmeeeee

- Mmmmme—-ey mmmmmmme—-ey mmmmme-e-ey

- Mmmmmmmaaaaaaah mmmmaaaaaah mmmmaaaaaaah

Explore the relationship of your lip surfaces to the vibrations. Don't think about "consonants." Don't listen. The wet part of your lips makes contact, and the muscles involved are minimal, stimulated by the vibrations. Make no unnecessary effort that could tighten the lips and kill vibrations.

Now, changing the energy quality, go faster:

- Mee-mee-mee mey-mey-mey mah-mah-mah

 And then feed in changing rhythms.

- Mee mee mee-mey mey mey-mah mah mah

- Mee mee mee-mey mey mey-mah mah mah (Repeat three times.)

- Mee mee mee mee mee

- Mey mey mey mey mey

- Mah mah mah mah mah (Repeat three times.)

- Mee mee mee mee mee mee mee

˘ ˘ ˘ ˘ ˘ ˘ /
Mey mey mey mey mey mey mey

˘ ˘ ˘ ˘ ˘ /
Mah mah mah mah mah mah (Repeat three times.)
And so on.

Play with whatever rhythmic patterns you choose as long as you can make a pattern that you can repeat clearly and accurately. Every other part of the body must be quite still and relaxed so that the lips can learn to be responsible and independent and the route from the brain to the lips becomes clearly defined.

Step 4 will take you through a similar pattern of exercises on "b." The same area of the lips is involved as for "m," but the quality of the relationship to the vibrations will be different—The "m" is sustained as compared to the "b," which is explosive.

Find the exact point of impact between vibration and lip surface for the "b" sound, which provokes a small explosive action.

STEP 4 Let your lips touch each other. Don't anticipate the sound. Be aware of your relaxed lips—teeth just apart behind them, tongue quite loose inside the mouth, jaw relaxed. Now think the sound of the letter "b." What muscles begin to respond? Don't say the sound yet.

If you do this slowly enough you may notice some unnecessary preliminary responses in parts of your mouth other than in your lips. For instance, it is not uncommon for the base of the tongue to tighten as a sort of springboard for the "b," which results in an almost imperceptible glottal grunt just before the consonant occurs. This is not a very economical or crystal-line rendition. Practice thinking the "b" directly onto your lips.

■ Think the sound "b."—Now lightly voice the "b."

The vibration should catapult forward off the lips in a tiny explosion of sound that is not trapped anywhere in the throat.

Feel and listen for the arrival point of the sound. If it is at all labored or hoarse, then there is too much tension in the channel for the sound to be free.

- Feel the tiny ball of vibrations fly forward off the lips.

- Play with that ball: buh-buh-buh

Change the shape of the ball to something flat and thin:

- Bee-bee-bee

Change the shape again:

- Bey-bey-bey

Change it again:

- Bah-bah-bah

Leave the lips loose to respond to your thought. Don't make the lips work hard.

Play with the explosions of vibrations thus:

- Bee-bee-bée bey-bey-béy bah-bah-báh

Then build the capability of lip response by applying the pattern of exercises followed for "m," increasing the pace and changing the rhythms.

Tongue (Front of Tongue)

We will leave the lips for a little and move to the blade of the tongue. I differentiate between the tip of the tongue and the blade of the tongue in order to emphasize that the most effective and natural parts of the articulating apparatus with which to produce "d," "t," "s," and "z" are the surface of the tongue just back from the tip and the upper gum ridge, which is the hard bony rim between the front top teeth and the dome of the roof of the mouth.

When the tongue, in repose, swells to fill the mouth cavity, its edges touch the teeth all the way round, and its surface touches the hard palate from front to back. The part of the front of the tongue that naturally meets the front upper gum ridge is the part to exercise for forward tongue consonants.

In order to isolate that area and strengthen it, here are some exercises that make exaggerated use of the tongue's muscles outside the mouth so that when it relaxes back into the mouth it can perform with greater ease.

STEP 5

■ Let the tongue slide loosely forward until the tip lies on the lower lip. Use a mirror to check that it is broad and thick and can lie there without any movement. If it is narrow and pointed, thin and flat, or moves, it is not relaxed.

■ Lift the front of the tongue up to touch the top lip and then bend it down to touch the lower lip as though there were a hinge about 1/2 inch back from the tip that gives precise mobility. Move it up and down, specifically touching top and bottom lip.

■ Move the tongue from side to side, outside the mouth, touching the corners of the mouth.

Make sure the jaw doesn't swing with it.

■ Alternate the last two movements several times.

■ Then stretch and relax the tongue, tip behind the bottom teeth.

■ Release the front of the tongue once more out on the lower lip. Then lift it as before to touch the top lip and, this time, find vibrations between the lip and the tongue to make the sound "l" as the tongue drops.

It is as though you were speaking with your tongue outside your mouth, saying "luh luh luh" with the front of the tongue and the top lip. Let the tongue touch the lower lip again after each "l" sound.

- Repeat this tongue-to-lip movement going through the sequence of vowel shapes previously used, all outside the mouth against the top lip, slowly and deliberately.

- Lee-lee-lee ley-ley-ley lah-lah-lah

- Then let the tongue slip inside the mouth and quickly and easily repeat the sequence, this time with the tongue patting the upper gum ridge for the "l"s:

  Lee-lee-lee -ley-ley-ley-lah-lah-lah

- Alternate the last two exercises:

  Outside the mouth slowly

  Inside the mouth quickly

It should seem that the "l"s inside the mouth happen without any effort because the tongue has relaxed after the exaggerated stretching work outside the mouth.

- Build the capability for quick, lively tongue response on "l" as you did with the lips on "b" and "m." Gradually increase the pace and add the changing rhythms.

- Now explore the quality of action needed in the tongue to produce "d." The blade meets the upper gum ridge and propels the vibrations forward, and the tongue drops away.

  Dee-dee-dee dey-dey-dey dah-dah-dah

The "d" strengthens and limbers the tongue even more than the "l" because of the stronger impact between the articulating surfaces needed to explode the vibrations for this strong consonant.

Note the similar quality of handling that the vibrations receive for "b" and "d." For a true result, it is essential that you really feel the vibrations between the surfaces. It is all too easy to have agile lips or a tongue producing what is in effect a heavy "p" or "t" while the vibrations of sound remain back in the throat.

- Follow the same instructions to explore the sound "nnn."

This is, obviously, in the same family as "mmm," a nasal consonant. The blade of the tongue is in contact with the upper gum ridge in the front of the mouth blocking the mouth exit so that the sound comes out through the nose. As soon as the blade of the tongue goes down, the vowels following the consonant can and must escape through the mouth.

- Nee-nee-nee ney-ney-ney nah-nah-nah

- Alternate the "mee mee mee" sequence and the "nee nee nee" sequence.

Tongue (Back of Tongue)

STEP 6 In order to exercise the third main articulating area, you must isolate an area where the back of the tongue makes contact with the back of the hard palate just in front of the uvula.

- Keeping the tip of the tongue firmly in contact with the back of the bottom teeth, yawn. In the middle of the yawn bring the back of the tongue up to touch the back of the hard palate just in front of the soft palate, interrupting the yawn to say "ng" as in the end of "sing."

- Repeat the yawn and lengthen the "ng," then take the back of the tongue away from the soft palate while continuing the sound that should automatically turn into "aah."

Using a yawn stretch without actually yawning, repeat the back of tongue movement up and down with sound to make:

- Ngng-aah -ngng-aah, etc. (The "g" is silent; the "aah" is a yawn stretch.)

This consonant is again in the family of nasal consonants.

Relax the mouth and throat. Exercise the back of the tongue with the same pattern of sounds as before:

- Ngee-ngee-ngee ngey-ngey-ngey ngah-ngah-ngah

- Alternate the lips, front of tongue, back of tongue sequences:

- Mee-mee-mee mey-mey-mey mah-mah-mah

- Nee-nee-nee ney-ney-ney nah-nah-nah

- Ngee-ngee-ngee ngey-ngey-ngey ngah-ngah-ngah

- Play with changing rhythms.

- With the back of the tongue, this time hitting sharply but lightly against the hard palate just in front of the soft palate, explode vibrations that have the same quality as "b" and "d." If you follow this instruction accurately and calmly you should arrive at the consonant "g," which belongs to the same explosive family as "b" and "d."

- Follow the by-now-familiar pattern of exercises from:

- Guh guh guh

- Through

- Gee-gee-gee gey-gey-gey gah-gah-gah

Making sure that the tip of the tongue stays relaxed behind the bottom teeth.

Make sure the jaw stays out of the way, relaxed and still.

STEP 7   Finally put together a sequence of exercises going from lips to front of tongue to back of tongue, to front of tongue to lips. This exercise should be used as regularly as brushing your teeth to keep the whole set of articulators agile.

From lips to front of tongue:

- Buh-duh-buh-duh-buh-duh

From front of tongue to lips:

- Duh-buh-duh-buh-duh-buh

Slowly, then gradually gathering speed, alternate starting with the lips and starting with the tongue.

Then from back of tongue to front of tongue:

- Guh-duh-guh-duh-guh-duh

From front of tongue to back of tongue:

- Duh-guh-duh-guh-duh-guh

Slowly first, then gathering speed, begin alternately with the back of the tongue and the front of the tongue.

From lips to front of tongue to back of tongue:

- Buh-duh-guh-duh-buh-duh-guh-duh-buh-duh-guh-duh

From back of tongue to front of tongue to lips:

- Guh-duh-buh-duh-guh-duh-buh-duh-guh-duh-buh-duh

Work it out slowly at first, then gather speed.

Precision and clarity are the criteria here.

Sigh the vibrations freely out from the center of the diaphragm through-out these exercises so that there is a steady stream of sound for the mouth to handle. These consonants can easily become clipped and dead unless you pay great attention to the connection of your voice with the articulating surfaces. As you become familiar with the "bdgd"s you may find them going into a railway train rhythm. Exploit that or any other rhythmic patterns that occur to enliven the exercise.

- Play with the "bdgd"s and their variants on scales, arpeggios, or songs always being aware of a sigh of sound from the center of the diaphragm that is not inhibited by the consonants but is handled by them.

- Explore your range from chest resonance to falsetto using "bdbd"s "dbdb"s, "gdgd"s, "dgdg"s, "bdgd"s, and "gdbd"s, all the way from the bottom to the top and back down, sighing out, without skipping any of the rungs of the resonating ladder.

- Improvise conversations using only "bd"s,"db"s, "gd"s, "dg"s, "bdgd"s, and "gdbd"s.

- Improvise questions and answers

- Improvise political arguments

- Improvise love scenes

- Improvise shopping expeditions, and so on, all expressed solely through these sounds.

While doing these improvisations, occasionally check with your partner or with a mirror to see whether your eyebrows are being unnecessarily active. Leave them relaxed. Make sure your head does not poke forward.

Often energy intended for the articulating muscles is picked up and rerouted through the eyebrows, the hands, the shoulders, or a nodding head. All movements in these areas should be regarded as extraneous for the moment, and expression channeled exclusively into the breathing area and the mouth. Eventually, hands and shoulders might enhance communication, but for now encourage responsibility in the lips and tongue and leave other areas relaxed. As I've mentioned before, movement in the eyebrows is almost always a substitute for lively articulation or soft-palate response; only a few specific feelings need the eyebrows for expression (a very incredulous question, considerable surprise, frowning). Excessive eyebrow raising always robs the voice. The brows go up instead of the pitch. They wiggle when lips and tongue should be the ones dancing.

STEP 8   Follow the patterns described in Step 5 with a combination of the nasal consonants.

- Muh-nuh-muh-nuh-muh-nuh
  Nuh-muh-nuh-muh-nuh-muh
  Nguh-nuh-nguh-nuh-nguh-nuh (The "g" is silent.)
  Nuh-nguh-nuh-nguh-nuh-nguh

- Muh-nuh-nguh-nuh-muh-nuh-nguh-nuh-muh-nuh-nguh-nuh

- Nguh-nuh-muh-nuh-nguh-nuh-muh-nuh-nguh-nuh-muh-nuh

Send all the "uh" sounds out through the mouth; only the consonants are nasal.

STEP 9   Follow the same patterns and rhythms of exercises whispering "p," "t," and "k."

These are the unvoiced equivalents of "b," "d," and "g," exploding breath this time instead of vibration.

No voice: whisper

- Puh-tuh-puh-tuh-puh-tuh-puh-tuh

- Tuh-puh-tuh-puh-tuh-puh-tuh-puh

- Kuh-tuh-kuh-tuh-kuh-tuh-kuh-tuh

- Tuh-kuh-tuh-kuh-tuh-kuh-tuh-kuh

- Puh-tuh-kuh-tuh-puh-tuh-kuh-tuh-puh-tuh-kuh-tuh

- Kuh-tuh-puh-tuh-kuh-tuh-puh-tuh-kuh-tuh-puh-tuh

With this exercise you can clearly check the freedom of the breath. It should not be heard in the throat but should lightly and transparently flick off the articulating surfaces. Nor should there be any sense of holding the breath back in attempting transparency. Sigh out with complete abandon from the center of your diaphragm and insist that the lips and tongue catch and deal with the breath as it flies through the mouth. If there is no tension in the throat and a genuinely free contact between breath and articulators, you may experience a fluttering sensation in the diaphragm. This is a useful guide to the purity of connection between the mouth and the center. The flutter is created by the quick, repeated, minute stops on the breath applied by the lips and tongue as they form "p," "t," and "k."

Be very sure that your tongue comes down sharply enough from the hard palate to create a clean, sharp "t" and "k." If the tip goes too far forward onto the teeth, you will hear a sibilant sound almost like a "ts"—the voiced equivalent would be "dz." The tongue, both at the front and the back, must drop far enough away from the palate to create a space through which the breath can escape freely, not scraping or hissing through a narrow crevice.

I will give only the briefest description of the other English consonants as they do not present much difficulty once the lips and tongue are free and strong. I will explain where they are commonly formed for those who want to check their own effective usage. For those who have a specific problem, there are many books that deal with the details of speech and speech defects that are outside the scope of this overview.

Other voiced consonants and their unvoiced equivalents

Lips:

- "V" and "F"

- "Vvvv" is formed between the bottom lip and the top teeth as sound vibrates the lip against the teeth.

- "Ffff" is the whispered equivalent, with a softer relationship between the lower lip and top teeth because breath provokes a gentler muscle response than vibrations.

Tongue:

■ *"Z" and "S"*

"Zzzz" belongs to the same family as "vvvv," which is categorized as fricative, and is formed between the front of the tongue and the upper gum ridge. To produce a really strong "zzzz" sound, try sticking the front of the tongue to the gum ridge, leaving the tip of the tongue just lightly touching the lower teeth, and insist that the thought of "zzzz" pushes a path of vibration between the adhering surfaces. You will probably create "dzzz" to begin with, but use that to create the strong vibration and then cut out the "d."

"Ssss" is the whispered, unvoiced equivalent of "zzzz." If the tongue is relaxed, a rich "s" sound should naturally occur in response to the thought "sss." A sibilant "s" is usually the result of tongue tension that pushes the tongue forward and onto the top teeth where it funnels the breath through the cracks between the teeth, creating a hiss or whistle, which can be very distracting to both the listener and the speaker.

There is no one correct place for the "s" to be formed as there are so many variations in individual mouth structure. The best thing to do is to use your ear to discover where an "s" that pleases you occurs in your mouth. Start with your tongue relaxed and thick in the floor of the mouth, and then find the bit that most easily comes in contact with the rim of the gum ridge before it ascends into the dome of the roof of the mouth. If the tip of the tongue stays relaxed and you release a strong stream of breath out between the tongue surface and the upper gum ridge, a clear "sssss" should result.

If not, put the tip of the tongue down below the bottom teeth to touch the lower gum ridge. Keep it there. Practice a strong connection between the blade and the rim of the upper gum ridge with:

■ Zzzzeee zzzzey zzzzaaa

With a long, clear, buzzing "z" sound.

■ Then think "zzzz," but whisper the zzzzeee zzzzey zzzzaa and listen for the result that should sound like a strong "sssss."

■ Now add vibration to the vowels "eee," "ey," "aa" while still thinking a whispered "zzzz" and you should arrive at a strong

- Ssssee sssssey ssssaa

With an "s" sound that is different from your habitual one. It is up to you to find out where the difference lies in your mind and your mouth and breath.

Tongue:

- *"TH" and "TH"*

The sounds "th" voiced, as in "the," and unvoiced, as in "both," belong to the same fricative family as "v/f" and "z/s" and are formed with the tip of the tongue trying to get out through a very small gap between the top and bottom teeth.

Tongue:

- *"J" and "CH"*

- *"ZJ" and "SH"*

- *"Y"*

- *"R"*

Maverick sounds made with the middle of the tongue almost rising as high as the dome in the roof of the mouth are: "j" and its unvoiced equivalent "ch"—plosives; "ZJ" (as in "pleasure") and its unvoiced equivalent "sh"—fricatives; and "y," which is a hybrid, half vowel, half consonant ("i"+ "uh"="y").

"R" is another maverick that answers to many rules and deserves a whole treatise. Here I will only express my personal opinion on two controversial points of usage and say that the American "r" should be restrained from pulling the voice back into the throat and the British actor-y "rrrr" should be banned as a trilled ornamental device in "classical" speech except for comic effect.

Lips:

"W" is another hybrid vowel/consonant ("oo"+"uh"="w"), and you have exercised this consonant in the sinus work.

There are all sorts of articulation games that can be played, and tongue twisters are very useful to exercise mental and articulative agility. Here are some very simple repetitions that you can practice.

STEP 10 I will give you a few examples of the repetition of a particular consonant in a little jingle, and then you can invent your own for all the other consonants.

■   *"B"*
    Billy Button Bought a Bunch of Beautiful Bananas
    Visualize Billy; picture the bananas; tell the story. As you go faster
    let the pictures speed up; the purpose of the exercise is not to get
    mechanical as you go faster but to increase the mental agility with-
    out separating words from meanings.

■   Practice now using arpeggios and go higher on each repetition:

Get someone to fire the following questions at you at the end of each phrase and respond immediately with the emphasis confined to the initial consonant:

■   Question: "Was it *Joe* Button?" Answer: "*Billy* Button bought a bunch...etc."

■   Question: "Billy Smith was it?" Answer: "Billy *Button* bought...etc."

- Question: "Billy *stole* the bananas?" Answer: "Billy Button *bought* ...etc."

- Question: "Did he only buy *one* banana?" "Billy Button bought a *bunch*...etc."

- "Were the bananas *rotten*?"

- "Did he buy *apples*?"

This may drive you a bit crazy but should stimulate the mind to deal with changing emphasis economically and at speed.

Go through the same process for "g"

- "G"
  Giddy Goddesses Gather together and Gossip in Garrulous Groups

- Add similar questions to it:

- "Were they *silent*?"

- "*Politicians* were they?"

- "Was this goddess *alone*?"

- "Were they discussing their *work*?"

- "Quite *monosyllabic* probably"

- "Just the *two* of them?"

- "D"

- Desperate Donald Died the Death of a Dastardly Drunken Dog

- "M"

- Marvelous Mammals Mimic the Murmurs of Mundane Minimal Men

- *"N"*

- Nubile Nellie Nibbled the Knees of Nervous Nautical Nerds

- *"L"*

- Lilly Langtry Lay on the Lawn and Languidly Lasciviously Laughed

You can use this pattern to invent jingles for "t"s, and "f"s, and "p"s, and "z"s.

You should also use the ever-practical Peter Piper.

- Peter Piper picked a peck of pickled peppers
  A peck of pickled peppers Peter Piper picked
  If Peter Piper picked a peck of pickled peppers
  Where's the peck of pickled peppers Peter Piper picked?

I like to use a whole scale for this tongue twister, which fits very neatly into the ascending scale and then the descending scale:

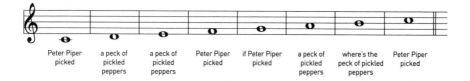

- Then speak it again, preferably in dialogue with someone else. Find ways of awakening more and more mental energy to justify increased speed. Let skepticism grow to righteous anger at the unlikely story of Peter Piper ever having had the energy to pick a whole peck of pickled peppers in the first place. Or take on Mrs. Piper's anxiety at the non-return of her husband with the peppers required for dinner. Or spread hasty, gleeful gossip about a possible scandal.

In this way you keep the agility of articulation constantly in touch with mental agility. You will discover that as long as you can think quickly enough, you will be able to speak as fast as you like. You will, however, only be able to think quickly enough if you maintain real relaxation throughout your body while your mind, your breath, your lips, and your tongue are stimulated. The more physical relaxation you sustain, the more mental focus you will be able to achieve.

Vowels

I will discuss vowels first in terms of fantasy. For years I believed that a voice scientist told me—and indeed that I had been shown with a special kind of laryngoscope—that vowel shapes are initially formed on the vocal folds themselves. Although I am now firmly informed that this is not so, I will persist in what I consider to be a creative mistake. My aim is to engender respect for vowels and a sensitivity of approach that will save them from distortion and colorless standardization.

There is intrinsic music in the basic physical nature of vowel sounds. It begins when the vocal folds assume approximations of the shape of the vowels conceived in the speech cortex, thereby changing the resonating pitch, whether on breath alone or with vibration. A simple demonstration will give a model of this process. Push your lips forward into a pout and blow breath through them. Listen for pitch. Now stretch your lips into a grin and blow breath through them. Listen for pitch. Be sure your tongue is completely relaxed so that breath goes directly onto the lips. You should hear a definite low sound when the lips are forward and a high pitch when they are pulled sideways. The vocal folds, in response to the thought "oh," form a round shape roughly similar to the lip pout, creating in miniature the shape for a low resonating path. In response to the thought "ee," the folds are pulled close together, and air or vibrations going through the resultant narrow space create a higher pitch with that vowel. The main categories of vowels change the shape between the vocal folds, creating embryonic differences in their innate pitch. The subtleties of vowel differences need the soft palate, the pharyngeal walls, the tongue, and the lips for refined modification and molding. On the vocal fold level, the shaping of vowels is deeply rooted in the involuntary nervous system. In the interest of preserving such subtle musicality, the subsequent modifications must be highly sensitive. Any tension that clutches the breath will change the intrinsic pitch that depends for its existence on a free voice.

This correlation of pitch and vowel does not mean that "ee" cannot be said on a low note or "oh" on a high one. The introduction of a chosen pitch or the influence of a mood that dictates another pitch is what creates the harmonics of an interesting voice. Try the word *sleep*. First as an irritated command to a naughty child: "Go to sleep!" There is a place in the vocal range where there is pure marriage between the "ee" and a middle-to-upper resonance. A single fundamental sound comes through that reflects both mood and vowel pitch. Now take the word *sleep* as though it were a hypnotic suggestion to be fed for its effectiveness through deep chest resonance. Listen for the low frequencies of the chest resonators harmonizing with a high frequency that is that of the vowel. This is the natural richness and texture of speech. It is easiest to hear the harmonies with "ee" where the pitch and the vowel are unambiguous. The sharper listening needed for other vowels is good training. Try *moon* first as a luxurious appreciation of a big, round, red harvest moon. The natural low pitch of "oo" merges with the image creating a fundamental deep resonance: "Look at the moon." Then try *moon* while quickly and excitedly pointing out the sliver of a new moon. The pitch of "oo" is low with harmonics coming in as the energy of the image carries the voice high.

This is a very analytical description of a process that can only work spontaneously. Thus, once more, the job is to render the muscles that pick up the motor impulses from the brain as free from tension and as subtle and sensitive as possible, which allows them to function involuntarily. The criterion for forming effective vowel sounds should be economy. Without economy there is no sensitivity, without sensitivity there is no subtlety, without subtlety there is little music. Therefore, if you can make vowels without the use of the jaw, you should do so. The jaw is unnecessary in the formation of vowel sounds, though its movement will add resonance to them. If you have to move a large jawbone around in order to achieve different sounds, you are expending more energy than if you move only the tiny muscles of the tongue and the lips.

Isolating the lips and tongue from the jaw is important for clear speaking, but if you take this principle to an extreme you might as well use one of the most pernicious props of the elocution brigade—the bone prop. This is an actual instrument about an inch high that the student is asked to place between the teeth and bite in order to keep the mouth open and the jaw immobilized while the lips and tongue perform diction exercises. A cork is sometimes used to provide an even greater obstacle. I am sure that the actor who trains his or her diction thus will never effectively perform any part in a play. The only way in which the lips and tongue can function in such conditions is with huge exaggeration; the diligent student will have to use gross mouthings, killing any hope of natural music in speaking. This method can also program jaw tension, which can lead to throat tension and breathing tension.

Let me repeat that clear diction comes from clear thinking. I have witnessed actors whose mouths are working elaborately, yet I have been unable to understand what they are saying. I have also witnessed actors who seem not to be articulating at all, and I can hear and understand everything. Ultimately the clarity of understanding is the result of clear and specific intentions on the part of the actor.

Thus, for me, the basis for work on vowels is primarily the freeing process that has been detailed for liberating, developing and sensitizing the whole voice so that it is capable of responding to specific thought intention. The ear can safely be trained to listen once you have a heightened awareness and a clear experience of the connection between yourself and your voice. Ear training then becomes a skill that enhances artistry rather than a way to judge yourself.

Louis Colaianni's book *The Joy of Phonetics* is a wonderful resource for vowel, accent, and dialect work. The underlying philosophy of *The Joy of Phonetics* is the same as that which permeates *Freeing the Natural Voice.* Colaianni has developed ways of extending freedom and sensuality from voice into speech so that one need no longer divide voicing from speaking. Any systemized work that I do on vowels is based on the vowel scale in W. D. Aiken's book *The Voice.* It is good for British sounds but needs some adjusting for American sounds. The great value of his work is that it is grounded in resonance and equates the vowel scale with the resonator scale.

I find, however, that less and less specific vowel work is necessary as the voice becomes freer and freer.

As voice becomes a medium for language in the next section of the work, you will expand your consciousness into physical exploration of vowels and consonants as vital components of words rather than as a discrete discipline.

WORKOUT

The following is a way of working through the whole sequence of voice exercises that have been taught so far. It emphasizes stimulated breathing and breathing power, an altered order of exercises, and a faster rhythm of work than before.

(1.)   General relaxation and physical awareness.
(2.)   Rib-cage stretching.
(3.)   Vacuuming the lungs.
(4.)   Four big sighs; six medium sighs; anticipation panting on center.
(5.)   Natural breathing awareness
      (Spend about ten minutes on 1 through 5.)
(6.)   Touch of sound
(7.)   "Huh-hummmmmuh"s on ascending and descending pitches at twice your normal speed:
      Huh-huh-mmmmmmm-uh
      Let the breath drop in fast with an awareness of the springy center created by the panting.
(8.)   Head and neck rolling and humming. Roll your neck fast in one direction, then a quick release inside for a new breath, then a fast roll in the other direction. (Faster means freer neck muscles and several more rolls to one breath.)
(9.)   Dropping down the spine on a hum. A quick drop down and up in one breath; release sound at the top. (Drop down giving in to gravity and bounce up from the bottom on the rebound.) Repeat several times with knee bounces, shoulder bounces, etc.
(10.) Shake your jaw loose—with sound.
(11.) Tongue exercises. Twice the speed and with a new rhythm.
(12.) Drop down, head downward, and do the tongue exercises on ascending pitches.
(13.) Stay upside down and pant loosely.
(14.) Start upside down on tongue exercises, then slowly build up your spine on "hee-yuh-yuh-yuh"s. (Quick releases for breath in between).
(15.) Rest.
(16.) The whole panting sequence. Slow—medium—fast.
(17.) Soft palate. Fast in and out on whispered "kah"s at the speed of medium panting. The inner behavior of the diaphragm is the same during this soft-palate exercise as during the six medium sighs of relief. Look for

cooperation between the source and the channel.

(18.) Call across an imagined valley on "hi-i-i" with the inner energy generated by (16).

(19.) Lengthen your neck and head back, open your throat. Slow panting on whispered "hah"s.

> Neck and head up: medium panting on whispered "huh"s; let the puffs of breath come straight from the center of the diaphragm to the roof of the mouth.
>
> Neck and head forward: fast panting on whispered "hee"s; let the breath come sharply from the center of the diaphragm onto the teeth.
>
> Reverse the order: forward, up, back, panting through the changing shapes.

(20.) Chest resonance

> Ha-ah-ha-ah-ha-ah

Mouth resonance

> Huh-huh-huh

Teeth resonance

> Hee-hee-hee
>
> Reverse the order and repeat several times.

(21.) Call to free yourself on "he-e-e-ey." Shake it all out.

(22.) Vacuum the lungs.

(23.) Do the whole sequence of panting.

(24.) Sinus resonance. Do these alternately massaging with your fingertips and moving the sinus muscles up and down, and alternately hanging head downward and standing upright. Mid- to upper-register pitches.

(25.) Nasal resonance. Do the fast panting with pleasurable anticipation, then use that energy to ping the vibrations into the nose bone, quickly across the cheekbones and freely out of the mouth.

(26.) Range from bottom to top on "he-e-ey." Range from top to bottom. Range from bottom to top releasing into falsetto.

(27.) Fast, excited panting resulting in an impulse that sends the voice into your skull on falsetto, "keee-eee."

(28.) Fast falsettos going higher and higher with gathering excitement and instantaneous release from excitement for the ingoing breath.

(29.) Deep chest "hey"s.

(30.) Range, loosening tongue on "huh-yuh-yuh-yuh" all the way from bottom to top and top to bottom;

> Range, loosening jaw with hands throughout the sound.
>
> Range, shaking whole body loose as sound travels from basement

to attic to basement.

Range, dropping down and up the spine several times on one breath.

(31.) Articulation. Limber up the lips and tongue without sound. Facial isolations. Corners of the lips forward and sideways on "wey," "willyou," and "willyouwait."

Range, on "wey wey wey . . ." from bottom to top and top to bottom.

Buh-duh-buh-duh-buh-duh duh-buh-duh-buh-duh-buh

Guh-duh-guh-duh-guh-duh duh-guh-duh-guh-duh-guh

Buh-duh-guh-duh-buh-duh-guh-duh-buh-duh-guh-duh

Guh-duh-buh-duh-guh-duh-buh-duh-guh-duh-buh-duh

Speak it—sing it on ascending and descending pitches. Do it through the range from top to bottom and bottom to top. Do it slowly, then as fast as possible—improvise rhythms.

Whisper:

Puh-tuh-puh-tuh-puh-tuh tuh-puh-tuh-puh-tuh-puh

Kuh-tuh-kuh-tuh-kuh-tuh tuh-kuh-tuh-kuh-tuh-kuh

Puh-tuh-kuh-tuh-puh-tuh-kuh-tuh-puh-tuh-kuh-tuh

Kuh-tuh-puh-tuh-kuh-tuh-puh-tuh-kuh-tuh-puh-tuh.

Add other articulation exercises.

(32.) Speak a poem or a speech; sing a song.

You should study and learn the sequence of exercises so that you can add variations to this workout without missing any elements. Make sure that the organic progression of energy release is maintained. You have a number of floor exercises to incorporate into the work, and you have swings and arpeggios to develop strength and freedom.

This sort of workout should leave you feeling very wide-awake, never tired. If you are tired it means you have been pushing and have ignored the intrinsic energy in reflex action. Never "breathe in," it is exhausting. Breath will "replace" naturally, and, with the panting exercises, you have been developing natural agility and restoring the speed of natural reflexes.

Part Three

The Link to Text and Acting

Words . . . imagery

Language began instinctually, physically, primitively. The extended roar of pain, hunger, pleasure, or rage was, over time, articulated into more detailed communication by muscles in the body responding to the demand of an evolving body-mind-intellect. The brain, needing to convey increasingly precise information, deployed muscles in the mouth to distinguish positive from negative reactions and gradually to describe objects and facts and handle the minutiae of language. It is inconceivable that when the mouth first started to make words it did so in a manner divorced from its familiar exercises of chewing, biting, kissing, sucking, licking, snarling, lip smacking, and lapping. All these were practical activities, with sensual rewards and palpable side effects of pleasure for most of them, and anger or fear for one or two. Words have a direct line from the nerve endings of the mouth to sensory and emotional storehouses in the body that include the nerve centers governing appetite.

That direct line has been short-circuited over the past three or four hundred years by the exponential growth in our dependence first on print and most recently on technology for communication. Whatever the benefits of these modes, they have shifted the bulk of information sharing from the ear to the eye. The eye's initial relationship with information is at a distance, outside the body; the ear, by its anatomical nature, receives information inside the body allowing internalization more readily. One could say that the eye objectifies while the ear "subjectifies." Information that enters aurally enters on vibrations that travel into the body. Visual information can bypass physical responses and easily move into the realm of assessment, appreciation, and judgment. Oral/aural communication is the stuff of an actor's life. Listening is life-blood, oxygen, food, and drink; when the actor listens, s/he answers from the body-mind. If you have been conscientious in following the exercises in this book you have done much to restore direct neurophysiological pathways for the voice to travel through the body, arousing physical, sensory, sensual, and emotional response. But there is still work to be done to reestablish the visceral connection of words to the body.

Words have become largely utilitarian in everyday life and are conditioned to run from the speech cortex straight to the mouth. They seldom pick up an emotional charge except under extreme provocation. Passionate rage, joy, love, or grief can break through convention and spark the ignition of visceral truth. But there is a vast territory of expression between utility and passion that can profit from visceral connection without waiting for extremity.

Awareness of the sensory nature of words must come before that of their informational purpose if we are to restore words to the body. This is not to say that intellect is to be ignored but that, in order to redress the balance between intellect and emotion, emotion must be given precedence for a little while. For a large part of any day, our voices are programmed to convey information, the dry facts and figures of making appointments, exchanging news, dealing with clients or officials. The "shopping list" part of the brain has commandeered language almost entirely to its use, while the emotional and imaginative parts have to struggle for their rights in it. Taking words back to their physical, sensory, and emotional sources is not difficult once a few examples have been given and the guidelines understood. The exercises in this lesson are experimental. They are intended to spark further experiments and fresh ideas and must not be seen as rule making.

STEP 1 You will explore the different effects that different vowel sounds can have on your feelings and on your body. The *feeling* of vowels and consonants reveals sub-verbal meaning in words. The *feeling* of vowels and consonants links us to the desire to communicate. The word *feeling* implies here both physical sensation and emotional affect.

Prepare your body to be a receiving instrument to be played on by the sound. You can lie, sit, or stand, but whichever position you start from, you must prepare with deep relaxation that will result in a state of unblocked physical awareness through which vibrations can flow. (To begin with, the supine position is the least tense, and therefore the most receptive.)

Center your attention in the solar plexus/breathing area. From that central area, sigh out a long, easy "aaah-aah."

- Picture the stream of sound flowing from the center of the torso, up through the chest and throat, out through the mouth, down the arms, out through the hands, down through the stomach, into the legs, out through the feet.

- Imagine the wide stream of "AAH-AAH-AAH" vibrations as energy that can move your body.

- Imagine that the electrical impulse for sound activates your body and your voice simultaneously.

On each "AAH-AAH-AAH" explore the feelings that are aroused by the sound and free those feelings through the sound.

Now think the sound

- EEEEEEEEEEEEE

- And feed it down to your central solar plexus/diaphragm area.

- Sigh out "EEEEEEEEEEEEE."

- Let it flow through your torso and your limbs. Let it stimulate your body into movement. Allowing your body to take in the intrinsic quality of "EEEEE," find out what differences there are between the mood of "AAH" and the mood of "EEE," and whether your body and your feelings reflect those differences.

- Now go through the same processes with "OOOOOOOOOOOO," as in "food."

- Feed the sounds into the central area, alternating with

- AAH-AAH-AAH

- EEEEEEEE

- OOOOOOOOOOO

- Change sequences.

- Be true to the form of each vowel sound.

If you have been experiencing these lying down, repeat the exercises standing, so that you let the sounds move your body through space.

STEP 2   Take three vowel sounds whose quality is intrinsically sharper, shorter, and more staccato than the first three.

- a (as in "cat")

- i (as in "hit")

- u (as in "cut")

- Taking each in turn, drop it into your diaphragm center and bounce it out of you as though the diaphragm were a trampoline.

- Pant with each sound.

- Bounce each vowel sound up and down your range.

- Find out how each makes you feel.

- Play these short, staccato vowels into your body to stimulate movement. It may be that only a small part of your body will be affected by the small sounds. The quality of movement will differ if the quality of "i" is different from the quality of "AAH-AAH-AAH."

STEP 3   Drop contrasting vowel sounds into your body one after the other to spark contrasting physical and vocal responses. For example:

- u

- AAH-AAH-AAH

- i

- OOOOOOO

- EEEEEEE

- a

- AAH-AAH-AAH

This is to develop vocal and physical flexibility of response. Vary the rhythm, always observing the contrast between short and long vowels.

There exists a very fine line here between a free sound/movement response, and the imposition of invention on the sound. Invention and creativity with sound belong in another kind of exercise. In these, the objective is to see whether your body and your voice are capable of receiving, and realizing fully, the innate character of a particular vowel sound. You are imposing your power of invention on sound if, in search of variety, you force "OOOO" to go high and staccato, and "i" to be deep and legato, when the one is intrinsically comfortable in deep resonators and slow, warm movements, and the other feels more at home higher up the range while moving your hands and feet. Your variety will be exercised in the wide variety of vowels.

I have used as examples only the most obviously contrasting sounds. As you explore the influence on sound and movement of subtly different vowels, such as the "e" in bed, "ey" in hate, "oh" in hope, "aw" in walk, "o" in hot, you will, if you persevere, develop the sensitivity of your muscles and your resonators so that they will naturally reflect the delicate nuances of color and music that are the stuff of words.

STEP 4   Now we move from the feeling of vowels to the feeling of consonants.

- Focus your attention into your mouth.

- Explore the physical sensation of "MMMMMMMMMMMMM" between your lips. Run it high and low, moving your lips.

- Let the vibrations of "MMMMM" feed from your lips down to your midsection to find out how you feel as your mouth is used by "M."

- Now explore "VVVVVVVVVVV."

- Let that consonant tell you its nature.

- Then let your tongue taste "NNNNNNNNNN" and "ZZZZZZZZZ."

- Taste them long and luxuriously, picturing a stream of vibrations forming an unbroken connection between the tongue and the upper gum ridge, and the solar plexus center.

- Play with "sssssssssss" and "fffffffffffff."

These involve breath and no vibrations of sound—they are "unvoiced."

How do they make you feel?

- Play with "B," "D," "G" (voiced), then with "k," "t," "p" (unvoiced).

Feel the staccato quality in contrast to the legato of the "M"s and "S"s.

- Play with contrasting staccato and legato consonants. (The vibrations of breath will explode from the staccato consonants in an unformed, neutral "uh" spoken with the voiced consonants, whispered with the unvoiced. The legatos need no vowel sound.)

Example: (Uppercased letters are voiced; lowercased letters are unvoiced, or whispered.)

- BUH ZZZ fff NNN kuh sss tuh DUH MMM.

- Make a collection of consonants and develop rhythmic patterns for them. Example: MMM kuh ZZZ fff tuh tuh DUH NNN (Uppercased letters are voiced; lowercased letters are unvoiced, or whispered.)

- Let a rhythmic pattern of consonants (such as the above) move your body.

STEP 5   Take two contrasting vowel/sound/feeling qualities and two contrasting consonant/sound/feeling qualities, for example, oo+a and ZZ+t, and mix them. (Underlined letters=long sounds; italicized letters=short sounds.)

- OO<u>OZZZ</u>t*A*

- ZZ*A*<u>OOO</u>t

- *tA*<u>ZZZOOO</u>

Elongate the long sounds, clip the short ones as small as possible.

- Improvise with range, volume, and rhythm changes on your vowel/consonant mixture.

- Play these through your body so that they become spoken music activating you to move. Don't sing; this exercise is to expand the potential in your *speaking* voice.

Let your body feel the different qualities of the sounds and respond to them. Try not to use the sounds to express your energy, but let the sounds use you.

- On the basis of Step 5 explore a mix of three or more contrasting vowels and three or more contrasting consonants. Put them together in clear rhythmic patterns so that they do not become gibberish. Exercise your body and your voice to respond to thought impulses of sound that are free from meaning.

- <u>ZZZ</u>*I*fff*A*<u>LOOO</u>*tAp*A*k*<u>EEE</u>

- *pU*MMMMMAAABOOO*ff*ISSIt*A*GOOGOONAA

- Use any combination you can put together that moves your mouth and your breath and your body to react with changing energies.

It is essential to these sound and movement explorations that the intrinsic characters of the different vowels and consonants are not ironed out by the rhythm or subdued by other energies. You will find that as you allow these sounds to play through you, they will stimulate energy by the impact of their vibrations. If your body is relaxed and your mind open, sound will immediately generate energy. It also offers a channel through which you can express pent-up feelings; you must decide whether you are going to use the exercise to release emotions or to stick to the rules of this particular exercise. The rules are that the differing energies generated by the different sounds feed right back into those sounds and serve them.

Here is an example to illustrate this.

- tIpItAZZOOOEEEE

- This might look roughly like this on a stave:

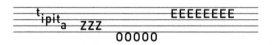

If you repeat it several times with rhythm and movement, it might become:

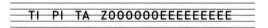

- Don't pound it into one note. This must be avoided. Also try to avoid releasing arbitrary excitement that will send the sounds away from their resonance homes.

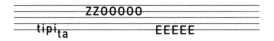

To tune your ear to the built-in music of vowels, whisper them. As you take away the resonance of your voice, you will clearly hear the pitch changes that occur as breath passes through your changing mouth-shapes.

STEP 6 Here now is a way to organize the intrinsic music of vowels with the resonating ladder. Vowels and resonance have their homes in the body. This is an energizing warm-up of embodied vowels and consonants. You will be moving through the vowel scale with a different consonant attached to the beginning of each vowel, starting with the lowest and working up to the highest. Each sound belongs in a different part of the body, and you should let each sound arouse energy, mood, feeling, or full-blooded emotion and then activate your body as it goes through you.

- Use your hands to shape, encourage, stroke, and pummel the sounds from your body, as though your hands too were speaking.

- Let the sound "ZZOOO" travel down into your pelvis and legs, moving you and them.

- Now imagine a huge mouth opening from your belly and let the sound "WO-O-Oe"—as in "woe"—emerge, moving you and the middle of your body.

- Picture the diaphragm/solar plexus attached to the bottom of your rib cage and let out a long-drawn-out "SHAW-AW-AW."

- Now put one fist on the center of your chest, over the breastbone, the other directly behind it between your shoulder blades. Feel as if the sound must break through your bones and let a sharp, strong "GOh"—as in "got"—burst out.

- Put both hands on your upper chest and start a long "MMMM," which opens into a wide, warm "AAAA" as your arms gradually lift out at the sides. Your heart releases its vibrations out through a wide, generous throat and through the expansion of your arms and hands.

- Put your fingers on your lips, and as if blowing a quick kiss, let out "FUh," as in "fun." Make it light and airy.

- Now your hands and your mouth are going to release a vague, misty, perhaps rather unsure sound, like a long, unformed sigh, "HU-U-U-H."

- Next, place your fingers on your cheeks and explode a sharp, strong, extrovert "BA"—as in "bat"—from your lips straight out through the middle of your cheeks. Let it be bright and confident and cheery.

- From there, move up to your cheekbones. Guide your fingertips to the hard, resonant cheekbone-ridge on either side of the bridge of your nose, let the blade of your tongue flick the syllable "DEh" —as in "deck"—forward and up, to spring jauntily, carelessly into the air.

- The upward journey of your thoughts has now reached the level of your eyes. Feel the bone structure circling your eye sockets. Picture the portholes of the eyes. Be aware of how fragile your eyes are and the protection that surrounds the "windows to the soul." An almost transparent flow of vibration can stream out at this level on "PE-EY-EY"—as in "pay"—expressing an open vulnerability, perhaps surprise, wonder, innocence, or even panic.

- Then take a quick hop up to a pinprick of sound, spitting off the middle of the forehead, "KI"—as in "kit."

- The final sound at the top of the scale that spirals out as though through a small hole in the crown of your head is "RRREEE-EE-EE." This should lift you off the ground with its sheer ebullient energy. It may be silly, ecstatic, trilling, or thrilling, but it can hardly be done without your smiling and jumping in the air.

Having gone all the way up, go all the way down. Let each sound arouse its different energy and mood. Make sure you allow each sound its true pitch and frequency. Let your breath be free and your spirit willing to be acted upon.

Here is the sequence, bottom to top, and then top to bottom:

Start here and go down.

RREE-EE	crown	RREE-EE
KI	forehead	KI
PE-EY	eyes	PE-EY
DEh	cheekbones	DEh
BA	mid-cheeks	BA
HU-UH-UH	mouth	HU-UH-UH
FUh	lips	FUh
MAA-AAH	heart	MAA-AAH
GOh	chest center	GOh
SHAW-AW	solar plexus	SHAW-AW
WWO-Oe	belly	WWO-Oe
ZZOO-OO	legs and pelvis	ZZOO-OO

Start here and go up.   **End here.**

To begin with, you should allow a new breath impulse for each sound. As you become familiar with this sequence, you can put together sound groups as though in sentences, but make sure they are fully embodied in sound and movement.

ZZOO WOe SHAW △
GOh MMAAAH △
FUh HU-UH BA DEh △
PE-EY KI RRREEE △
RRREE KI PE-EY △
DEh BA HU-UH-UH FUh △
MAAAH GOh SHAW WOe ZZOOOO

Then graduate to:

ZZOO WOe SHAW GOh MMAAA △
FUh HU-UH BA DEh PE-EY KI RRREE △
RRREE KI PE-EY DEh BA HU-UH-UH FUh △
MAAAH GOh SHAW WOe ZZOOOO

And finally:

ZZOO WOe SHAW GOh MMAAH FUh HU-UH BA DEh PE-EY KI RR
REE △

RRREE KI PE-EY DEh BA HU-UH-UH FUh MAAAH GOh SHAW WOe
ZZOOOO

This scale that integrates vowels, resonance, body, and energy should warm
you up through a wide spectrum of sounds and pitches. The scale provides
an aerobics of the inner self that vitalizes language and brings incarnated
life to any text.

STEP 7   Using Steps 1 through 6 as models for anatomizing words, choose
a word that is onomatopoeic and play it into your body, ignoring
its sense as much as possible.

■ Examples:

Splash   ratatat   murmuring   susurration   whip

If you were to take the word *splash* you might go through the following
processes:

■ Feel "S" in your breath released from your center, hissing between
the front of your tongue and the upper gum ridge.

■ Feel "P" in the tiny puff of breath exploding from between the wet
parts of your lips.

■ Feel "L" as liquid vibration between your tongue and gum ridge.

■ Feel "A" as staccato, bouncing from the diaphragm, glancing off the
roof of the mouth and out into the air.

■ Feel "SH" in the air softly foaming out between the middle of the
tongue and the roof of the mouth.

■ Take them slowly, one by one, with a new breath for each.

- Then gradually speed up the sequence until they join together in one breath with physical awareness dominating.

- Admit the sense and/or picture conjured up by the collection of sounds.

- Drop the word-sense into the center of your body and see what it makes you feel.

Let the sense of the word and the vibrations of the word play on you.

- Explore the sound, the sense, associations, and feelings with movement.

STEP 8   Take a word with a representational picture.

- Example:

Wind	butterfly	clouds	sky	
Earth	stone	rock	brick	
Sea	waves	stream	river	ocean
Fire	flame	blaze	sparks	

- Close your eyes to see the picture clearly in your mind's eye.

- Drop the image into your solar plexus breathing center.

- Allow your feelings to respond to the image as breath flies in.

- Let the feelings find sound. As the sound releases out through your mouth, your lips and tongue mold it into the original word. Let the word serve the image. Let the feeling *need* the word to express itself.

STEP 9   Take a word with an emotional image.

- Example:

  Love   rage   giggle   sorrow

- Drop the word deep down into your body and see what happens. If you give yourself time, you may find that associative images grow out of what the word means to you, or that the meaning makes direct contact with your feelings. Again let your breath merge with the feelings that flow back out through the word.

STEP 10 Find words with more abstract images

- Example:

  Purple   red   blue   yellow   jagged   round

  Darting   transitional   whimsy   flimsy

  Stolid

- Let these words form their images and associations and feelings in you. Let the feelings be expressed through breath, voice, and the word as you speak it.

STEP 11 Explore action words

- Example:

  Run   subside   explore   live   die   fight   go   fly

  Murder   comfort   placate

STEP 12 Play with small words.

- Example:

  For   and   to   it   if   such   now   which   what

  How   or   but   against   unless   since

  If you give each word time, it will assert its independent character, which can create its own abstract shapes in the mind's eye. Normally subdued by the more powerful images to which they are attached in a sentence, their separate qualities can add nuanced, vivid color to inflection. They have dramatic influence on thought, opening doors, turning corners, creating or breaking relationships.

STEP 13 String together a sequence of the words you used in Steps 8 though 11 in any order without making sense.

- Example 1:

  Butterflies   blue   giggle   murmuring

- Exercise your ability to let one image (representational or abstract) follow another in sequence and to let feeling flow in response from image to image. You may hear or see the image in your head and beam the image down to your middle. Or you may directly see the image in the center of your body.

- One after the other let each word/image/feeling find accurate reflection in your voice. Slowly first, to be sure of precise, moment-to-moment connection, then faster without letting one word rob another of its independent character. Don't, for instance, let "blue" color "butterflies" or "giggle" affect "murmuring."

- Make some sense grammatically out of the words. Example:

- "The murmuring blue butterflies giggle."

- Now, as you put "blue" and "butterflies" together they will form a new image from the two separate ones, but the composite picture is more powerful by virtue of the strength of the components. Add "murmuring" and the three make one whole, mobile picture; the "giggle" comes in and breaks the picture up, changing the feeling.

- Example 2:

  No sense—blaze ocean ratatat rage yellow

  Grammatical sense—"The ratatat ocean blazes into yellow rage."

- *Ocean* is one picture. *Ratatat* added to *ocean* changes the picture. *Blaze* is one picture. *The ocean blazes* is a new picture. *Rage* might be red when it is alone but it has to yield to the *yellow rage* of the *ocean.*

The point of this exercise is to allow individual words to influence your voice, giving a phrase or sentence more life than just what it gets from the overall sense. The first example has, deliberately, little sense to it, but it does convey the information that those butterflies were giggling. The general feeling of the sense is giggly and that can be the one tone to emerge from the sentence. In that case the fact that they were murmuring and were colored blue could be immaterial. In the second example the general impression is of anger, but there are descriptive specifics in the picture that can be communicated if the voice is sensitive to the influence of *ratatat, yellow,* and *ocean.*

Memories of kindergarten poetry speaking—"The sun is in the sky," pointing heavenward, voice with an upward inflection, "And the earth is down below," looking down, dropping the voice—may give one pause. But these exercises are designed to start moving the voice from within, to make it come alive to a sensory and imagistic inner world. Once it is made flexible and sensitive you can return to the job of communicating textual sense but with your voice now susceptible to paratextual influences. The extremes of color and image will serve the sense inflection, but sense need no longer be the sole inflection in your speech.

About Texts . . . art

Some General Observations

The focus of this book is the *voice* as an instrument of communication distinct from that of *speech*. Once the natural voice is free, it will be expanded for artistic potential in all arenas. Most theatre performances make use of the voice in some way, though there are certainly theatre pieces that are more or less, or completely, without words. Contemporary dance theatre may be vocal, and puppet theatre makes use of extended voice, but both of these are elaborations on the mission of an actor's voice training, which is to bring the text of a play faithfully to life. The ultimate aim of this work is for the voice to be supremely well prepared to translate the written text of a play into spoken language. The actor works on voice and speech as a collaborator in the service of the play. "From page to stage" is a pithy phrase that is accomplished by transforming and resurrecting the word from dead print to an embodied, flesh-and-blood presence.

The etymological root of the word *text* is the Latin *texere*, which means "to weave" or "to fabricate." The word *textile* comes from the same root. A text is a tapestry of ideas woven with words. The actor must translate the written tapestry into a spoken story through voice, and the art of acting lies in the actor's ability to intuit the feeling behind the idea that is expressed in words. The actor's vocal craft will determine the level of intuitive skill with which s/he can probe the text for the originating feelings.

Western theatre is primarily verbal and text-based. In order to fulfill the demands of Western dramatic literature, actors must develop an appetite for language and a wide understanding of texts. In the final pages of this book I will offer some ideas as to how to approach a text. Text work of this kind is not analytical; it is not the "table work" that often precedes active rehearsal on a play. It is the actor's private and personal absorption of the words of a play deep into the body-mind where the seeds of meanings can be sown, take root, and grow organically. Out of the intelligence of the body-mind spring surprising truths, as opposed to the more predictable fruits of rational frontal-lobe thinking where decisions are made and results are preconceived and controlled.

The Cartesian way of thinking, which has been boiled down to an over-simplified adage of "I think, therefore I am," has never been convincing to performing artists. It is obvious to those of us who work in the psycho-physical field that it is "I am, therefore I think." Antonio Damasio's book *Descartes' Error* maps the communication routes between mind and body and delivers neurobiological proof that being must be the ground for thinking. I have quoted Damasio previously, and I turn again to his second book, *The Feeling of What Happens,* as we begin the adventure of language, text, and words. His description of the way language works has an authenticity and elegance I am unable to emulate.

> Language—that is, words and sentences—is a translation of something else, a conversion from nonlinguistic images, which stand for entities, events, relationships and inferences. If language operates for the self and for consciousness in the same way that it operates for everything else, that is, by symbolizing in words and sentences what exists first in a nonverbal form, then there must be a nonverbal self and a nonverbal knowing for which the words "I" or "me" or the phrase "I know" are the appropriate translations, in any language. I believe it is legitimate to take the phrase "I know" and deduce from it the presence of a nonverbal image of knowing centered on a self that precedes and motivates that verbal phrase.
>
> The idea that self and consciousness would emerge after language, and would be a direct construction of language, is not likely to be correct. Language does not come out of nothing. Language gives us names for things.
>
> Given our supreme language gift, most of the ingredients of consciousness, from objects to inferences, can be translated into language, and for us, at this point in history and the history of each individual,

the basic process of consciousness is relentlessly translated by language, covered by it, if you will. Because of this, it does require a major effort to imagine what lies behind language, but the effort must be made.

(From *The Feeling of What Happens* by Antonio Damasio, pp. 107-108)

The mental effort the actor must make in taking the printed word and transforming it into the spoken word is to still the clamor of the rational brain and give the word time for the image of print to dissolve and transmute into the nonverbal images, feelings, states of being, desires, and memories that lie beneath. A word or a phrase or a sentence is like a pebble that, when thrown into the pool of the body-mind, sets up ripples that disturb the waters. The waters? Physical, sensory, sensual, and emotional energies. Then, when the energies become insistent and need to be released, the water turns to vibration and becomes voice. The nonverbal now has access to words, readymade—retained and shaped by the brain but not controlled by it. The voice work you have been doing on your journey through this book prepares you to meet words in this way.

Ideally, voice work should feed organically into "acting," "speaking a text," or plain "speaking" without conscious application of technique. If the work to free the voice has been deeply absorbed, the person will be naturally freer; the person and the voice will have become unified. In many instances a natural connection happens. Someone will go from a voice class to an acting class and experience a totally new freedom that is only partly to do with the voice. It might seem superfluous to mention the advantage of doing a warm-up before going on stage or into rehearsal, but there are actors who are still surprised at how well a rehearsal or performance went after having first done a voice workout. It should also be said that the majority of serious actors always warm up physically and vocally for up to an hour before every performance. (Only gifted exceptions can walk in off the street and onto the stage and give an electrifying performance with no preparation. No young actor should make them exemplars.) The aim of a warm-up is not just to produce a well-tuned instrument but to reopen the road leading into and out of the creative sources.

When an acting "moment" hits the pay dirt of truth, voice and words know how to behave. Contemporary acting training uses exercises and improvisations to guide, shake, or trick the student into a nonverbal, instinct-based state of being where impulses are generated and acted upon without thinking about them. Genuine states of being can be experienced, the routes to them gradually familiarized and a craft developed that takes some of the haphazardness out of the creative process. However, an actor needs as many keys to the truth as possible, and knowing how to read a text in depth and connect language with breath and voice will provide a golden key to hang on the chain of craft.

A continuing theme in the voice work throughout this book has been the use of images. There have been accurate anatomical images and specific imaginative images. The central nervous system governs the whole organism through continuous streams of images be they auditory, olfactory, tactile, visual, impressionistic, or figurative. Images in voice work help to reconnect the acts of listening and speaking to the whole organism. Listening is no longer attached just to the ear. Speaking no longer suffers under the dictatorship of the mouth. Embodied listening and speaking involve the whole person from feet to skull. The body is all ears. The body is one big mouth.

From this ground of experience we can devise processes that accelerate our entry into the understanding of a text. The intelligence of the whole body is infinitely greater than the intelligence of the frontal lobes, and when the word becomes flesh the speaker is led to the threshold of understanding.

The Welsh poet Gwyneth Lewis says:

> The way forward for me lay in using a different part of myself to judge between true and false. The best way I can describe it is moving down from my head and into my stomach. The head is where all your fancies, recollections, gripes and projections are endlessly rehearsed. It's a Virtual Reality gallery dedicated to your personal preoccupations. Although the pictures are vivid—no, compelling—this area has no way of distinguishing between fantasy and truth, because both look just as convincing. The head, then, is very good at trying out possibilities, versions of reality, and totally unable to make moral choices between them.
>
> The stomach doesn't work visually, but viscerally. It "sees" in the dark, but if listened to carefully, gives reliable guidance. It ties itself in knots when you're lying, and tells you what to do even before you have worked out why that should be right. Like a dog it is instinctive in its likes and dislikes and its decisions are invariably sound. The head tells you what could be, the stomach tells you what is.
>
> When you're used to leading your life with your head, it's hard to move down and learn to see with another part of yourself. But the insights that come with the effort to do so are startling.
>
> (From *Sunbathing in the Rain: A Cheerful Book about Depression* by Gwyneth Lewis, p. 233)

When you're used to leading your life with your head, you are probably also used to reading a text with your head. Even those who live more stomach-centered lives nonetheless read with their heads, thinking of texts as somehow separate from life. Moving down into the stomach—and lower—in order to read will reward you with all sorts of insights.

In addition to voice work and whatever acting techniques have been developed by the actor for his or her own personal approach to this multi-faceted art, I would like now to offer some simple techniques designed specifically for delving into the text itself.

Some General Ideas and Ways of Approaching the Text

Reading with the Head: The Linear Habit

I invite you to enter a test to determine your relationship to a printed text. Pick up a poem or a speech from a play. Look at the text printed on the page. What is the first thing you do?

In ninety-nine percent of first reactions to a page of print, the reader will skim quickly through to the end in order to find out what it means: that is, what the plot is and who the characters are.

Why do you want to know what it means? So that you can be in control of the situation; so that you can be intelligent about the content; so that you can immediately make some decisions about how to speak the text. Your head rules. Your head tells you that it is dangerous not to know. You are in the grip of the linear habit. Linear reading will give you rational information—with maybe a hint of the underlying forces.

As an actor, however, you must redirect your energies and demand that what comes off the page goes vertically down into the well of your psyche to mingle with the underground rivers of your unconscious mind.

How to Arrest the Linear Habit

Think of the words on the page of a script as seeds.
Think of your body-mind as fertile ground.
Let the seeds of the words impregnate you.
Give them time to gestate, to germinate.
When they become full of the desire to be alive, to be spoken,
allow them be born again in words.

Words must drop down into the solar and sacral centers to become

Images   feelings   intimations
Intentions   descriptions   memory
Potential   action   energy

These swirling forces merge with breath and the *inner reactions and impressions are focused into impulse and the need to speak.*

Breath becomes vibration.

Internal streams of consciousness find the order of words.

The mouth answers the need to articulate, and *the embodied language expresses a truth that is born from the marriage of the printed words with the speaker.*

I know that this is a convoluted description of a process that we take for granted. We all can read, but what I am asking here is, "What kind of conditioned reading are we engaged in?" Horizontal, linear reading will keep us within the safe confines of our controlling, inventive forebrains. Vertical reading will lead us into the creative chaos of unpredictable responses from sensory, emotional, and physical landscapes of being and biography. The forebrain will keep us safe, but safety and comfort are the refuge of the creative coward. The actor must crave insecurity, the unknown, the uncharted boundaries of the imagination, because traveling along that edge leads to the promised land of creativity.

Rehabilitating Reading

When we talk we are not aware that we are seeing what we say as images. The images run by too quickly. The image has become impulse.

We say to ourselves or someone else: "I wonder if I have time to run to the supermarket for some milk before I go to work." "I'll pick up the laundry on my way home." "I'll just have time to feed the cats before going out to meet..." All of these are mundanely informational yet all have images attached. I have students who say they are not visually oriented; they are aural, or tactile. But given these small daily events to dwell on, they recognize what image is and can develop the visual sense to balance the others.

More abstract discussion is still imagistic: "I'm feeling really down today." "I don't know what to do." "Everything seems pointless." In a logical extension from this familiar mood to the equally familiar existential question "What is the meaning of life?" images abound in impressionistic embraces of color and shape. Mood and emotion, sensation and action are all registered in the organism in a stream of images.

When we talk we have some purpose behind what we say. When we study a text we must sink beneath the obvious purpose of the words to the underlying need, the personal, character-driven desire that is initially experienced in images. We must slow down the whole process so that we imprint the psyche, the organism, slowly and painstakingly with the images that preceded the words.

Once those images have been planted, impulses are born. Words spring forth again. If the planting has been true, then the words will be spoken as truth. The actor will no longer "see" the images s/he has so painstakingly imprinted on the psyche. The body-mind mechanism is set in motion, and impulses automatically fire the involuntary voice and speech musculature.

The truth of the result depends on the depth of the planting.

The planting can be deepened by using the anatomical and inner landscape pictures with which you are now familiar.

How to Rehabilitate Reading

When you are first learning lines, do not use the word *memorize*. It has a busy, fast utilitarian ring to it, and *memorization* tends to use photographic memory of the text: in your mind's eye you know if you are at the top or the bottom of the page and even when the page is turned. You tend to set up a kind of TelePrompTer™ just behind and above your eyes that, in effect, you read. This method of learning very quickly imprints speaking inflections that become hard to eradicate. The speaking becomes mechanical and devoid of human content.

The old-fashioned term "learn by heart" tells you what you need to be doing when you learn. You need to absorb the words of the character you are playing into your inner landscape. You need to be breathing the words in so that the underlying thoughts become feelings and the cellular make-up of your body starts to rearrange itself in response.

Exercise: A simple way to start is by lying flat on your back with your script on the floor beside you. Assuming that you have warmed yourself up vocally and physically, your awareness of self will be energetically alive in the lower part of your body.

- Lazily lift the script so that you can see a few words.

- Put the script down. Let the ingoing breath take the words down into the lower spaces and keep breathing naturally as the words turn into images, feelings, potential action, mood, question, etc.

- When the words are no longer seen as print, speak them on an outgoing release of sound.

Continue with the ensuing words, alternating the supine position with the diagonal stretch, the semifetal position, the folded leaf, and the banana stretch.

Learn your words lying on the floor.
Learn your words on an outgoing, free sound—don't learn them in a whisper.
Keep exploring images, feelings, associations.
Let the words find new meanings with every repetition—don't settle for an interpretation.
Let the different positions of your body deliver up different responses to the words.

Don't hold back—let your voice out as you learn.

- When you are tired of the floor, shift your physical position; speak your words in a squat, on all fours, or with your head downward. Plant the words deeply as you speak them.

- When you eventually stand, make sure that you are still dropping the words down into the middle and lower parts of your body.

Move your pelvis as you speak.
Bounce your knees as you speak.
Bounce your shoulder blades as you speak.
Shimmy, undulate, walk, jump, and stretch as you speak.

Don't make any decision about HOW the words are to be spoken. Find out WHAT they are saying and WHY you are saying them.

The physical shifting will help dislodge any premature interpretation while opening up "unpreconceived" levels of thought and idea. Throw caution to the winds and let your voice out as you think and feel your way through the text. This is pure and active research.

Reminder: Speaking involves thought/feeling impulse, the desire to speak; breath; vibration; resonance; articulation. The muscles that are engaged are on the muscular-skeletal, involuntary level, triggered by images.

Here is another way of thinking about the process of absorbing and speaking a text, a kind of mnemonic:

The 3 M's to be nurtured are:

Mind   Middle   Mouth

These are the areas to be stimulated—the mind (body-mind experiences), the middle (solar plexus/diaphragm, sensitive to image and impulse), the mouth (lips and tongue, equally sensitive). The lips and the tongue think and feel. They do not merely articulate.

The 3 M's to be banished are:

Muscling   Manipulation   Mastication

It is all too easy to let the *muscles* take over. When they do, they kidnap the truth. "Believe me, or else," "I'm telling you loud and clear," "You gotta believe me!"

In real life the muscles very often get involved in emotional expression to the point that the muscular experience says, "Anger *is* the tightening of the fists and shoulders, the clenching of the jaw, the bunching up of the stomach muscles. Grief *is* the clamp-down in the throat, the contortion of the face muscles, the constriction in the chest." But such muscle behavior is most often the habitual response to emotion that has developed, in fact, from the *suppression* of the emotion. When a performance demands free expression of emotion, the actor's subsequent fight to get past the habitual suppression creates extra muscle work. The effort can convince the performer that this is really real, really powerful, really effective emotional delivery.

True emotion rides on the winds of breath and on sound waves reverberating through the magnifying caverns of the inbuilt resonators of the body. Obviously, muscles are strongly involved in the expression of strong impulses—a two-year-old in the grip of a tantrum is proof of that—but there is a big difference between emotional energy *moving through* those muscles and being *held in* them. There is a graphic difference in authenticity when those muscles are stimulated powerfully from inside out rather than grasping, manipulating, and actively wielding the power.

To play eight performances a week, the artist who is portraying emotion must know how the flow of such energies goes through the body. The performer who photocopies the everyday neural displacement of emotional expression will quickly succumb to exhaustion and strain.

Some Specific Observations about the Texts in Their Own Right

Clearly there is no one simple rule that can serve to illuminate and bring to life all texts in all plays. Different periods, different geography, different societies are captured in differing textual styles and require differing approaches.

For example, the work that you must undertake to do justice to Shakespeare's text is specialized. You must understand how to absorb an English that is four hundred years younger than the English we speak today. You must learn how to read meaning from clues encoded in figures of speech, the iambic pentameter and its irregularities, and the structures of verse and prose, and all of this within the context of an Elizabethan world picture. There are many books that will provide the detailed information you need to enter into the Shakespearean adventure. My own book *Freeing Shakespeare's Voice: The Actor's Guide to Talking the Text* is one of them.

Plays that come under the heading of "classical," from the Greeks to Shakespeare to Boucicault, use heightened language and very often poetry to convey the heightened experience of epic stories. The story telling is in the words. The performance relies on the dramatic enactment of language through strongly delineated characters. The information is on the surface of the page.

Modern drama is usually said to begin with Ibsen, Strindberg, and Chekhov. Here the English-speaking actor must struggle with translations but also with the fact that now s/he must enter the realm of subtext. Language is still heightened and often poetic, but the characters' inner lives drive the action more than the story they reveal in words.

Shakespeare's dictum in *Hamlet* Act III scene 2, "Suit the action to the word, the word to the action," is perfect advice for playing the classics. But he goes on to say, "...with this special observance: that you o'er step not the modesty of nature. For anything so overdone is from the purpose of playing, whose end, both at the first and now, was and is to hold as 'twere the mirror up to nature, to show virtue her own feature, scorn her own image, and the very age and body of the time his form and pressure [*impression*]." This qualification leads us from the mandate for theatre in Shakespeare's time to our mandate for modern drama, contemporary drama, and whatever may come in the future.

Ibsen and Chekhov were holding their mirrors up to their time, which was beginning to reveal psychological and personal dramas, a split-level existence that had gone unacknowledged or unrecognized in earlier times. The label "modern" spreads from Ibsen to playwrights such as George Bernard Shaw, Arthur Miller, and Tennessee Williams. Their words delve into the substrata of society and relationships, and also give the people whose lives they chronicle rich language with which to express their conflicts and desires. Language is still a component of identity in modern drama.

When today's playwrights hold the looking and listening mirror up to contemporary nature they reflect a society that has lost its language identification tag. In film and television, language is very often the tip of the iceberg as far as character is concerned. Words can be mere signposts to where the action is. In theatre, music and technology and soundscapes and special effects often do what words did in the past. Conflict, which is the lifeblood of theatre, may well now manifest itself as dissociation—a human being's life-saving ability to remove him or herself from extreme pain. The language of dissociation may be eloquent and often verbose, but it floats above a hidden life. Today's actor must dig into the subsoil of today's stage inhabitants to tap motivation and action. The energy comes from under and behind the words; it is subverbal, infraverbal, paraverbal.

The contemporary voice is, in general, a restricted voice, and the everyday range of sounds used by English speakers is small. Four or five notes may well suffice for most verbal communication. The fact that three or four octaves of speaking notes are available, that they are capable of expressing the full gamut of human emotion and all the nuances of thought, and yet that they are hardly ever used is evidence of how much we, in Western society, suppress what we are thinking and feeling.

Listening in to these labels, "contemporary," "modern," "classical," we may hear that the "modern" voice was less adversely influenced by technological communications systems than our "contemporary" voices are, and more positively influenced by social systems that fostered vocal communication: family meals, singing and recitation as homegrown entertainment, open-air speeches and political debates, story telling, education that encouraged learning poems and speaking them individually or in chorus, and a respect for, even a veneration of, literature. The range and the power of voices were central to the life of a community.

Listening in to classical texts we can hear how free and wide-ranging the classical voice was. The huge stories told by the Greeks call for huge vocal and emotional capacity. The stories can only be told in poetic language that treads on the skirts of melody and trips into chant or song whenever the choruses carry the tale. Shakespeare, Marlowe, Jonson, Webster, and Ford in England; Moliere, Racine, and Corneille in France; Gozzi and Tasso in Italy; and de Calderon in Spain give evidence of European societies that were lavish in their expenditure of language and vociferously well equipped to celebrate the expense.

Well-nourished by a diet of songs, poems, and stories still rooted in a thousand-year-old oral tradition, all classes of society exercised the full range of voice for practical purposes. In the fields and cottages, women and men called, cajoled, wailed, and wassailed. In the streets of the cities, they hawked their wares at full volume. In schools and universities, men and boys recited their lessons in stately Latin according to the rules of rhetoric. John Donne, whose sermons filled the cathedral of St. Paul to capacity, is said to have had a voice that rose and reverberated round the great dome and was heard by the overflow crowd clustered outside among the surrounding gravestones. Ship captains threw their voices up with the wind into the sails where ship boys tugged at ropes; armies were lashed into battle by the tongues of their leaders; kings and queens, noblemen and women harangued their subjects with a forceful eloquence that made good use of the melodious range of their voices exercised daily by singing motets and madrigals and canons and cantonets.

I have no doubt that the ring and range of these voices can still be heard if we learn to listen well. This is the classical range of voice. We need to cultivate a kind of imaginative time and space travel machine with built-in listening sensors that can pick up the ancestral voices. The imagination must be fed by reading and historical research, but then it must trust its own ethereal ears and eyes.

There is a charming story told about Gugliemo Marconi, the physicist who invented radiotelegraphy and the short-wave wireless. His discovery of electromagnetic wave technique forms the basis of nearly all modern radio functions. Perhaps this is an apocryphal tale, but it serves as a good stimulus for the historical imagination. In his old age—he died in 1937—he was asked whether he was still engaged in new research. "Of course," he answered. He was asked what was occupying his scientific interest at this point in his life. He answered that, based on the fact that sound waves never end but continue forever out into the universe, he was working on the development of technologies that could tune into words that had been spoken in the past. "What words, in particular, from centuries of speech, would you like to hear?" was the next question. His answer was "The Sermon on the Mount."

Perhaps our ancestors' voices are still surfing the eternal billows; perhaps Jesus is yet blessing "The poor for they shall inherit the earth." There are those who say that our ancestral memory is stored in the limbic region of the brain. One way or another we have the ability to tune in to the past, and the words of classical texts provide reliable probes for the actor to deploy in the search for the sounds of past voices.

Within these very broad categories of dramatic texts—classical, modern, and contemporary—there are all sorts of variations and exceptions to the categorical rule. The distinctions are intended to serve as general guidelines to more specific examination.

Tuning in to the Text
. . . imagination

At this juncture in your approach to understanding a text you will be enlisting the intellect as a guide. The intellect can provide a kind of checklist for the investigative imagination: What are you listening for? Have you covered this angle, or that? Are you sure you know why you're saying these words?

The intellect must not, however, be allowed to be an autocrat. The intellect guides the imagination to impulse, emotion, sensation, and sound, and it has a powerful responsibility if it is not either to be drowned in emotion or to rise up in self-defense and stifle anarchic impulse. It must mold all that emerges from the creative source into shapes that have sense and meaning. Initially the intellect can whisper suggestions in your ear that guide your explorations; ultimately it is a conduit, not a controller.

Here now are some ways to sensitize your textual antennae. Once you have worked with reference to this checklist often enough, you will automatically *read* any text with an ear for its particular style and content. These checkpoints straddle the border between text and acting, but they can and should be part of an actor's homework on a text, before interacting with others in the rehearsal process.

Checklist:

Transitions:
Thought transitions, transitions in the subject matter, transitions in the argument, transitions in the activity

The Six Eternal Questions:
Who, where, when, what, why, how

The Five P's:
Personal, psychological, professional, political, philosophical

Dynamics:
Dynamics of the text, dynamics of the character, dynamics of the event

Rhythm:
Rhythm of speech, rhythm of character, rhythm of the scene

What Are Transitions?

Transitions are thought-changes that are often signaled by words such as *if, but, or,* and *though,* and always by punctuation.
Transitions are emotional shifts.
Transitions are shifts of direction in the action.

What Are the Six Eternal Questions?

(1.) Who: Who is initially answered by the Five P's. And then it is answered by "To whom are you talking?" "Who else is there?"
(2.) Where: Where asks questions such as, "Where are you as you speak?" "Where are you coming from?" "Where are you going?"
(3.) When: When asks questions about the time—year, month, day, time of day or night; or season—the time in relation to events.
(4.) What: What asks questions about the content of your speech; the content of the argument, the events.

(5.) Why: Why asks questions about your motive. Why are you saying what you are saying? The first four questions also help you discover *motive.* Why also asks why you use the particular words you do? The character could have simply said "X" but chose to say "Y."

(6.) How: How asks questions about tactics and strategies—psychological, behavioral, and physical.

What Are the Five P's?

(1.) Personal: Personal facts are all of those about the speaker's life: age, gender, ethnicity, family situation, tall, short, fat, thin, educated or not, etc.

(2.) Psychological: Psychological facts tell whether a person is happy, depressive, aggressive, melancholic, and what childhood experiences informed the personality along with other formative personality experiences.

(3.) Professional: Professional facts tell what position the person holds in society; how s/he earns a living, for instance.

(4.) Political: Political facts explain within what political context s/he lives. Where does s/he belong in the socioeconomic structure. Is the character involved or not involved in politics, etc.

(5.) Philosophical: Philosophical facts are those such as religious or not religious; believes in God or does not; follows a spiritual practice of any kind; searches for existential meaning; animist; lives only from day to day, etc.

What Are the Components of Dynamics?

Pace is a component of dynamics.
(fast, faster; slow, slower; somewhere in between fast and slow).
Pitch is a component of dynamics.
(high, higher; low, lower; middle of the range)
Volume is a component of dynamics.
(loud, louder; soft, softer; mid-volume)

What Are the Components of Rhythm?

Dynamics are a component of rhythm.

Emphasis is a component of rhythm and involves strong emphasis juxtaposed with weak emphasis.

Regularity, irregularity, syncopation are all components of rhythm.

Rhythm, dynamics, and transitions all depend for artistic execution on a person's well-developed sensitivity to contrast.

The actor must know the answers to the six eternal questions and those posed by the five P's. The actor must be the master of all the information even though the character may not know nearly as much.

I repeat the point I made earlier: *These checkpoints straddle the border between text and acting, but they can and should all be part of an actor's first encounter with a text when s/he is alone, before interacting in a rehearsal process.*

Once the private work has created its own harmonic reservoir of fact and fancy, association, memory, motive, music, and rhythm, it can then meet, mingle, and alchemize with the fresh ingredients coming from others.

Applying this long checklist may seem laborious, but with practice— the repetition of labor—the intellect extends its centripetal awareness and "reads" with greater breadth and depth.

The Haiku

I am going to use one particular kind of poetic text for a demonstration of how to use the ideas I have outlined. I hope this illustration will act as a guide for work on other texts. If I were to try to give examples of how to approach two, three, or twenty different styles of writing, I would have to cover them all, which would be impossible within the limits of this book.

The haiku is a perfect miniature gymnasium for exercising one's text talents. The basic attributes of a good haiku are that within seventeen syllables there are at least three images that arouse three different emotional responses.

I use only haiku that have been anointed as classics in the Japanese tradition. This means that we must use translations and in English the seventeen-syllable rule yields often to an accurate expression of feeling and image. I work with haiku because so much happens within so few words that class-room time is used in a very economical way. I use classic haiku because they have stood the test of time and are packed with power. They are emotionally and psychologically potent and they only work when the speaker is ready to be acted upon, not actively "doing." They are thus good, compact text and acting exercises.

The other great lesson the haiku teaches is that to enter its truth you must imagine the author. You cannot speak them without joining with the poet on some imaginative plane. The origin of haiku writing is lost in Japanese antiquity, but the golden age of haiku arrived in the seventeenth and eighteenth centuries. I have chosen five from this period. They are to be found in *An Introduction to HAIKU, An Anthology of Poems and Poets from Basho to Shiki*. The translation and invaluable commentary are by Harold G. Henderson. Henderson says this of Basho, who is considered the great classic master of haiku:

…Consciously or unconsciously, Basho put into most if not all of his later haiku all the meaning that anyone can find, and probably much more. The more one reads them, the more one finds depths in each single one, even in those that seem most trivial. One gets the feeling that they are somehow all parts of one whole. Japanese who have had the same experience have explained it by saying that Basho was so imbued with the spirit of Zen that it could not help showing in everything he wrote. This is quite possibly true, but as an explanation it suffers from the fact that nobody has yet been able to define what "the spirit of Zen" actually is. Zen illumination (satori) is apparently a strong emotional experience for which there are no words. It has been called a "realizing of reality." About all that non-Zen people can do is observe its effects on Basho and on his poems. Among the qualities which are often considered as indicative of his Zen are a great zest for life; a desire to use every instant to its utmost; an appreciation of this even in natural objects; a feeling that nothing is alone, nothing unimportant; and an acute awareness of relationships of all kinds, including that of one sense to another.

What follows is a painstaking examination of what it takes to bring life, breath and presence to a text (in this case a haiku) and thus to elucidate its meaning. Once you understand the process, it goes quite fast. In order to understand though, I must lead you through the process at a snail's pace.

The poets who wrote the following five haiku are respectively Oni-tsura (1660–1738); Sodo (1641–1716); Basho's pupil, Joso (1661–1704); Issa (1762–1826); and Basho himself (1644–1694).

STEP 1

■ Please copy each of these haiku onto a separate sheet of paper in capital letters with a large space between each line. Make two copies of each.

Green fields of grain

A skylark rises

Over there

Comes down again

My hut in spring

True there is nothing in it

There is everything

"I've just been

To the lake bottom!"

That is the look

On the little duck's face

A man   just one

Also a fly   just one

In the huge living room

Clouds come from time to time

And give to men a chance to rest

From looking at the moon

STEP 2   Haiku #1

**Green fields of grain
A skylark rises
Over there
Comes down again**

- Arrest your linear habit: tear the poem up so that each word is torn away from its neighbors. You will have a small pile of scraps of paper, each with one word on it.

- Lie down on the floor. Pick up a scrap of paper randomly. Hold it above your face so that you can see the word on it. Let the word go deep into your body with your breath. Let it turn to image, or emotion, or action, or abstract shape. Give the images time and space to grow and become vivid.

- Put the paper down so that you are no longer reading it.

- Let the feeling that comes from the imagined word inhabit your breath and generate the vibrations of sound. Let the imagination in your body come into the word as you speak it.

- Let the energy of the sounds and the images activate your body as you speak the word.

- Continue with each word individually until the pile of paper is finished.

- Let each word enter you, your breath, and the touch of sound more than once, so that you really see it, taste it, touch it, and find its meaning.

STEP 3

- Take your second copy of the haiku and tear each line away from the others.

- Lie down on the floor and let each group of words enter into your body and imagination by way of your breath. Let the group create new pictures, pictures that are made vivid because you have already imaged the words separately. Now that they are related one to another, they form something new.

- Let the pictures turn into words.

- As the separate lines gather energy from your imagination and from the feelings triggered by the images, let them bring you up to standing. Let your body be activated by the images.

- Continue to be active physically as you enhance the details. (The lines are now in the right order.)

Green fields of grain

- Be scrupulous in the accuracy of your image:

> The color.

> More than one field.

> Not grass—but grain.

Green grain tells you something about the season—late spring, summer.

Stay with the image of the fields—know how you feel.

- Now let the next image *happen*.

A skylark rises

- The image changes—the feeling changes.

This is a transition.

- Be accurate in the image: a skylark is a small bird with vertical take-off and an ecstatic song.

Over there

The distance has significance and qualifies the feeling of the previous image.

This is another transition, on a smaller scale.

- Stay with that image—know how you feel.

- Let the next image *happen*.

Comes down again

What is the feeling that comes with this new image? Register the new emotional transition.

STEP 4   This is not just a pretty nature poem. The poet's observation of a specific moment in nature comes from the perspective of his emotional and psychological state of being at the time. A significant moment of being heightens perception. The heightened language of poetry illuminates the scene and the feeling behind it. The speaker's task is to enter that first creative moment and deduce the poet's inner state. Then the speaker must resuscitate the moment by finding an equivalent state of being in his or her own life.

In order to find the poet's creative moment, you must turn to the Six Eternal Questions and the Five P's. (Not necessarily *all* of them will be relevant.)

(1.) Let the images happen again with thought-feeling transitions:

Practice seeing them simultaneously *outside* and *inside* your body. (*Outside* gives the actual scene; *inside* leads to the emotional significance.)

(2.) Picture the poet, in his time and place, in relation to the images:

Who? Who is he? Or she?
Where? In the fields? standing at the door of the house?
When? What time of day? What time of year?
What? What is going on in the poet's life right at that moment?
Why? Why does the poet suddenly perceive the fields and the skylark in such a way that a haiku *must* be written?

(3.) Now put yourself in the scene in place of the poet. Find an equivalent view that you know *or* an imaginary one. Ask yourself the same questions.

(4.) The Five P's will help flesh out answers both for the poet and for yourself. For example:

Personal: What age is the poet? How old am I? Why are we out in the countryside?

Psychological: A feeling of youth and promise comes with the picture of the young grain. A stab of excitement comes as the skylark erupts out of the field—something thrilling will happen soon in my life. But it is a long way off. And as the skylark descends, so does my hope.

Professional: This promise, this hope, and the subsequent disappointment are familiar in the ups and downs of my professional life.

And I am always falling in love and then falling out again. Is it the poet's professional or personal life that is the background for this haiku? And mine?

Political: This *could* have a political story behind it, but I think that would be a red herring, so I will ignore the political.

Philosophical: The poet and I both know that life is full of expectation and disillusion, and we know that each experience of this is as fresh as the first time.

STEP 5 Now that there is some content that needs to be expressed, the speaker can become gently aware of how the images and feelings change. In other words, the speaker can look for the dynamics that are intrinsic to those images and feelings. Be careful, though, in expressing these transitions. There is a danger that the intellect will "hear" interesting dynamics and apply them: faster here, higher there, slower and quieter to finish. If the intellect dictates the dynamics, the resulting expression will be dead.

(5.) Dynamics

Green fields of grain

> With all the content from the previous work, these words need a bit of amplitude—they will probably emerge with some weight and quite slowly.

A skylark rises

> The speed of the ascent sparks the voice into a different energy from the "green fields"—the voice may go a little higher, the words may come faster.

Over there

> The distance, the remoteness, the sounds of the vowels all make the delivery slower, the words perhaps stretch a little, perhaps go lower in pitch.

Comes down again

> The feeling drops and the voice drops with it. The heavy beat of "comes down" is like that of a bass drum. "Again" trips to the final thump of meaning.

(6.) Rhythm

> The rhythms of the haiku emerge from innate qualities within the dynamics of image, feeling, and word.

> Be aware also that in this haiku nearly every word has a strong emphasis and that among the sixteen syllables there are only five weak syllables.

STEP 6   Speak the haiku. Experience the three emotional shifts that come in reaction to the three major image shifts.

STEP 7   Haiku #2

> **My hut in spring**
> **True there is nothing in it**
> **There is everything**

■   Follow the same process as for the first haiku. Tear the words apart from one another. Absorb them into your reservoir of images, emotions, and actions. Speak each one with the imagination embodied in the word as you speak.

■   Tear the lines away from one another. Absorb them. Let them activate your body as they release out of you.

■   Put the lines in the right order. As you see and speak the images, practice seeing them simultaneously *outside* and *inside* your body. (*Outside* gives the actual scene; *inside* leads to the emotional significance.)

> Go through the Six Questions and the Five P's.

At this point a student will often come up with a picture that is personal but inaccurate. It might be a picture of a beach cottage that is sparsely furnished, and in this case "There is everything" means "But that's quite OK." But the personal must give way to the poet's words. It is a "hut" and it has "nothing" in it. The speaker must begin to use imagination and see not a log cabin in the Adirondacks with Ikea furniture, but a bare hut.

The first speaking of the haiku can often leave students baffled and thinking, "So what?" The words are flat and the facts are not very interesting. But a poet wrote these words, and his relationship to his hut must become the students' if they are to understand the haiku's meaning. If the hut is really a bare hut and they accept that they own it, they can start to imagine where it is, what it looks like, and why they own it, and ask questions about their relationship to it.

The significance of "spring" is easy to ignore yet the poet sees his hut suddenly made vivid by that season of the year. And so I, too, at the mention of spring must evoke an image that tacitly sets it against the other seasons. Perhaps in winter the hut is closed up because it's too cold to inhabit. By the time summer comes, I've become used to it and hardly look at it when I go in. In the fall I find that it gets damp and chilly. But spring reminds me of everything I love about the solitude of my time in my hut. It seems pretty clear that I don't invite other people to my hut.

What about "nothing" and "everything"? Is it the solitude, the silence that make up the "nothing"? What happens to me when I am alone and silent in my hut? And then, in spring do I smell the blossoms and feel the breeze? Do I find myself thinking, "I am content; I am full; this is everything"?

From the Five P's we need to draw on the philosophical for deeper levels of this haiku. If my hut is, in fact, me, then it is possible that I am finding a way to express those moments when I renew my spirit, and in meditation come to a state of nothingness that opens into a profound sense of self and fulfillment.

■ Speak the haiku going from specific image to specific image, letting each image find its specific emotional, personal response. Let reverberations from the past, from the poet's inspiration, resound.

STEP 8 Haiku #3

> "I've just been
> To the lake bottom!"
> That is the look
> On the little duck's face

Follow the same process as for the first and second haikus. Your inner ear and eye should be hearing and seeing more as you continue.

Compare your reading with my example below. Mine is not necessarily correct, but it may open up more possibilities for you to explore.

"I've just been

I've been somewhere but I don't know how to describe it

To the lake bottom!"

My equivalent of the lake bottom is a dark world of wonder, or some fabulous trip of fantasy—or, by contrast, a sense of drowning in a pit of despair.

That is the look

On the little duck's face

I envision a little duck who dived down for the first time to the bottom of the lake and has just surfaced, shaking drops of water from its head and looking around with pride and the delight of "Aha! I survived!"

I see the poet plunged in gloom walking along the edge of the lake; suddenly the duckling breaks up through the water. It looks quite surprised; it looks as if it is smiling, laughing. The poet feels a weight lift from his heart and he says, "But I'm alive! I survive!"

The rhythms are choppy: "lake's bottom," "little duck," "that is," "on the," echoing the splashing duck movement with sharp "k's" and "t's.".

STEP 9   Haiku #4

> **A man just one**
> **Also a fly just one**
> **In the huge living room**

Follow the same process as before. The more transitions you can find, the better. For instance "a man" is the first image; when you add "just one" the image is modified into something a little odd, maybe even slightly menacing. Balanced with the next image, "a fly—just one," the oddity grows. Don't run these phrases together. Feel the tension between the contrasting images and the repetition of "just one."

Explore the scene with the questions of where you are and where the poet is in relation to the man and the fly. Are you, and is the poet, the man? Are you looking in through the window? Is the living room just a living room?

Remember: there must have been a strong psychological or emotional reason for the poet to see this scene and transform it into a haiku.

Please do your own work on the haiku before continuing to read.

When I explain to you my reading of this haiku, you must remember that it is not the correct reading. It is mine.

> I am struck by the amount of space in the picture and by the silence—broken, perhaps, by the buzzing of the fly, but perhaps the fly is silent, clinging to the wall or the ceiling. I see the man and the fly looking at each other. Something about the scene pushes beyond the domestic, and the huge living room suggests life itself, or the world. The man and the fly now become the last living creatures. Will the man kill the fly or the fly kill the man?

This interpretation does not come from my head; it gradually swims up through misty images and questions that won't settle for immediate or comfortable answers. Extremes start to become attractive. A haiku that has lasted for three or more centuries was conceived in some kind of extremity, otherwise the potency of the images would have faded.

This is text groundwork for actors. It must become familiar turf before moving into the more complex territory of performance.

You must be able to experience emotional imagination in the body. You must be able to express the incarnated emotional imagination in words if you are to speak classical texts and poetic texts truthfully.

Note that I say "you must be able to." This fullness of expression is not an aesthetic rule for classical or poetic texts. Once you are free from your personal limitations of expression, you can choose to contain language within a variety of chosen styles of speaking.

STEP 10 Haiku #5

> **Clouds come from time to time**
> **And give to men a chance to rest**
> **From looking at the moon**

Clouds come from time to time

> My first impression is that the clouds are gray; dark clouds suggest moments of sadness or depression.

And give to men a chance to rest

> Oh! *these* clouds are comforting, peaceful.

From looking at the moon

> The clouds float across the moon in a night sky.
>
> What does the moon connote? Love; madness; dreams and aspirations; sleeplessness?

I now know that it is nighttime, that the poet and I can't sleep. We are in love, or in the grip of an obsession, or concocting brilliant and unlikely dreams of future glory. The moon reflects our lunacy. And every now and then, thank heaven, we remember times in the past when a disastrous love affair failed, an obsession dissolved, or an ambition was thwarted, and it was quite a relief really. The clouds of reality are restful. But the moon comes out again from behind the clouds—the obsession grips us again.

Clouds come

The rhythm is weighted and quite slow—the tone rather dark.

From time to time

This qualifies and slightly lightens the effect of the first image. The vowels are brighter but still long.

And give to men

This is a transition to the personal human world from an indifferent natural world. Both are on a universal scale. The rhythm quickens slightly as the vowels shorten and the question "What can clouds give men?" moves the energy forward.

A chance to rest

"Chance" lifts the voice a little with its hopeful potential; "to rest" lets the voice settle gently down.

From looking at the moon

The haiku doesn't quite finish; the brightness of the moon unsettles us with its lunatic insistence.

The *rhythm* of this haiku is different from the others not only because the rhythm of the content is different but because in this one the major words are interspersed with many small, short words.

Clouds come from time to time

And give to men a chance to rest

From looking at the moon

You are searching for meaning: gazing at the moon. You can fall in love with this poem. You might feel you're going crazy trying to get to the bottom of it.

Is the moon perhaps your voice? Is it hard to understand your voice?

Are you working on a role? Searching for the character?

Let the clouds come for a little. Go to sleep. Turn your mind off. Let go.

The next time you look at the moon you might suddenly really see it.

The next time you speak this haiku you might really get the feeling behind the meaning.

The next time you work on your voice it might be whole and free and absolutely yours.

Appendix

Excerpted from
Anatomy and Physiology of the Voice and Choral Pedagogy
By Robert Sataloff, M.D., D.M.A.

The human voice is remarkable, complex, and delicate. It is capable of conveying not only sophisticated intellectual concepts but also subtle emotional nuances. Although the uniqueness and beauty of the human voice have been appreciated for centuries, medical science has begun to understand the workings and care of the voice only since the late 1970s and the early 1980s. Although it is not necessary to master detailed scientific information about anatomy and physiology to sing [speak] in a healthy fashion, at least a basic understanding of the structures and functions is helpful....

Anatomy

What Is the Larynx?

The *larynx* (voice box) is essential to normal voice production, but the anatomy of the voice is not limited to the larynx. The vocal mechanism includes the abdominal and back musculature, the rib cage, the lungs, and the pharynx, oral cavity, and nose. Each component performs an important function in voice production, although it is possible to produce voice even without a larynx (e.g., in patients who have undergone laryngectomy [removal of the larynx] for cancer). In addition, virtually all parts of the body play some role in voice production and may be responsible for voice dysfunction. Even something as remote as a sprained ankle may alter posture, thereby impairing abdominal muscle function and resulting in vocal inefficiency, weakness, or hoarseness.

The larynx is composed of four basic anatomic units: *skeleton, intrinsic muscles, extrinsic muscles*, and *mucosa*. The most important parts of the laryngeal skeleton are the *thyroid cartilage, cricoid cartilage*, and two arytenoid cartilages. Intrinsic muscles of the larynx are connected to these cartilages. One of the intrinsic muscles, the *vocalis muscles* (part of the *thyroarytenoid muscle*), extends on each side from the arytenoid cartilage to the inside of the thyroid cartilage just below and behind the *"Adam's apple,"* forming the body of the vocal folds (popularly called the *vocal cords*). The vocal folds act as the *oscillator* or *voice source* (noise maker) of the vocal tract. The space between the vocal cords is called the glottis and is used as an anatomic reference point. The intrinsic muscles alter the position, shape, and tension of the vocal folds, bringing them together (*adduction*), moving them apart (*abduction*), or stretching them by increasing longitudinal tension. They are able to do so because the laryngeal cartilages are connected by soft attachments that allow changes in their relative angles and distances, thereby permitting alteration in the shape and tension of the tissues suspended between them. The arytenoids are also capable of rocking, rotating, and gliding, which permits complex vocal fold motion and alternation in the shape of the vocal fold edge. All but one of the muscles on each side of the larynx are innervated by one of the two *recurrent laryngeal nerves*....This structure runs a long course from the neck down into

the chest and then back up to the larynx (hence the name "recurrent")...
The remaining muscle (*cricothyroid muscle*) is innervated by the *superior laryngeal nerve* on each side...It produces increases in longitudinal tension important in volume projection and pitch control. The "false vocal cords" are located above the vocal folds; unlike the true vocal folds, they do not make contact during normal speaking or singing.

What Happens Above the Larynx?

The *supraglottic* vocal tract includes the pharynx, tongue, palate, oral cavity, nose, and other structures. Together, they act as a *resonator* and are largely responsible for vocal quality (or timbre) and the perceived character of all speech sounds. The vocal folds themselves produce only a "buzzing" sound. During the course of vocal training for singing, acting, or healthy speaking, changes occur not only in the larynx, but also in the muscle motion, control, and shape of the supraglottic vocal tract.

What Happens Below the Larynx?

The *infraglottic* vocal tract serves as the *power source* for the voice. Singers and actors refer to the entire power source complex as their "*support*" or "*diaphragm.*" Actually, the anatomy of support for phonation is especially complicated and not completely understood, and performers who use the terms *diaphragm* and *support* do not always mean the same thing. Yet, it is quite important because deficiencies in support are frequently responsible for voice dysfunction.

The purpose of the support mechanism is to generate a force that directs a controlled airstream between the vocal folds. Active respiratory muscles work together with passive forces. The principle muscles of inspiration are the diaphragm (a dome-shaped muscle that extends along the bottom of the rib cage) and the external intercostal (rib) muscles. During quiet breathing, expiration is largely passive...

Deficiencies in the support mechanism often result in compensatory efforts utilizing the laryngeal muscles, which are not designed for power source functions...

Physiology of the Voice

How does it all work together to make a voice?

What do the brain and nerves have to do with voice production?

The physiology of voice production is extremely complex. Volitional production of the voice begins in the cerebral cortex of the brain. The command for vocalization involves complex interaction among brain centers for speech and other areas...The "idea" of the planned vocalization is conveyed to the precentral gyrus in the motor cortex, which transmits another set of instructions to the motor nuclei in the brain stem and spinal cord. These areas send out the complicated messages necessary for coordinated activity of the larynx, the chest and abdominal musculature, and the vocal tract articulators. Additional refinement of motor activity is provided by the extra-pyramidal and autonomic nervous systems. These impulses combine to produce a sound that is transmitted not only to the ears of the listener, but also to those of the speaker or singer...Tactile feedback from the throat and muscles involved in phonation also helps in the fine-tuning of the vocal output, although the mechanism and role of tactile (sense of feeling and touch) feedback are not fully understood.

How Is Sound Produced?

Phonation—the production of sound—requires interaction among the power source, oscillator, and resonator...

During phonation, the infraglottic musculature must make rapid complex adjustments because the resistance changes almost continuously as the glottis closes, opens, and changes shape. At the beginning of each phonatory cycle, the vocal folds are approximated, and the glottis is obliterated. This permits infraglottic pressure to build up, typically to a level of about 7cm of water, for conversational speech...Because the vocal folds are closed there is no airflow. The subglottic pressure then pushes the vocal folds progressively further apart from the bottom up until a space develops and air begins to flow. *Bernoulli force* created by the air passes between the vocal folds and combines with the mechanical properties of the folds to begin closing the lower portions of the glottis almost immediately, even while the upper edges are still separating. The principles and mathematics of

Bernoulli force are complex. It is a flow effect more easily understood by familiar examples, such as the sensation of pull exerted on a vehicle when passed by a truck at high speed or the inward motion of a shower curtain when the water flows past it.

The upper portion of the vocal folds has strong elastic properties that tend to make the vocal folds snap back to the midline. This force becomes more dominant as the upper edges are stretched and the opposing force of the air diminishes because of the approximation of the lower edges of the vocal folds. The upper portions of the vocal folds are then returned to the midline completing the glottic cycle. Subglottal pressure then builds again, and the events repeat...

Pitch is the perceptual correlate of frequency. Under most circumstances, as the vocal folds are thinned and stretched and air pressure is increased, the frequency of air pulse emission increases, and pitch goes up...

The sound produced by the vibrating vocal folds, called the voice source signal, is a complex tone containing a *fundamental frequency* and many *overtones*, or higher *harmonic partials*....

How Is the Sound Shaped?

The pharynx, the oral cavity, and the nasal cavity act as series of interconnected resonators...some resonators are attenuated and others are enhanced. Enhanced frequencies are then radiated with higher relative amplitudes or intensities. Sundberg had shown that the vocal tract has four or five important resonance frequencies called formants. The presence of formants alters the uniformly sloping voice source spectrum and creates peaks at formant frequencies. These alterations of the voice source spectral envelope are responsible for distinguishable sounds of speech and song.

How Do We Control Pitch and Loudness?

The mechanisms that control two vocal characteristics—fundamental frequency and intensity—are particularly important. Fundamental frequency, which corresponds to pitch, can be altered by changing either the air pressure or the mechanical properties of the vocal folds, although changing the latter is more efficient under most conditions. When the cricothyroid muscle contracts, it makes the thyroid cartilage pivot and increases the distance between the thyroid and arytenoid cartilages, thus stretching the vocal folds. This increases the surface area exposed to subglottal pressure and makes the air pressure more effective in opening the glottis. In addition, stretching the elastic fibers of the vocal folds makes them more efficient at snapping back together. As the cycles shorten and repeat more frequently, the fundamental frequency and pitch rise. Other muscles, including the thyroarytenoid also contribute.

Vocal intensity corresponds to loudness and depends on the degree to which the glottal wave motion excites the air molecules in the vocal tract. Raising the air pressure creates greater amplitude of vocal fold displacement from the midline and therefore increases vocal intensity. However, it is not actually the vibration of the vocal fold, but rather the sudden cessation of airflow that is responsible for initiating sound in the vocal tract and controlling intensity. This is similar to the mechanism of the acoustic vibration that results from buzzing lips. In the larynx, the sharper the cutoff of airflow, the more intense the sound.

Conclusion

The vocal mechanism includes the larynx, the abdominal and back musculature, the rib cage, the lungs, the pharynx, oral cavity, and nose. Each component performs an important function in voice production. The physiology of voice is extremely complex, involving interaction among brain centers for speech and other areas. Signals are transmitted to the motor nuclei in the brain stem and spinal cord, coordinating the activity of the larynx, the chest and abdominal musculature, and the vocal tract articulators. Other areas of the nervous system provide additional refinement. Phonation requires interaction among the power source, oscillator, and resonator. The sound produced by the vocal folds, called the vocal source signal, is a complex tone containing a fundamental frequency and many overtones. The pharynx, oral cavity, and nasal cavity act as a series of interconnected resonators. They shape sound quality and enhance audibility by creating a [singer's] formant. Specific anatomic adjustments control fundamental frequency and intensity....

Acknowledgments

For the 1976 edition of *Freeing the Natural Voice* I gratefully acknowledged the Ford Foundation for making it possible for me to take a year away from teaching in order to write the first edition of this book, and the Rockefeller Foundation for the five weeks they granted me at the Villa Serbelloni where the atmosphere made writing possible.

For this revised and expanded edition I thank the Columbia University School of the Arts and Dean Bruce Ferguson for awarding me a semester's creative leave in order to revise my textbook. I gratefully acknowledge Marjorie Hanlon, Julie Sheehan, Joanna Weir, Andrea Haring, and Fran Bennett for their invaluable editorial help. I remain indebted to Tom Shipp for his contribution to the description of "How the Voice Works," which stands more or less unchanged from the 1976 edition, and to Dr. Robert Sataloff for giving me permission to use excerpts from his writings to augment the anatomical picture.

I also dedicate this edition to all the teachers of *Freeing the Natural Voice* who have undergone my rigorous teacher-training programs and who love this way of working on the human voice.

Kristin Linklater
New York City

www.kristinlinklater.com